FINALS

CONTRACTS

CORE CONCEPTS AND KEY QUESTIONS

Second Edition

T. Leigh Hearn, Esquire
Series Editor

© 2009 by Kaplan, Inc.

Published by Kaplan Publishing, a division of Kaplan, Inc.
1 Liberty Plaza, 24th floor
New York, NY 10006

Printed in the United States of America

10   9   8   7   6   5   4   3   2   1

ISBN13: 978-1-60714-092-4

Kaplan Publishing books are available at special quantity discounts to use for sales promotions, employee premiums, or educational purposes. Please email our Special Sales Department to order or for more information at kaplanpublishing@kaplan.com, or write to Kaplan Publishing, 1 Liberty Plaza, 24th floor, New York, NY 10006.

CONTRACTS

I. BASICS

A. DEFINITION OF A CONTRACT: A contract is an agreement between two or more parties that is enforceable at law. In determining whether there is a contract, courts look for (1) an offer, (2) an acceptance, and (3) consideration.

1. **The Sources of Contract Law:**

   a. **Common law:** Contract law is governed by state law, and most contracts are governed by the common law. While you may be learning case law from many states, your professor is unlikely to test you on a specific state's law. Instead, you will be learning majority and minority rules, and your exam questions will expect you to utilize all of the law from all of the cases you have studied, no matter what state the particular case may be from. Most of the time, the jurisdiction of an exam question will not be a particular state. For example, a common exam "jurisdiction" is Erehwon, which is "Nowhere" spelled backwards.

   b. **The Uniform Commercial Code (UCC)**—While the common law covers most contracts, in your first-year contracts course, it is fairly likely you will also study Article 2 of the UCC, which governs the sale of goods.

   The important thing about the UCC is that it attempts to speed up the nature of commerce. Consequently, it gets rid of a lot common law requirements that might slow down commercial deal-making.

   It is helpful to think of the UCC as a toggle switch—either it's on or it's off (you can't go halfsies). For example, hiring someone to walk your dog is clearly a service contract, and such contracts are governed by the common law. However, buying a drill at the hardware store is clearly a contract for the sale of goods.

   However, in some transactions, it might be harder to tell whether the contract is for services or the sale of goods. In such a case, look for the dominant idea behind the transaction.

   EXAMPLE: Amani goes to the store and buys a new set of tires, which the store installs on her car. Is this a UCC contract for tires, or a common law contract for the installation service? Clearly, Amani went to the store in the first place to buy tires, so this contract would be covered by the UCC.

   c. **The Restatement (Second) of Contracts:** Although the Restatement is extremely influential, it is not actually "law" in and of itself. It is a "textbook" written by a group of legal scholars setting out what the common law of contracts seems to be. Importantly, while the Restatement is based on judicial decisions, it does not necessarily reflect what the most common rule is in a particular situation; sometimes, the drafters of the Restatement may actually be advocating a minority rule that they feel other jurisdictions should follow.

d. **Why do the sources matter?** On your exams, the differences among how the common law, the UCC, and the Restatement approach a particular matter is likely to be a primary issue on your exams. Consequently, many of your answers may evaluate a particular issue under the common law, then under the UCC, and finally what might happen if the Restatement rule were followed.

2. **There Are Three Types of Contracts:**

   a. **Express contracts:** When parties enter into an agreement either orally or in writing.

      EXAMPLE: Dr. Jimmy says, "I will mend your arm for $1,000." Mary Frances replies, "I accept."

   b. **Implied-in-fact contracts:** When the parties' actions imply the existence of a contract, although no words were written or spoken.

   c. **Quasi-contracts:** When there is no contract at all, but it would lead to "unjust enrichment" if one party received a benefit without compensating the other party. These are sometimes referred to as "implied-in-law" contracts (as opposed to "implied-in-fact" contracts).

      EXAMPLE: Dr. Jimmy finds Mary Frances lying unconscious in the street with a broken arm. Dr. Jimmy mends Mary Frances's arm and later demands a fee. In these circumstances, Dr. Jimmy is entitled to the reasonable value of his services, even though there was no contract between the parties. *See Richard A. Posner, Economic Analysis of the Law 151-152 (5th ed. 1998).*

B. OFFERS

An offer is an objective manifestation by the offer or of the intent to enter into a bargain that creates a power of acceptance in the offeree. To be enforceable, an offer usually requires a statement of essential terms: (1) the parties; (2) the subject matter (*e.g.,* bananas); (3) the price (*e.g.,* $300), and (4) the quantity (*e.g.,* 10 bushels). This makes sense, because otherwise the offeree would have no idea what he or she is accepting, and the court would have no idea what sort of remedy might be appropriate if one of the parties breaches the contract.

NOTE: The "offeror" is the person who proposes the bargain. The "offeree" is the person who has the power to create the contract by accepting the offer.

1. **Objective:** A reasonable, prudent person would believe an offer was being made. Even if the offeror is secretly joking, what matters is what someone watching the communication would think. Consequently, the setting of the offer is important (*e.g.,* a statement in a business letter is more likely to be an offer than a similar one at a keg party).

EXAMPLE: As a joke to see whether Lyda has any extra money in the bank, Jerry offers to sell Lyda his car. Lyda accepts. The two parties work out the terms of the contract, write it out on the back of an envelope, and sign it. The next day, Lyda attempts to enforce the agreement. Even if Jerry was only joking and did not subjectively intend to sell the car, a contract was formed because Lyda reasonably believed the offer was serious. *See Lucy v. Zehmer, 84 S.E.2d 516 (Va. 1956).*

2. **Manifestation:** The offer needs to be communicated to the offeree, and the offeree cannot accept an offer he or she doesn't know about. Don't get confused if your professor refers to a "meeting of the minds"—coincidence doesn't count.

   EXAMPLE: Daniel, a bookshelf maker, mails Kerry, a bookstore owner, a written offer to sell her 10 bookshelves at $100 each. Unaware of Daniel's offer, Kerry mails Daniel an offer to buy 10 bookshelves at $100 each on the same day. At this point, there is no contract because neither party knows of the other's offer. *See Restatement of Contracts Section 23.*

3. **Intent:** The immediate intent to enter into a bargain, as opposed to a promise to make a promise or preliminary negotiations and "invitations to deal." In determining whether the parties are merely making preliminary negotiations, look for language like "I am looking for ...," "Would you be interested ...," "Would you pay ...," or "Would you consider ...?" Such language is likely to be simply a negotiation, not an offer.

   EXAMPLE 1: Dooner says to Sepulveda, "I would like to sell you my house next week for $200,000." There is no offer, because by saying, "I would like to sell you my house next week," Dooner does not intend to form a present bargain with Sepulveda.

   EXAMPLE 2: Johnson asks François, "Would you consider selling me your motorcycle for $250?" François replies, "I could not accept less than $400 for it." Neither of these statements is an offer. By their wording, they are merely preliminary negotiations. *See Elkhorn-Hazard Coal Co. v. Kentucky River Corp., 20 F.2d 67 (6th Cir. 1927).*

4. **Essential Terms:** Under the common law, if the offer did not contain all of the essential terms, the offer would fail for indefiniteness.

   a. **Modern view:** Under the modern view, courts try to uphold the intent of the parties by using "gap fillers" for any missing terms. When both sides of a transaction are silent as to a particular term, courts will fill it in with a reasonable term. A reasonable term is one consistent with the past dealings of the parties or with the custom and usage of the particular industry or trade if the parties know or could be fairly expected to know that custom or usage.

i. **UCC approach:** The UCC has abolished the common law formation rules respecting attempted contracts for the sale of goods.

    (a) The UCC is satisfied by formation "in any manner sufficient to show agreement, including conduct by both parties which recognizes the existence of such a contract."

    (b) The failure of the parties to specify one or more essential terms by their words or deeds is not fatal under UCC 2-204(3). "[A] contract for sale does not fail for indefiniteness if the parties have intended to make a contract and there is a reasonably certain basis for giving an appropriate remedy."

ii. **Restatement approach:** Restatement (Second) of Contracts Sec. 32(2) recommends that the common law evolve in the direction of the UCC reforms.

    (a) The omission by the parties of the content of an essential term need not be fatal "… if the terms (which can be ascertained from their dealings) provide a basis for determining the existence of a bargain and for giving an appropriate remedy."

iii. **Limitation on the ability of any court to imply a "reasonable term":** Neither the evolving common law nor the UCC is willing to make a better bargain for the parties than they appear to have consciously attempted.

    (a) If the parties did attempt an overt bargain with respect to a term, but did so in a confusing or ambiguous manner, a reasonable term cannot be implied and the bargain fails due to indefiniteness.

        (1) Therefore, true silence, with respect to a term, is required.

iv. **Requirements and output contracts:** Although not specific in the sense that they set forth identifiable numbers, these contracts are no longer deemed to be too indefinite to be enforced.

    (a) **Original common law position:** Originally, the common law refused to find enforce an agreement that measured the quantity term by the seller's output or the buyer's requirements.

    (b) **Modern common law position:** The common law has abandoned this position and now upholds such bargains. There are two specific types:

        (1) **Requirements contract:** In a requirements contract, the quantity is everything a buyer may need in the good faith course of its business. **In contract law, "good faith" means honesty and fair-dealing with no subjective intent to act wrongfully.**

(2) **Output contract:** The quantity is everything the seller can produce in the good faith course of its business. Importantly, the seller does not guarantee any minimum quantity.

(c) **UCC position:** UCC 2-306(1) specifically allows requirements and output contracts, but also specifically includes language stating that the quantity can't be unreasonably disproportionate to prior dealings or any stated estimate.

v. **Open price terms:** The common law required a price term, or the contract failed for indefiniteness. Some courts still follow that rule. In other circumstances, the court will imply a good faith attempt to set a price and will supply a reasonable price if one is not agreed upon.

(a) **UCC approach:** The UCC adopts a more liberal attitude than the common law. Under UCC 2-305, the parties, if they so intend, may form a present contract for sale even though the price is not fixed. They have the following options:

(1) **Silence:** If the parties are silent about price, the court will interpret their mutual silence as consent to trade at a commercially reasonable price.

(2) **Later agreement:** The parties may leave the price to be agreed upon in the future. In this case, present contract is formed although both parties, and a reviewing court, will have to await future events to ascertain the price term.

(3) **Defined mechanism:** The parties may agree to have the price fixed by some agreed-upon term setting machinery (such as a quotation to appear in the next issue of a designated trade journal).

(i) If the agreed upon machinery should fail to set the future price, the earlier intent of the parties determines whether the contract fails.

(ii) If it appears that they intended to form a contract despite the failure of the price mechanism, a court will supply a reasonable price.

(iii) If they appear not to have intended a contract unless their agreed upon term setting machinery worked, there is no contract.

> **EXAMPLE:** Farmer Job offers to sell Farmer Ned "300 bushels of corn at the same price as that quoted tomorrow in the *Iowa City Kernel* newspaper." Farmer Ned accepts. The next day, the *Kernel* quotes the price of a bushel of corn as $20. As a result, the contract is for 300 bushels of corn for $6,000.

5. **Termination of Offer**

a. **Duration:** An offer terminates either by (1) death, insanity, or legal incapacity of the offeror; (2) revocation; (3) rejection; (4) counteroffer; (5) supervening illegality; (6) destruction of the subject matter of the bargain; or (7) lapse of time. Once an offer terminates, an offeree can no longer accept it to create a contract, unless the offeror *revives* the offer.

EXAMPLE: Egan offers to sell Ullom his horse for $500. Ullom responds, "No way. That horse is terrible." This terminates the offer, and the offeree can no longer accept it. However, if Egan says something like "Why don't you think about it until tomorrow?" the offer is revived and the offeree's power to create a contract by acceptance is restored.

i. **Death, insanity, or legal incapacity of offeror:** This is only at the offer stage. After the offer is accepted, the death of the offeror will not terminate the contract (at that point, the offeree may be able to enforce the contract's terms against the offeror's estate).

ii. **Revocation:** The general rule is that any offer can be revoked by the offeror at any time prior to its acceptance. There are two ways an offeror can revoke an offer: direct and indirect.

(a) **Direct:** Offeror directly tells offeree that the offer is revoked.

EXAMPLE: Wesley says, "Hey, Frances, I'll sell you my comic book for $5." Before Frances can respond, Wesley shouts, "Nope! Too late! Changed my mind!"

(b) **Indirect:** The offeree is put on notice that he or she can no longer accept the offer.

EXAMPLE: A famous rock band asks you to be their lead singer for a new world tour. You decide to think about it overnight, buy some spandex, and practice some high kicks. The next day, you read an article in the paper that says Rock Enroll is the new lead singer and that the band is playing the EnormoDome that night. At this point, you can't yell, "I accept!" You have been put on notice that the power of acceptance has terminated, and the offer is dead.

iii. **Rejection:** If the offeree says "No," the offer is terminated.

iv. **Counteroffer:** If the offeree changes the terms of the offer before agreeing to the bargain, the offer dies. In this situation, be careful that the offeree is not simply making an *inquiry*. An inquiry would be something like "I don't know, would you take less money?" In an inquiry situation, the offeree is simply looking to see if there is room for negotiations.

EXAMPLE: Walter offers to sell Lee his lawnmower for $50. Lee responds, "I'll give you $45 for it." In this situation, what has happened is that Lee has rejected Walter's offer and made a new offer of his own.

v. **Supervening illegality:** Before the offer is accepted, a change in the law makes the bargain illegal.

EXAMPLE: Pollard Inc., a United States general defense contractor, offers to sell 100 surface-to-air missiles to the Country of Erehwon. The next day, the United States declares war on Erehwon and makes any contract with the country illegal.

vi. **Destruction of the subject matter of the bargain:** Remember, this is at the offer stage. There are special rules once a contract is formed regarding which party has to bear the loss.

vii. **Lapse of time:** This is generally very fact specific. It can be written into the terms of the offer itself (*e.g.,* "This offer must be accepted by Saturday, January 17."), or it can depend upon the subject matter of the bargain. For example, if I make an offer to sell stock, the lapse of time could be a microsecond before the market changes. If I offer to sell you my watch, the time for acceptance could be much longer.

(a) **End of conversation rule:** Generally, if an offer is made in conversation, and nothing is done with the offer before the conversation ends, the offer is terminated.

EXAMPLE: Emerson, a carpenter, is walking down the street when he runs into Mahone. Emerson says, "Hey, I'll fix your broken deck for $200." Mahone responds, "That seems fair." At that point, Mahone's neighbor, George, peeks over the fence, and the three of them start talking about the Red Sox. Nothing further is stated about the deck. The next day, Mahone calls Emerson and says, "I accept your offer." At this point, Mahone can no longer accept the offer because the offer terminated when their conversation did. Basically, the lifespan of an offer in this situation is what would be reasonable, and if an offer just pops up in conversation, it would be reasonable that it terminates and can no longer be accepted when the conversation ends.

viii. **Exceptions:** There are several exceptions to the rule that an offer is freely revocable.

ix. **Option contract:** An option is a promise to keep an offer open for a stated period of time. Under the common law, such an option has to be supported by its own separate consideration. In upholding an option contract, courts will accept nominal consideration (for example, $1 to hold open an option to buy a $1 million yacht) or even sham consideration (where consideration is recited in the option contract, but is never actually given).

EXAMPLE: Jose sends Vladimir a letter that states, "I offer to sell Vladimir my farm for $1 million. In consideration of $1, receipt of which is hereby acknowledged, this offer will remain open for 45 days." Even if Vladimir never gives Jose the $1 consideration, a valid option to purchase the farm has been created.

x. **Promissory estoppel:** In some situations, even if there is no additional consideration, an offer will be held open if the offeree relies upon it to his or her detriment. The important question in such situations is whether the offer was deliberately made with the reasonable expectation of inducing the offeree to rely on it, he or she did act or refrain from acting in justifiable reliance, and he or she suffered some detriment as a result.

EXAMPLE: Yiyun writes to Tracy and offers to sell Tracy her mobile hot dog stand for $20,000 and states that the offer will be held open for a week. In preparation for going into the mobile hot dog business full-time, Tracy quits her job the next day. If Yiyun tries to revoke the offer the day after Tracy quits, but before the week is up, Tracy can ask the court to enforce the promise under the doctrine of promissory estoppel.

xi. **Construction bids:** There is a special rule that applies to construction contracts.

xii. **How construction contracts work:** In a construction contract, a general contractor makes a bid to build something (for example, a house). In making his or her bid, the general contractor usually collects bids from subcontractors who will be doing some of the smaller parts of the overall job (for example, the roof, the plumbing, the wiring, the drywall). The general contractor collects the bids, adds in overhead and profit, and then makes his or her offer to the offeree (for example, the homeowner).

xiii. **General contractor has the right to rely on the subcontractor's bid:** If a general contractor relies on a subcontractor's bid in making his or her bid, this creates an option contract. This means that once the general contractor submits his or her bid, the subcontractor cannot withdraw his or her bid.

xiv. **UCC Firm Offer Rule:** Under UCC 2-205, an offer can be unrevokable even if there is no additional consideration to hold it open if: (1) the offer to buy or sell the goods is made by a merchant (someone who buys or sells goods as his or her trade or profession), (2) the offer is in a writing signed by the offeror, and (3) there is an assurance to the offeree that the offer will be held open. If these conditions are met, the offer will remain open for the time stated or a reasonable time if no time limit is included.

EXAMPLE: Soungjae's Furniture sends to Oswald's Outlet Mall the following letter: "Soungjae's Furniture offers to sell to Oswald's Outlet 35 new SuperLux Couches at $250 per couch. This offer will remain open for 90 days." The letter is signed by Soungjae. Because the offer is made by a merchant, is in a writing signed by the offeror, and contains an assurance it will be held open, the offer will remain open for 90 days without any further consideration.

6. **Other Special Situations**

   a. **Advertisements**

   Generally, advertisements are considered invitations to deal rather than offers that create a power of acceptance in an offeree (this makes sense, considering advertisements are sent out to the general public, and could result in an infinite number of contracts for the offeror). However, if the advertisement is definite in its terms, leaves nothing to negotiate, seems objectively reasonable, and is unlikely to be overaccepted, a court may find the advertisement is an enforceable offer.

   EXAMPLE 1: A clothing store places an advertisement in the newspaper that says "Saturday 9 a.m. Sharp 3 Brand New Fur Coats Worth to $100 First Come First Served $1 Each." Portele is first in line on Saturday morning and gives the store $1. A contract has been created. *See Lefokowitz v. Great Minneapolis Surplus Store, 86 N.W.2d 689 (Minn. 1957).*

   EXAMPLE 2: While watching Saturday morning cartoons, Kurt sees an advertisement on television for Jitter Cola. The ad focuses on Jitter Points, a promotion where people are encouraged to drink Jitter Cola and collect the bottle caps for valuable prizes. The ad shows all the different things a person can trade in Jitter Caps for, such as 5 caps for a water gun, 10 caps for an action figure, and 15 caps for some music downloads. At the end, the ad shows a happy teenager landing a fighter jet on the roof of his high school, a jet the commercial implies he got for 1 million caps. Kurt collects 1 million caps, and tries to collect the jet. Jitter Cola refuses to give him one. Since the ad is indefinite, capable of being accepted by an infinite number of people, and clearly a joke, Kurt is not entitled to the jet. *See Leonard v. Pepsico Inc., 88 F.Supp.2d 116 (1999).*

   b. **Auctions:** Whether placing an item up for auction constitutes an offer or not depends on whether the item is offered "with reserve" or "without reserve." If an item is auctioned "with reserve," the offeror is merely inviting buyers to make an offer. If the item is auctioned "without reserve," the offeror is extending an acceptable offer that can lead to the formation of a contract.

C. ACCEPTANCE

1. **Overview**

   a. There are no mandatory words or acts that constitute an acceptance of an offer and formation of a contract.

   b. An acceptance consists of an expression of present, unequivocal, unconditional assent by the offeree to each and every term of the offer.

   c. This expression must be communicated to the offeror at a time prior to revocation or termination of the offer.

2. **Elements of Acceptance**

   a. The person seeking to accept an offer must be the offeree.

      i. **Status of an offeree:** Only a person intended by the offeror may effectively accept.

         (a) Unlike rights acquired under the terms of an existing contract, the status of offeree may not be assigned to someone else.

      ii. **Offer extended in an advertisement:** Unless restricted by the terms of the advertisement if a court finds that the advertisement was an offer (see above), the offer may be accepted by any person who has acquired knowledge, directly or indirectly, of the terms of the offer.

         EXAMPLE: After Ikenna loses his watch, he places "Reward" posters all over his school, offering $25 to anyone who returns it. Since there is no limitation on who can accept, anyone who finds the watch can claim the reward.

      iii. **Offer extended to an agent:** An offer extended to a disclosed agent may be accepted either by the agent or by the principal.

         EXAMPLE: The Dartmouth Rangers Professional Hockey team offers Smitty $1 million a year for the next three years. Either Smitty or his designated agent can accept the offer.

      iv. **Offeror's mistake as to identity of offeree:** If the dealing is face to face, an offeror must accept the consequences of his or her own mistake as to the identity of the offeree.

         (a) Acceptance by the person to whom the offer was extended forms a bargain unless the other party has subjective knowledge that the offeror has mistaken him for another.

         (b) If the dealing was not face to face, but conducted through some instrumentality such as the mails or telecommunications, courts have been more sympathetic to the protest of the offeror that his or her offer reached the wrong person.

    (c) If the offeror can demonstrate prejudice should he or she be held to the bargain, and the party who wrongly believes that he or she is the offeree has not changed position in reasonable reliance on the offer, many courts will permit the offeror to refuse to recognize the acceptance.

b. The content of the offeree's response must express agreement as to the exact terms of the offer.

    i. **Mirror-image acceptance:** At common law, the content of an effective acceptance must be a literal mirror image of the terms of the offer, and only those terms This is commonly referred to as the "mirror image rule."

        (a) If the offeree seeks to vary the offer by even the most minute addition, deletion or substitution, there is no acceptance.

            (1) Worse, the attempt to do so is regarded as a "rejection" terminating the outstanding offer and leaving only a counter offer of the terms as modified by the offeree on the bargaining table However, a mere inquiry will not violate the mirror image rule. See Termination of Offer above.

            EXAMPLE: Theodore offers Rosanna 25 apples from his tree for $10, payment to be made on delivery. Rosanna responds, "I accept, but I have until the day after delivery to pay you." In this situation, Rosanna's acceptance violates the mirror image rule, and no contract is formed.

c. The offeree must communicate acceptance to the offeror during the life of the offer.

3. **Acceptance Under the UCC**

  a. **The UCC position:**

    i. UCC 2-207 does not require a mirror-image acceptance, but only a "definite and seasonable expression of acceptance."

    ii. UCC 2-206 allows an acceptance through "any medium reasonable under the circumstances."

    iii. Therefore, under many circumstances in which no bargain would have been formed at common law, there will be a contract under the UCC.

    Even so, the offeror may still make an "iron clad" or "take it or leave it" offer by making an offer which explicitly limits acceptance to the exact terms of the offer. Importantly, the UCC does not limit any party's ability to reject, counter offer, or exclude different or additional terms from the contract. The UCC is intended to aid contract formation, not to force it upon the parties.

b. **Impact of additional or different terms in a purported acceptance of an offer to purchase or sell goods:**

   i. As stated above, under the common law's mirror-image rule, any attempts to add or change the terms of the offer meant that there was no valid acceptance.

   ii. Under UCC 2-207(1), between merchants, unless the offeree has clearly conditioned his or her acceptance upon the offeror's assent to these additional or different terms (in which case, the offeror is faced with an explicit rejection and counteroffer), the acceptance still creates a contract.

c. **Determining whether additional terms become part of the contract:** An "additional" term is a term that covers some matter that was not included in the original offer. For additional terms, the important question is whether the offeree's additional terms are a "material" alteration of the offer. If they are not, they are deemed consistent and become part of the contract. If they are a material alteration, a contract is still formed, but only on the terms of the original offer. See UCC 2-207(2)(b).

d. **Objection to additional terms by the offeror:** If the offeror objects to the inclusion of consistent additional terms within a "reasonable time," the resulting contract is once again reduced to the terms of the original offer only. See UCC 2-207(2)(c).

e. **Test for materiality:** UCC 2-207(2) does not define the phrase "materially alter." As a general rule, "materiality" depends upon whether the term is one the parties likely understood to be a significant part of the exchange.

   i. In practice courts appear to test the offeree's terms against the content of the offer looking for significant shifts in:

      (a) economic advantage;

      (b) allocation of the elements of risk inherent in the proposed transaction; or

      (c) prejudice to remedies which would otherwise apply in the event of breach.

   ii. Courts also determine materiality by deciding whether a merchant in the position of an offeror would be surprised or suffer hardship in the event the term or terms added by the offeree were to be included unless she objected, they pose a material alteration. *See* Comment to UCC 2-207.

f. **Determining whether different terms become part of the contract:** A "different" term is one that contradicts some term in the offer. Importantly, there is a discrepancy between UCC 2-207(1) and UCC 2-207(2). While UCC 2-207(1) refers to both "additional" and "different" terms, UCC 2-207(2) only refers to "additional" terms. In the context of different terms, the courts have dealt with this problem in three distinct ways:

g. **No difference:** Some courts treat different terms in the exact same way they treat additional terms. Consequently, whether they become part of the contract or not depends on their materiality.

h. **Different terms can never be part of the bargain:** Some courts find that since different terms are not mentioned in UCC 2-207(2), they can never become part of the bargain whether material or not.

i. **"Knockout rule":** Some courts find that the different terms "knock each other out" of the contract. Consequently, neither term is included. In that case, a court may default to the general provisions of the UCC as a gap-filler.

j. **Determining the moment of formation:** Classical contract analysis envisioned two distinct formation patterns.

    i. **Bilateral contracts:** If the offer and acceptance each contained a promise of performance, the exchange of the promises themselves formed the contract. An important issue in bilateral contracts is whether the performance is "divisible" into discrete parts. If performance is divisible, there could be an issue as to whether the breach of one promise contained in the agreement is "material" or "total." See Breach below.

    ii. **Unilateral contracts:** In a unilateral contract, the offer is a promise, but the offeree can only accept through full performance of his or her duties and obligations under the contract.

    EXAMPLE: Champ offers Kelly $25 if she walks across the Brooklyn Bridge. Kelly responds, "I promise to walk across the bridge." At this point, Kelly has not yet accepted the offer.

k. **Bilateral formation:** In a bilateral contract, both the offer and acceptance are in the form of a promise.

    i. Communication of the offeree's assent is not a problem if the offeror and the offeree deal face to face.

    ii. If they deal at a distance, the time between dispatch and communication raises a legal issue about the when the acceptance became effective.

        (a) **Concept of implied authorization:** Under the common law, the offeree was always impliedly authorized to communicate his or her acceptance by the same means used by the offeror (for example, if the offeror sent his or her offer by mail, the offeree can accept by mail).

iii. **The "mailbox rule":** For most of history, the only practical means of acceptance were mail or hand delivery. Therefore, an acceptance was deemed effective as soon as it was dispatched by the offeree (putting the risk of loss or delay on the offeror).

(a) **Mailbox rule as default:** The mailbox rule was only the default rule. If the offeror specified that he or she required actual notification, or her his requirement controlled.

EXAMPLE: Rosemary sends Hannah a letter stating, "I hereby offer to sell you my old car for $100. Please notify me of your acceptance by April 21." Hannah mails her acceptance on April 21. In this case, since Rosemary wrote "notify me," the mailbox rule does not apply and Hannah's acceptance is ineffective.

(b) **Today's "deposited acceptance rule":** Because so many means of communication exist today, an offeree is impliedly authorized to use any reasonable channel for communicating his or her acceptance. If he or she does so, the acceptance is still effective upon dispatch.

(c) **UCC rule:** UCC 2-206 expands the modern concept of implied authorization.

(1) Unless otherwise unambiguously indicated by the language or circumstances, an offer to make a contract shall be construed as inviting acceptance in any manner and by any medium reasonable in the circumstances.

(d) **Rule not available where the offer has been re-enforced by an option contract:** A majority common law view (supported by the Restatement) holds that the exercise of an option requires the offeree to give actual notice of acceptance to the offeror within the time optioned.

1. **Silence as acceptance:** Silence does not constitute acceptance under either the UCC or the common law.

EXAMPLE: Nelly Nefarious emails 10 million people this offer: "Unless I hear from you tomorrow, you have agreed to buy 10 pencils from me at a cost of $10 per pencil." Clearly, the courts would not enforce such an offer.

i. However, there are exceptions to this rule when the offeree was under a "duty to speak."

(a) **Previous dealings:** If the offeror and offeree have a recent history of prior transactions in which the offeree has allowed his or her silence to be treated as an acceptance, a repetition of the identical offer met by the offeree's silence will create a bargain.

(b) **Conduct of the offeree in retaining the goods:** If an offeree consciously retains goods that were tendered under the terms of an explicit offer, his or her conduct, coupled with a failure to express any objection to the offer, may be treated as an effective acceptance.

(c) **Distinguished from quasi-contractual liability:** If the offeree's conduct plus a failure to object to the terms of an explicit offer is treated as an effective acceptance, the terms of the offer control.

(d) **Unsolicited goods—a statutory exception:** Under federal law (as well as the law of several states), any unsolicited merchandise mailed with a request for payment or a charitable contribution may be treated by the recipient as a gift.

   (1) In such circumstances, the recipient has no liability to the sender in either contract or quasi-contract.

m. **Crossed communications:** Under the majority view, while acceptance is effective upon dispatch, a revocation by the offeror is only effective upon receipt by the offeree.

   i. Therefore, if an offeree dispatches his or her acceptance before receiving communication of a revocation, the acceptance controls and a contract is formed.

   EXAMPLE: Tasha mails Keith an offer to sell him her comic book collection. He receives the offer on July 27 and immediately mails his acceptance. On July 28, before she has received Keith's acceptance, Tasha calls Keith and tells him she doesn't want to sell her comics after all. At this point, since Keith's acceptance is in the mail, it is too late to revoke her offer.

n. **Rejection followed by acceptance:** Rejections must be communicated to be effective.

   i. Therefore, if an offeree first rejects, then accepts, a conflict arises.

   ii. In this circumstance, the first communication *received by the offeror* controls.

   (a) If the acceptance arrives first, a contract is formed.

   (b) However, if the rejection arrives first, a belated acceptance is too late. The offer has been revoked by the received rejection.

o. **Unilateral formation:** An offer for an act or forbearance instead of a return promise creates a unilateral contract.

    i. Under the common law, an offer for a unilateral contract can only be accepted when performance is ***complete.***

    EXAMPLE: Texas Tim offers Cowboy Chris $5,000 if he can ride one of Texas Tim's wild horses for 30 seconds. Cowboy Chris jumps on one of the horses and starts riding. After 10 seconds, Texas Tim yells, "I revoke!" Because an offer for a unilateral contract can only be accepted by completed performance, Cowboy Chris still has to ride the horse for another 20 seconds to accept the offer and create an enforceable contract.

    ii. An offeree who elects to begin performance as a mode of acceptance must notify the offeror within a "reasonable time" of such commenced effort or else the offeror may treat his or her offer as having lapsed before acceptance.

    iii. **Old common law:** Under the old rule, because an offeror may revoke an offer prior to proper acceptance, the offeror could revoke at any time before the performance was complete.

    iv. **Modern rule:** Modernly, the offer becomes irrevocable once the offeree begins performance. Restatement (Second) Section 45.

    EXAMPLE: Alice asks Jorge to paint her house. Jorge paints the entire house, and just as he is finishing up the last few paint strokes, she grabs his brush away and yells, "I revoke! I don't have to pay!" While Jorge still has to finish painting the house, Alice cannot revoke the offer, nor can she try to stop him from completing performance.

    v. **Mere preparation:** Preparing to perform is not enough to render the offer irrevocable.

    EXAMPLE: As in the example above, Alice asks Jorge to paint her house. Jorge buys paint, some new brushes, and a new tarp. Before he starts to actually paint the house, Alice tells Jorge that she has decided to paint her house herself. Since Jorge was merely preparing to perform, the revocation is effective.

D. CONSIDERATION

1. **Definition:** "Consideration" is defined as a bargained-for exchange of something of legal value. This thing of legal value can either a benefit or a detriment. Importantly, courts do not generally question the adequacy of the consideration, and the value of the consideration does not necessarily have to be economic.

2. **The Bargained-for Exchange Element**

   a. **Exchange:** It is necessary that the consideration proffered by each party be in exchange for the other's consideration. Thus, two independent promises that are unrelated will not constitute consideration.

   b. **Motive is irrelevant:** It does not matter what the motives are of the persons exchanging promises.

      i. Thus, even if a person was already planning to do or refrain from doing something, a promise to act in that way will still constitute consideration if made in exchange for other valid consideration.

3. **Gifts Distinguished From Consideration**

   a. If one party bestows a gift on another, an item of substantial value may change ownership. However, gifts are not consideration because the bargained-for exchange element is missing.

      i. The test is whether the act or forbearance benefits the gift-giver in any way. If it does, a court may consider a "gift" to be sufficient consideration to create a contract.

      ii. A restriction on a gift will not constitute consideration. Because the person who received the gift had no right to the gift, the restriction is not a legal detriment to the person giving the gift.

      iii. **Bargain favored over gift:** In doubtful cases, the objective theory of contract formation favors the finding of a bargain if the offer has induced the offeree to change position in a way that was both foreseeable to the offeror and detrimental to the offeree.

4. **Situations Involving no Consideration**

   In the following situations, there is no consideration to support a contract.

   a. **Past payment or value:** Prior completed payments or transfers of things of value do not constitute consideration. The crucial element of bargain is missing if the promisor is acting based on a service or benefit conferred by the promisee in the past. The bargain element requires a conscious exchange at the time the promise is given.

      EXAMPLE: Sven offers Mick "$500 in consideration for the good work you did for me last year." Under these circumstances, there is no consideration supporting Sven's offer.

   b. **Pre-existing duty not consideration:** Traditionally, agreement to perform a pre-existing duty is not consideration.

EXAMPLE: Officer Pascarella is called to the scene of a burglary. As Officer Pascarella takes the victim's statement, she says, "I'll pay you $100 if you catch the guy!" There is no consideration to support the victim's offer because Officer Pascarella, as a police officer, already has a pre-existing duty to apprehend the burglar.

i. **Existing debts:** An agreement to pay a portion of an existing valid debt is not consideration to support a contract. However, an agreement to pay a debt that is no longer enforceable can constitute valid consideration.

ii. **Modifications of existing contracts:** A modification of an existing contract where only one party changes his or her obligations may fail for lack of consideration. Generally, new consideration is required to modify a contract under the common law.

   (a) **Equitable modifications may be consideration:** In certain situations where a party to a contract requires additional time, money, or a relaxation of performance standards to complete his or her duties under a contract, a modification to the existing contract can count as consideration if:

   (1) The party making the request had made a good faith attempt to perform his or her contract duty, and

   (2) He or she met with unforeseen and unforeseeable difficulties that threatened substantial hardship unless an adjustment was made.

   (i) If both of these factors are present, a concession by the other party is binding, and he or she would be equitably estopped from later seeking to avoid honoring it by claiming a lack of consideration.

   EXAMPLE: On May 1, Tito agrees to dig a new fish pond in Jessica's backyard in time for her husband's birthday on June 16. Tito gets halfway done when two weeks of torrential rains make it impossible for him to finish the job by the 16th. He asks Jessica for an extension until May 30. She agrees. The original contract has now been modified with the new completion date.

c. **UCC solution:** Under UCC 2-209(1), parties to an existing contract are free to modify its terms, and such modifications do not require any further consideration to be binding.

   i. While the reason prompting the modification need not be unforeseeable, the modification demand must have been made in "good faith." (See the above entry for Requirements and Output Contracts for a definition of "good faith.") While the other party does not have to agree to the modification, if he or she does agree, the modification is binding.

d. **Accord and satisfaction:** This is a "modification" or settlement of an existing claim where a creditor agrees to accept less than what the debtor actually owes the creditor. The "accord" is the settlement agreement, and the "satisfaction" is the rendition of the new performance.

    i. If a creditor asserts a payment obligation that the debtor contests in good faith, the creditor's claim is **unliquidated.** "Unliquidated" means that the monetary value of the debt is unfixed and uncertain. This is the opposite of a "liquidated" debt. Here, if the debtor has a good faith belief that the debt the creditor is claiming is wrong, the amount of the debt is uncertain because the two sides are in dispute.

    ii. **The accord:** In order to have an accord and satisfaction, there must be a good faith dispute between the debtor and creditor. This dispute may involve the binding nature of the debt, the amount owed, the time of payment, or the type of alleged obligation. Secondly, the parties must make an agreement whereby the debtor promises to make a payment and the creditor promises to modify the original claim.

        (a) The debtor's position need not be a certain winner in litigation. It is sufficient if he or she has it in good faith, and a reasonable person would consider the issue debatable.

    iii. The satisfaction: This is the performance of the terms of the accord (for example, the debtor makes the promised payment and the creditor executes a written release of the original claim).

        (a) Upon satisfaction, the original debt is discharged.

    iv. **Status of the original creditor's claim pending satisfaction:** Once the disputed debt has been reduced to an accord, the original claim is suspended.

        (a) If satisfaction is accomplished, it is discharged.

        (b) If the debtor breaches the accord by refusing to honor its terms, the aggrieved creditor may choose between two causes of action.

            (1) He or she may assert that the original claim is now revived (and take his or her chances of winning a court case challenging the debtor's original grounds for the dispute), or,

            (2) He or she may commence an action for breach of the accord and ask a court to enforce the debtor's modified promise. While this is likely to be worth less, it might be easier to win because it is free from the dispute that surrounded the original claim.

e. **Token consideration:** Although nominal consideration still appears in many contracts, token consideration or sham consideration will not make an otherwise unenforceable gift enforceable as a contract. In such situations, the court will look to the overall substance of the agreement and find that no contract was formed.

f. **Moral consideration:** A moral obligation is not consideration because it also lacks the element of bargain and, for that reason, is not "valuable" because the bargain element is missing.

EXAMPLE: Bob's boss tells him that he will receive a big bonus this year because of all the good work Bob has done. Bob is justifiably happy and excited about the extra money. Without more, this statement is unenforceable for lack of consideration.

g. **Illusory promise:** If, at the formation stage of the contract, one of the parties does not incur a legal detriment because he or she retains an unlimited election to perform or not, his or her promise is illusory.

EXAMPLE: Woodrow promises to buy Theodore's antique bat for $2,000. Theodore responds, "I promise to sell you the bat unless I decide to change my mind." Since Theodore has the unlimited discretion to change his mind and not sell Woodrow the bat, there is no consideration to support the agreement because Theodore hasn't really promised to do anything.

   i. **Performance cures illusory promises:** If a party who retained complete discretion over whether he or she would perform does in fact perform, his or her complete performance cures the lack of consideration that had previously defeated the formation of a contract.

      (a) At the moment the discretionary performance has been tendered, the other party is contractually bound to carry out the terms of his or her own promise.

      (b) However, if an obligation is illusory, part performance does not cure the want of consideration, and the other party remains at liberty to ignore it while refusing his or her own performance.

      EXAMPLE: Rishmil offers to sell Frank all the books in his law library for $3,000. Frank agrees to buy the library unless he changes his mind. Rishmil delivers a few of the books, and Frank gives him $100. Rishmil brings another load of books, and Frank decides he doesn't want to buy the library after all. At this point, any alleged contract is unenforceable for lack of consideration.

   ii. **Contract obligations of minors and mentally disabled adults:** A person must have the capacity to enter into a contract, and under the law, minors and mentally disabled adults do not have such a capacity. In most states, a minor is a person under 18 years of age. While attempts to enter into such contracts are not illusory, the contractual promises of minors and mentally disabled adults are voidable. "Voidable" means that the attempted contract is in effect unless the minor or mentally disabled adult chooses to exercise his or her rights to terminate the agreement (on the other hand, a contract unsupported by consideration is "void," meaning there was no contract in the first place and neither party can enforce the relationship).

(a) **Necessaries:** However, a minor or mentally disabled adult is liable for "necessaries." "Necessaries" include food, shelter, clothing, and anything else necessary for the person's health, comfort, or education. Even so, the minor or mentally disabled adult will only be liable for the reasonable value of those services.

EXAMPLE: 16-year-old Britta is driving home from her grandmother's house when a sudden blizzard shuts down the roadway. She pulls over and checks into the Memory Motel. Realizing that Britta has no place else to go, the Memory Motel charges her four times the normal room rate. In this case, since a room is a "necessary," Britta is liable for the cost of the room, but only at its normal rate.

iii. **Conditional promises:** Conditional promises are not illusory if the promisor lacks the power to prevent the satisfaction of the condition.

(a) Such promises carry with them the elements of valuable consideration even if the odds of the conditional liability ever occurring are quite long.

EXAMPLE: Tobias offers to sell Sofia his beloved farm. However, Sofia has had several years of financial problems, has been unemployed for four years, has declared bankruptcy three times, and owes $125,000 on her credit cards. The sales agreement authorizes Tobias to check Sofia's credit score and cancel the agreement if Sofia's score is not over 760. Although Sofia's financial circumstances make such a score highly unlikely, this condition does not make the promise illusory.

5. **Legal Detriment**

a. **Basic concept:** Part of the idea of consideration is the idea of legal detriment. Unless there is "legal detriment" on both sides of an exchange, there is no contractual relationship.

b. **Legal detriment defined:** Each party to the exchange must change his or her legal rights or liabilities by a promise, act, or forbearance.

i. In a bilateral bargain, each of the exchanged promises or sets of promises must obligate the respective promisor to undertake some act which, but for this bargain, he or she was not legally obligated to perform.

ii. If the subject matter of the exchange features a promise to forbear some act or course of conduct, it must be an act which, but for this bargain, the promisor was legally at liberty to pursue.

EXAMPLE: William's uncle promises to pay William $5,000 if he refrains from drinking, smoking, swearing, or gambling until he turns 25. While refraining from these things might actually benefit William's health and well-being, the fact that he gives up his legal right to do these things counts as a legal detriment sufficient to constitute legal consideration. *See Hamer v. Sidway, 124 N.Y. 538 (1891).*

c. **Economic adequacy not relevant:** Bargained-for legal detriment, and not any economic factor, imparts "value" to valuable consideration.

   i. As long as any element of bargained-for legal detriment can be identified on both sides of the exchange, courts are not interested in identifying economic gain from the contract.

   ii. Thus, the adequacy of the consideration is left to the judgment of the parties, not the courts.

   EXAMPLE: In the example above, William's uncle receives a sufficient benefit simply by having William fulfill his expressed wishes.

d. **Promises to forbear from litigation:** Courts have long recognized that the threat or initiation of groundless litigation can be an effective terror tactic that has frequently prompted the victim to buy his or her peace.

   i. **Settlements:** Courts therefore favor out-of-court settlements.

   ii. **Old rule:** The early rule was that a promise to forbear to sue was consideration only if the party making it had a subjective good faith belief in the merit of the claim and it was at least legally colorable (meaning that a reasonable person could believe in its validity).

   iii. **Modern rule:** The modern rule, embodied in Restatement (Second) Section 74, is more tolerant of bargains that preclude or dispose of litigation.

      (a) Under this rule, the promise to forbear or abandon the prosecution of a legal claim is valuable consideration, even if it is uncertain, as long as the party making the give up claim has an honest, subjective belief in the claim's merit.

E. **ALTERNATIVES TO CONSIDERATION**

   1. **Revival of Discharged Obligations:** Some legal obligations can be discharged through a statute of limitations or a bankruptcy.

a. **No new consideration required:** Common law courts have long held that a new promise concerning that discharged obligation is enforceable without new consideration.

b. **Terms of revived promise:** Any revived obligation is on the terms of the new promise.

c. **Necessity of writing:** Some states require that the new promise to pay the debt be in writing.

d. **Revival of voidable contracts:** As stated above, promises of minors and mentally disabled adults are "voidable," meaning that such people may choose not to carry out their obligations under the contract.

   i. **Ratification:** Even after a minor or mentally disabled adult has chosen to void a contract, the minor or mentally disabled adult can make a new promise to uphold his or her end of the bargain after he or she has reached the age of legal majority (usually 18) or has recovered from the mental disability. In this case, the voided obligation has been "ratified." This ratification can be either express or by conduct.

   EXAMPLE: Scooter, a professional skateboarder, signs an endorsement contract with Wicked Cool Boards when he is 16 years old. Three weeks after his 18th birthday, Scooter cashes a $10,000 check from Wicked. He keeps performing under the contract, but decides he can get a better deal with another company six months later. At this point, he has ratified the original agreement, and can no longer try to void it by claiming he was a minor when the contract was signed. *See In re The Score Board Inc., 238 B.R. 585 (D.N.J. 1999).*

   ii. **No new consideration needed:** As such, it is enforceable according to the terms of the new promise without new consideration.

2. **Special Rule for Enforcement of Promises Against an Estate:** Some courts have held that an estate is liable to continue payments made pursuant to a promise only supported by a moral obligation when all of the following criteria have been satisfied:

   a. the deceased promisor had received a material benefit during his or her lifetime that motivated the subsequent promise,

   b. the promisee thereafter began performance according to the terms of his promise,

   c. the promisor died without ever evidencing an intention to repudiate the promise, and

     d. there were no superior moral claimants to the benefits of his or her estate.

        i. **Restatement position:** Restatement (Second) Section 86 advocates a cautious approach toward enforcing promises grounded on moral obligation.

        (a) The basic requirement is that the promisor must have acted in recognition of the receipt of some prior benefit from the promisee.

        (b) However, liability is generated only to the extent "necessary to prevent injustice."

        (c) Subsection (2) adds a further qualification: The promise is not binding if the promisee conferred the benefit as a gift or, for other reasons, the promisor has not been unjustly enriched.

3. **Promissory Estoppel:** In the event that there is no consideration to support a contract, the agreement can still be enforced under the doctrine of promissory estoppel.

    a. There are three elements to promissory estoppel under Restatement (Second): Section 90

       i. The promisor should reasonably expect his or her promise to induce reliance,

      ii. The promise does induce in fact the promisee's detrimental reliance, and

     iii. Justice requires enforcement of the promise.

> **EXAMPLE:** Amie agrees to buy Maria's old mansion in order to turn the land into an amusement park. They sign an agreement in which Amie promises to obtain a loan for the new construction. Following the signing, Amie urges Maria to demolish the mansion to make room for the new park. Maria demolishes the mansion, but Amie is unable to find a lender willing to lend her any money and attempts to get out of the agreement. At this point, Maria is entitled to recover under promissory estoppel for her foreseeable, definite, and substantial reliance on the contract. *See Wheeler v. White, 398 S.W.2d 93 (1965).*

II. DEFENSES TO CONTRACT FORMATION

A. OVERVIEW:

1. **Defenses Fall Into Five General Categories:**

    a. Defective formation

    b. Capacity

c. Societal prohibition

d. Coercion/deception

e. Form

Layered on top of those categories are two other contractual concepts: real versus personal defenses.

2. **Real Defenses:** Any defense which, if established, would render the attempted contract void.

   a. Put simply, there never was a contract.

   b. Real defenses may be asserted at any time.

3. **Personal Defenses:** These do not preclude the formation of a contract.

   a. However, if asserted in a timely manner, they render the obligations of the party asserting the defense "voidable." See the contracts of minors and mentally disabled adults above.

   b. Personal defenses do not arise unless they are asserted by the party who has the defense.

   c. Third persons may not raise them, and a court will not take independent notice of their existence.

   d. Personal defenses may not be asserted against an assignee of a contract obligation who paid value for the assignment and had neither notice nor knowledge of the defect. See Assignments and Delegation below.

B. **FORMATION AS A DEFENSE:** Any defect in the formation of a contract may be used in litigation to avoid liability.

   1. **Ambiguity as a Defense:** Ambiguity arises when the parties form a contract using a word or phrase which has more than one reasonable meaning.

      a. **Different meaning:** To assert ambiguity, each party must attach a different meaning to the ambiguous term.

      b. **Essential term:** If the ambiguity does not extend to an essential term, there is still a contract because the agreement does not go against the reasonable commercial expectations of the parties.

      c. **Attribution of fault:** If an essential term is ambiguous, formation is precluded unless fault can be isolated in one of the parties.

i. **Equal responsibility:** If the parties are either equally at fault or equally blameless in failing to define a word or phrase that has more than one reasonable meaning, no contract is formed.

ii. **One party at fault:** If one of the parties is at fault and the other is innocent, a contract is formed.

(a) **Meaning attributed:** The innocent party's meaning is read in to the ambiguous term.

EXAMPLE: Big Mike promises to "take care of" Al if Al helps Big Mike write his memoirs. Here, Big Mike's promise is too ambiguous to be enforceable. *See Baer v. Chase, 392 F.3d 609 (3d Cir. 2004).*

2. **Mistake:** In mistake cases, the problem is that the words do not accurately convey the parties' subjective intent.

a. **Mistakes of the parties:** There are two types of mistake: mutual mistake, where both parties are mistaken about some essential term, and unilateral mistake, where only one party is mistaken.

b. **Mutual mistake:** A mutual mistake occurs when both parties to the contract are mistaken about some essential term, usually during the formation stage.

i. **Two factors govern judicial reaction to such fact patterns:** (1) the significance of the mutual error and, (2) the point in time at which it is discovered.

ii. **Mutual mistake must go to the "very heart of the exchange:"** If it does, each party may invoke it as a basis for avoiding the obligations of the fatally flawed bargain. Restatement (Second) Sec. 152.

EXAMPLE: Yo Yo agrees to buy an antique Stradivarius violin from Branford. After Yo Yo brings the violin home, he discovers it is not a real Stradivarius. When Yo Yo calls Branford, he claims that he thought it was a Stradivarius. Since the fact that the violin is not a Stradivarius goes to the heart of the exchange, the contract is void by mutual mistake.

iii. **Mutual mistakes of minor consequence are legally irrelevant:** If the mutual mistake of assumed fact does not involve a fundamental assumption of both parties regarding either the subject matter or rights of the owner, it is not a threat to the bargain. In this case, the contract will be enforced.

EXAMPLE: Using the above example, assume the Stradivarius is real. However, Yo Yo thought Branford would restring and tune it before turning the violin over. Branford thought he was just selling the Stradivarius as is. If Branford gives Yo Yo the violin without restringing or tuning it, such a mistake does not go to the heart of the bargain.

iv. **Future or unknowable conditions or events:** While a mistake about a present fact can invalidate an exchange, a mistake in guessing what will happen in the future is never grounds for relief.

   EXAMPLE: Believing gas prices will reach $10 a gallon, Teresa buys a truck full of gasoline at $8 per gallon. A month later, prices drop to $2 per gallon. Such a mistake can never be grounds to invalidate the contract.

v. **Timing:** A party seeking to overturn an executed contract must be prepared to prove that the mistake was discovered within a reasonable time following execution of the contract.

vi. **Equity of recission:** The proper remedy in the case of a mutual mistake is recission. "Recission" means the contract is canceled, and neither party retains rights against the other.

c. **Unilateral mistake:** If, at the formation stage, only one of the parties is mistaken with respect to material facts concerning the bargain, there is no immediate threat to formation.

   i. **Two types:** There are two types of unilateral mistake.

   (a) **Mechanical miscalculations:** Typical examples involve a bidder who makes an error in math, misreads plans or specifications, or fails to carry a decimal point. If, at the formation stage, a party miscalculates, whether such a miscalculation precludes formation or provides a defense to enforcing the terms of the resulting bargain depends upon the state of mind of the other, non-mistaken party.

   (b) **Expectation:** If the non-mistaken party has formed a commercially reasonable expectation upon the terms to which the blundering party apparently consented, the blundering party is bound.

   (1) Remember that a cardinal principle of modern contract law is to protect the commercially reasonable expectations of the parties.

   (2) However, the law does not sanction the behavior of a party who would take advantage of what he or she knows or should know was the miscalculation of another. Importantly, one party is not allowed to "snap up" a mistake made by another party.

   (3) **Objective test:** In order to qualify as possessing a commercially reasonable expectation, the non-mistaken party must have been reasonable in his or her mistake and subjectively unaware that the bargain with the other party was "too good to be true."

(4) **Errors of business judgment:** A party guilty of only an error in business judgment will be bound by the contract, even if the other party knows that the mistaken party has made such an error.

d. **Mistakes of third-party intermediaries:** If, at the formation stage, one party employs some third party to handle communication of the offer or acceptance, the potential for mistake is broadened to include those mistakes made by the intermediary.

    i. Whether a third-party's mistake provides a bar to formation or defense to enforcement of the terms actually communicated will turn upon whether the recipient of such a message has developed a reasonable expectation.

        (a) If the recipient knows, or as a reasonable person ought to know, that the message cannot be accurate, he or she has no reasonable expectation predicated on its content.

        (b) In such circumstances, the sender may avoid liability on the terms communicated by either denying that a bargain was objectively formed or claiming a personal defense against its obligations.

        (c) However, if the recipient has formed an innocent and reasonable expectation based upon the third party's words or actions, the sender is bound by the terms communicated.

C. **PRECEDENT BREACH:** If, subsequent to formation, one of the parties materially breaches the terms of his or her promise, the other party need not perform.

D. **DEFENSES ROOTED IN SOCIETAL OBJECTION TO THE BARGAIN**

1. **Illegality:** If the subject matter of the bargain or the participation of one or both of the parties is "illegal," whether the contract is enforceable depends upon the time and nature of the offense.

a. **Time:** Whether illegality will (1) preclude formation, (2) discharge obligations on a theory of excusable non-performance, or (3) render the attempted bargain void depends upon whether the illegality existed before and after the attempted contract.

    i. **Prior illegality:** If the illegality existed prior to the attempted formation, the bargain is void.

    ii. **Effect on an offer:** As stated above, if an offer becomes illegal after it is made, the offer is invalid.

    iii. **Effect on a fully formed contract:** Illegality that arises after formation but prior to performance discharges the parties' duties of performance under the theory of impossibility. Basically, performance under the contract is now "impossible" because a party's performance would violate the law.

iv. **UCC policy on substituted performance:** Under UCC 2-614, if an agreed-upon means or manner of payment fails because of domestic or foreign governmental regulation, the seller may withdraw unless the buyer can provide a commercially equivalent and legal substitute payment.

   (a) Such policy is consistent with the UCC's desire to promote the formation and performance of commercial agreements.

E. UNCONSCIONABLE BARGAINS

1. **Definition:** An unconscionable bargain is one that is so unfair and grossly one-sided as to threaten important social values. The object of contract remedies is compensation of the aggrieved party, not punishment of the party in breach.

   a. **Unconscionable terms:** In general, freedom of the marketplace allows the parties substantial discretion in setting the terms of their bargain.

   b. **Limitations:** Most states, as well as provisions of the UCC, determine that certain important protections are not to be diminished or eliminated in the context of a bargain.

      i. **Stipulated remedies clauses:** If, at the formation stage, the parties include a stipulated remedy that goes beyond compensation, the clause is unconscionable. See UCC 2-718(1). These are known as unenforceable penalty clauses.

      EXAMPLE: Sunny's Cupcakes agrees to provide Carol's Catering as many cupcakes as Carol's may need in its catering business. The contract provides that if Sunny's fails to provide enough cupcakes, Sunny must pay Carol's $10 million in damages. Since this clause is unlikely to bear any relation to actual damages, the clause is an unenforceable penalty.

      ii. **Limitations on consequential damages:** Similar to a penalty clause, UCC 2-719(3) states that any attempt to *limit* the award of consequential damages for breach of a contract in the sale of consumer goods is prima facie unconscionable. Courts find that consumers are unlikely to have the power or inclination to bargain regarding such terms, and public policy demands that the producers of consumer goods cannot so easily protect themselves from damages caused by their defective goods.

      EXAMPLE: Tim's Toasters is a manufacturer of toasters for large retail stores. Inside the toaster box is a clause that states, "Tim's Toasters' liability for any damages is limited to a refund of the cost of this toaster." Such a clause is unconscionable, since the potential damages from a defective toaster could be much more than the toaster's cost (for example, if the toaster caused a fire that burned down the consumer's home).

(a) Such limitations in other contracts for the sale of goods may be unconscionable, but there is no presumption that this is so.

c. **The attempted disclaimer of warranties:** UCC 2-314 and 2-315 create implied warranties that any goods sold shall be merchantable and, if the buyer has permitted the seller to select goods to meet the buyer's disclosed requirements or needs, that they are fit for that purpose.

    i. UCC 2-316 permits modification or exclusion of these implied warranties.

    ii. However, consumer protection legislation in many states has made the attempted elimination of such implied warranties unconscionable.

2. **Consequences of Substantive Unconscionability:** Unlike most defenses, which either preclude formation or render the obligations of a contract voidable, the remedy for unconscionability is to sever (or eliminate) the unconscionable clause or clauses while enforcing the balance of the bargain. See UCC 2-302(1).

F. **PUBLIC POLICY AS A DEFENSE:** Even if not illegal, some contracts may be deemed to violate public policy, either because of their subject matter or because one of the parties should not participate in such an agreement.

1. **The Concept of "Public Policy":** If, at the formation stage, one of the parties seeks to gain an objective which threatens the values or institutions of society, a court will declare an offense to public policy.

a. **Examples:**

    i. Covenants in restraint of trade offend society's interest in the freedom to exploit talent and economic resources.

    ii. Covenants that directly encourage or promote tortious interference with a non-contracting party.

    iii. Contingent fee agreements for obtaining the passage of special legislation or rulings by government agencies because such agreements tend to promote the corruption of the political process, if not the personnel of government.

b. **Consequences of determination that the terms of a bargain violate public policy:** Just as courts have remained flexible in their formulation of the offense, they have remained pragmatic as to the nature of an appropriate response.

    i. Faced with a proven offense to public policy, a reviewing court may (1) hold the entire agreement voidable or (2) simply sever the offensive term or terms, while leaving the balance of the agreement to stand.

G. DEFENSES BASED ON DECEPTION

1. **The Common Law Distinguishes Three Types of Fraud:**

   a. real fraud,

   b. fraud in the inducement, and

   c. fraud in the execution.

2. **Real Fraud Defined:** Any deceptive strategy that has the consequence of preventing the victim from realizing that a contract is even in contemplation.

   EXAMPLE: Steven asks Corwin, a major movie star, to sign an "autograph." Steven hands Corwin a folded piece of paper. Corwin signs without unfolding it. It turns out the paper is actually a contract to star in Steven's new movie. Under these circumstances, Corwin has not promised to star in Steven's new movie.

3. **Fraud In the Inducement Defined:** Where a victim is aware that a contract is in contemplation, but his or her consent to the bargain is seduced by lies or deliberate half-truths.

   a. Fraud in the inducement is a personal defense, meaning the victim has the choice whether or not to void the contract.

      EXAMPLE: Attorney Al believes that Slippy McGee has a weak slip-and-fall case against a local grocery store. Even so, Attorney Al tells Slippy he thinks the case is "great" and a "sure winner" in order to get Slippy to sign a contract with him to litigate the case.

4. **Fraud In the Execution Defined:** The victim trusts fraudulent party to reduce the an oral agreement to writing and, acting on his or her assurance that he or she has faithfully done so, signs that writing without reading it. Later, the victim discovers the writing is different from the oral agreement.

   a. **Negligence of victim as a bar to judicial relief:** Under these circumstances, wishing to emphasize the importance of reading documents before signing them, courts have refused to allow such victims to recover.

H. DEFENSE BASED ON DURESS

1. **Duress Defined:** Duress is coercive force used or threatened against the victim to induce consent.

   a. There are two types of duress recognized at common law: physical and economic duress.

      i. **Physical duress:** Actual force or threat of death or bodily harm.

    ii. **Threatening a third party:** Coercive acts or threats of such acts to a third party can be deemed physical duress.

      (a) They are actionable if directed at those near or dear to the victim and their consequence was to "overmaster the will of the victim."

    iii. **Consequences of physical duress:** Evidence of physical duress will void the contract, and the proper remedy will be recission.

    EXAMPLE: Big Tony tells Schmidt, "Sign this construction contract, or I'll break your son's legs." A contract signed under these circumstances is void.

  b. **Economic duress:** Economic duress is far more problematic for the victim.

    i. **Elements:** To show economic duress, the victim must prove each of the following elements:

      (a) The other party was guilty of some illicit act or threat of an illicit act against the victim's property or business interests that created the pressure upon the intended victim.

      (b) This illicit pressure left the victim with no reasonable alternative but to submit to the terms insisted upon by the other party.

      (c) **Lack of economic duress:** Economic duress does not exist in a fact pattern where one of the parties is in desperate need of the subject matter and the other takes advantage of that to drive a harsh, one-sided bargain.

      EXAMPLE: Because of a medical emergency, Melvin needs to sell his house to raise some quick cash. Aware of his problem, Lily offers to buy Melvin's house at 40 percent less than the listed price.

      (d) **Consequences of economic duress:** In such circumstances, the victim may properly refuse to perform. However, if the bargain has been fully performed, rescission and restitution are both appropriate remedies. "Restitution" occurs when a court orders the other party to restore the exchanged property or its monetary value.

  c. **Undue influence:** The defense of undue influence is established when a victim is able to convince a court that he or she has been subjected to "overpersuasive pressure" by the other party.

    i. **Consequences of undue influence:** If the bargain that resulted from the assertion of over-persuasive tactics has not been performed yet, the victim may properly refuse to perform. However, if the bargain has been fully performed, some courts have allowed rescission.

I. ADHESION CONTRACTS

1. **Definition:** An adhesion contract is a take-it-or-leave-it proposition extended by a party in a superior bargaining position to a weaker party who needs the subject matter. Usually, adhesion contracts come about when one party has another party sign a "standard" or "form" contract.

   EXAMPLE: Caitlyn goes to Noah's car dealership to buy a new car. She finds a car she likes, and Noah presents her with a standard contract. The standard contract contains many clauses regarding repair, warranty, and other issues, leaving only the price open for negotiation. Caitlyn signs the deal and drives the new car off the lot. Ten days later, the steering wheel falls off, causing Caitlyn to be injured in an accident. When Caitlyn sues Noah, Noah points to a clause buried in the fine print of the contract that limits Noah's liability to replacement parts. In this case, the limitation of liability would be ineffective. *See Henningsen v. Bloomfield Motors Inc., 161 A.2d 69 (1960).*

2. **Unconscionability:** Adhesion contracts are not per se unconscionable, but neither are they "bargains" in the true sense of the word.

3. **Oppression:** "Oppression" occurs when the dominant party proposes terms that are grossly out of line with market expectations or that seek to curtail protections otherwise accorded parties, especially consumers.

4. **Usury or Inflated Prices:** Commonly deemed "unconscionable" are price or credit terms that greatly exceed general market expectations or statutory ceilings.

5. **Collections:** When a creditor is particularly brutal in trying to collect a debt, he or she may be deemed oppressive, especially if the consumer is unsophisticated.

6. **Unfair Surprise:** "Unfair surprise" occurs when the dominant party uses terms that are not in accordance with customary marketplace expectations and does not clearly disclose these terms to the other party at the formation stage.

7. **Consequences of Unconscionability:** If an agreement is unconscionable, Courts can:

   a. refuse to enforce the entire contract,

   b. limit the application of the unconscionable clause or clauses while enforcing the remainder of the bargain, or

   c. condition judgment for the dominant party upon its ability to prove that the weaker party was actually aware of and understood the clause or clauses and subjectively assented to their terms.

J. STATUTE OF FRAUDS

1. **Definition:** The Statute of Frauds provides that certain categories of contracts will not be enforceable unless they are in writing and signed by the party against whom enforcement is sought. Not with standing this apparently clear rule, the Statute of Frauds is rife with exceptions.

2. **Oral Contracts Otherwise Allowed:** Unless the subject matter of a contract is within the Statute of Frauds, an oral contract is enforceable.

3. **Typical Subjects:** Although the list can vary by state, in general, the subjects covered include:

   a. **Contracts that cannot be performed within one year:** An agreement that, by its terms, cannot be performed within one year from the date of formation. However, if there is any possibility—*no matter how unlikely*—that performance could occur within a year, the subject matter is not within the Statute, even if performance in fact takes longer than a year.

      EXAMPLE 1: Giorgio signs an employment contract to work for Big Motors for two years.

      EXAMPLE 2: Super Insurance orally agrees to insure Patrick's house against tornados for six years, and Patrick agrees to pay a weekly premium. Since it is possible, even if unlikely, that a tornado might destroy Patrick's house and Patrick might pay up the entire policy within one year, the agreement does not fall under the Statute of Frauds. *See Rest. 2d, Sec. 130.*

   b. **A promise to answer for the debt or default of another:** Contracts involving a guarantee or suretyship must be in writing and signed by the promisor.

   c. **Marriage:** An agreement made upon consideration of marriage must be in writing and signed by the promisor.

   d. **Real property agreements:** The sale or transfer of an interest in land must be in writing.

      i. Agreements for the lease of real property for one year or less are normally not within the Statute.

   e. **Executors and administrators:** An agreement made by an executor or administrator of an estate to personally pay for the decedent's debts.

   f. **Wills and trusts:** An agreement which, by its terms, is not to be performed within the lifetime of the promisor must be in writing.

   g. **The sale of goods:** Contracts for the sale of goods for the price is $500 or more fall within the UCC 2-201[1], the UCC's special formulation of the Statute of Frauds.

KAPLAN) *pmbr*

    i. As stated above, there are three important exceptions.

        (a) **Full performance and acceptance:** If the seller has tendered the goods and the buyer has accepted them, the buyer's oral promise to pay the agreed price is fully enforceable.

            (1) So, too, is the seller's oral promise to deliver goods if the buyer has submitted payment and the seller has retained it.

        (b) **Special order goods:** If the subject matter of an oral contract is goods made at the order of the buyer and not suitable for ordinary resale, the buyer's oral promise to pay for them is enforceable once the seller has made a substantial beginning in their manufacture or commitments for their procurement.

        (c) **Between two merchants:** If there is an oral agreement between two merchants, a written confirmation of the contract's terms sent by one party and received by the other who knows, or has reason to know, of its contents, satisfies the Statute unless written notice of objection is given within 10 days.

4. **Requirements of the Statute:** The essential terms of above-listed types of agreements must be in writing.

    a. **Essential terms defined:** The following are essential terms under the Statute of Frauds.

        i. The parties,

        ii. The subject matter,

        iii. The time for performance, and

        iv. The price.

    b. **Formality and intent:** The writing need not be formal or prepared with the subjective intention of satisfying the Statute.

        i. The writing or writings can be quite informal; for example, notes and letters are readily accepted.

        ii. Even a series of writings may be used if they are physically attached or refer to a writing bearing the signature of the party against whom enforcement is sought. For example, if the party to be charged pays by check, the signature on the check can be used to satisfy the Statute of Frauds.

        iii. **Signature need not be formal:** Modern cases regard a printed letterhead or a rubber stamp as sufficient.

5. **Consequences:** If the one party fails to satisfy the Statute, the other party may have a legal excuse not to perform.

   a. **Timely assertion:** If the party being sued does not raise a Statute of Frauds defense in a "timely manner," he or she waives it.

      i. Assertion is timely if it is contained in a responsive pleading (usually the answer to the complaining party's lawsuit).

6. **Third Parties:** Because the defense is personal in nature, the Statute of Frauds may not be raised or relied upon by third parties.

7. **Estoppel and the Statute of Frauds:** Some courts have applied both promissory and equitable estoppel concepts to preclude the party against whom enforcement is sought from asserting the Statute of Frauds as a defense.

   a. **Promissory estoppel:** If the a party specifically promised to reduce the oral contract to writing and breached that promise as well as the underlying oral contract, some courts have held that the other party may assert reliance and recover under promissory estoppel.

   b. **Equitable estoppel:** If the consequence of allowing a litigant to assert the Statute of Frauds would be to leave that party unjustly enriched, fundamental fairness will require that he or she be estopped from hiding behind the Statute.

      i. Other courts have even extended this doctrine to cases in which there was no enrichment of the party to be charged, but obvious impoverishment of the party who had relied on the oral contract.

   c. **Restatement position:** Restatement (Second) Sec. 139, adopts a middle course. It sanctions enforcement of the oral promise if:

      i. the promisor should have expected the promise to induce reliance on the part of the promisee or a third person,

      ii. there has been reliance, and

      iii. injustice cannot be avoided except by enforcement of the promise.

8. **Part Performance:** If one party sues for specific performance or injunctive relief, the court may accept proof of part performance by the other party of the terms of his or her oral promise as an evidentiary substitute for a signed writing.

   a. However, the performance must "unequivocally" refer to the contract and not merely the possibility of some understanding between the parties.

K. PAROL EVIDENCE RULE AND SIMILAR RULES

1. **The Rule Defined:** Evidence of a prior or contemporaneous agreement is inadmissible if it would vary or contradict the terms of a totally integrated writing.

2. **The Rule in Litigation:** The Parol Evidence Rule is a defense to the enforceability of a contract term. Once the Rule is invoked, the trial judge will make the following determinations:

   a. **Integrated writing:** Only written instruments intended by both parties as the final expression of the terms of their contract are protected by the Parol Evidence Rule.

      i. **Integration determined from the written instrument:** The most convenient way to reflect parties' intentions as to the writing is simply to state this intent in the body of the writing.

         (1) Such a recitation is customarily referred to as an "integration clause."

            EXAMPLE: A contract contains a clause that states, "This agreement is fully integrated."

      ii. **Integration determined from extrinsic evidence:** Relevant evidence may be introduced to establish that the parties regarded the written instrument as the final and complete embodiment of their contract.

      iii. **Lack of integration:** If the agreement is not integrated, it may be varied or contradicted by any extrinsic evidence which the court elects to credit.

   b. **Extrinsic evidence must be "parol":** Extrinsic evidence is any oral or written evidence which lies outside the four corners of the written instrument. However, the rule only excludes "parol" evidence.

      i. **Timing is relevant:** Evidence that would tend to prove a promise or understanding given or arrived at prior to or contemporaneous with the formation of the integrated writing is "parol" in nature and thus potentially excludable. The idea is that if the parties intended a promise or understanding to be contained in the final contract, they would have included it.

      ii. **Subsequent agreements:** Agreements that arise after the integrated writing are not covered by the Parol Evidence Rule and are therefore admissible.

3. **Forbidden Impact:** Parol evidence is precluded only if it would add to, vary, or contradict the content of the integrated writing. Again, it is the trial judge who determines if a proffer of parol evidence would have one of these forbidden impacts.

a. **Ambiguity:** Parol evidence may be freely used to clarify an ambiguity in the terms of the integrated writing. Ambiguity need not be evident on the face of the instrument.

b. **Creation of ambiguity:** Parol evidence may be used to clarify an ambiguity, not to create one.

c. **Trade dealings:** Parol evidence may be admitted to prove trade custom or course of dealings as between the parties.

d. **Defined terms:** Parol evidence may not be admitted to clarify a term which is defined within the integrated writing.

e. **Proof of fraud:** Evidence that otherwise would be barred by the Rule is still admissible to prove fraud or duress in making of the agreement.

f. **Conditions precedent:** Evidence showing that the entire agreement was subject to an oral or written condition precedent that had to be satisfied before it was to attain the status of a contract is admissible.

   EXAMPLE: Toshi, the owner of a sushi restaurant, contracts in writing with Fishco to buy 50 pounds of tuna. At the time the contract was signed, Toshi said orally to Fischo, "We have the understanding that Kifune, our chef, has to approve the quality of the fish before I pay you." If Toshi later refuses to accept and pay for the fish, evidence of the oral agreement for Kifune's approval is admissible to show the contract was subject to a condition precedent.

g. **Proof of partial integration:** If the parties intended the writing to govern certain, but not all, terms of the bargain, the Rule protects only those subjects intended to be completely covered. Consequently, the balance of the agreement may be freely contested by extrinsic evidence.

   i. **Traditional four corners test:** Courts used to require that the integrated writing appear to be incomplete within its "four corners." In such a case, a trial judge would look at the document only and determine whether it seemed complete on its face.

   ii. **The UCC position:** UCC 2-202 follows a more liberal approach. The official comment declares that the UCC rejects the assumption that because a writing has been worked out which is final on some matters, it is to be taken as including all the matters agreed upon.

4. **Existence of a Collateral Agreement and Its Terms:** In a partial integration fact pattern, the proffer of parol evidence is based on the theory that while the parties made one agreement, they intended that only certain of its terms appear in the integrated writing. They may then argue that the parties made a separate oral agreement at the same time as the written one.

a. **Limitations on the use of the collateral agreement exception:** If a party wants to introduce evidence of a collateral agreement, he or she must clear three hurdles:

    i. The evidence must prove the existence of a second agreement that is "collateral in form," meaning that it has a subject matter of lesser importance than the subject matter of the contract reflected in the integrated writing.

    ii. No term of the alleged collateral agreement may contradict any provision of the integrated writing.

    iii. The subject of the alleged collateral agreement must be sufficiently distinct from that of the integrated writing that it would be natural that persons in a writing frame of mind would not have included it as "part and parcel of a single bargain."

    EXAMPLE: The Caseys sign a written agreement to buy a beach house from the Abernathys. At the same time, Mr. Abernathy orally agrees to remove an abandoned bath house on the other side of the road. Here, evidence of the collateral agreement would not be allowed because taking down the bath house is so closely related to the sale of the property that one would expect it to be contained in the writing. *See Mitchell v. Lath, 160 N.E. 646 (N.Y. 1928).*

b. **Binding nature of collateral agreements:** Collateral agreements, to be binding, must have all the elements of an independent contract, including separate consideration.

III. CONDUCT BEFORE AND DURING A CONTRACT

A. CONDITIONS

1. **Conditions Defined:** A condition is a contingency that: (1) must be satisfied before the parties are obligated to perform, or (2) the happening of which will extinguish one or more contractual obligations.

2. **Conditions Precedent:** A condition precedent is any contingency that must be either satisfied or excused before one party must perform. Although there are no "magic words" to create a condition precedent, the test is whether one of the parties has basically stated that he or she will not be bound under the promise unless a specific condition occurs. See Parol Evidence on the previous page for an example.

3. **Conditions Concurrent:** The impact of a condition concurrent is the same as that of a condition precedent. It, too, has inserted some contingency that must either be satisfied or excused before the parties are obligated to perform.

    a. **Distinction:** The distinction between conditions precedent and concurrent has to do with scheduling the respective performances of the two parties.

      i. Satisfaction of a condition precedent excuses the performance of one party. It has no impact upon the duty of the other.

     ii. The term "conditions concurrent" is most often used when a contract provides for the exchange of one performance for another. If the contract fails to include a sequence of performance, most courts hold that performances capable of being performed at the same time are conditions concurrent to each other. For example, a buyer's duty to pay and a seller's duty to give the goods to the buyer are conditions concurrent. Generally, the buyer and seller make the exchanges simultaneously.

4. **If the Contract Is Silent as to Schedule of Respective Performances:** If the performance of one of the parties will take time, or requires several stages to accomplish, the party who must perform over time must perform before the other party is required to perform.

5. **Specified Condition:** If the terms of the bargain fix a date for one of the parties' performances, but say nothing with respect to the time of the other's performance, the party with the certain date must perform first. Otherwise, the other party will not be required to perform.

6. **Conditions Subsequent:** Conditions subsequent terminate what had, until the condition was triggered, been an enforceable duty of performance. If the terms of the bargain specify that a factual development will extinguish what had, until that moment, been a current requirement to perform, the condition is subsequent in nature.

    a. **Rarity:** Conditions subsequent are relatively rare, but they are present when one of the parties has declared to the other that he or she is not liable for performance if a certain fact occurs.

    EXAMPLE: Dalton signs a written agreement to buy Corinne's farm. Dalton intends to build a new apartment building on the land. In the contract, the parties include a clause that Dalton will not be liable under the contract if he fails to get the proper zoning permits. The town, which is trying to limit growth, decides not to give Dalton the necessary permits. At this point, Dalton's duty to buy the farm is discharged.

7. **Distinguishing Covenants from Conditions in a Contract:** The distinction between covenants and conditions is critical.

    a. **Covenants:** Covenants (promises) determine what must be performed in order to discharge contract duties.

      i. Thus, the failure of a promisor to perform the duties created by an unconditional covenant is a present breach of contract.

b. **Conditions:** Conditions determine when and if the duties defined in covenants must be performed.

i. If conditions are unsatisfied, there is no duty to perform. Because conditions occur outside of the parties' performance, failure to satisfy a condition is never a breach of contract.

8. **Intent of the Parties:** At the formation stage, a party is perfectly free to attach any conditions to his or her contractual duties.

9. **Consideration:** There doesn't have to be any consideration to support the promise as long as there is some possibility that the condition will be satisfied and the parties will be obligated to perform.

10. **Role of Business Customs:** If the bargain is between merchants, the customs, of the relevant market are useful in deciding whether a reasonable person would have appreciated the presence of a condition.

11. **Key Terms:** Certain terms or phrases indicate the presence of conditions. Terms such as "upon condition" are obviously best at alerting the other party. Others, such as "provided that," "unless," or even "if" may signal the introduction of a condition.

a. **Ambiguity:** If the phrase is ambiguous as to whether it is that of a covenant or a condition, in the interests of fairness, it will be interpreted as a covenant.

12. **Promissory Condition:** This term is used to describe a condition that is within the control of the promisor.

a. Such a promisor must use best efforts to achieve the objective of the bargain, and thus satisfy the condition. For example, in the example in Conditions Subsequent above, Dalton would be required to use his best efforts to acquire the correct zoning permits.

13. **Personal Satisfaction:** A contract calling for the personal satisfaction of the one of the parties as a condition precedent to performance may be valid under certain circumstances.

a. **Illusory construction disfavored:** In general, courts will not interpret contracts to obligate one party to pay only if he or she chooses to do so. Such a construction would defeat the entire goal behind contract formation.

b. **Good faith:** Where a condition is predicated on personal satisfaction, a good faith requirement is read in.

i. **Objective standard:** Even if the if a party says that he or she is not satisfied, objectively quantifiable attributes of operative fitness, mechanical utility, or structural completion will be evaluated under an objective, or "reasonable person," standard.

ii. **Subjective standard:** If the subject matter is "personal," or a subjective matter of taste or aesthetics, this term is literally construed. The party will not have to perform if, in good faith, he or she is not subjectively satisfied.

EXAMPLE: Countess Nevermind hires Van Ink, a famous portrait painter, to paint her portrait. The contract states that Countess Nevermind will pay for the painting only if she is personally satisfied. Van Ink paints an astonishingly beautiful portrait, but Countess Nevermind tells Van Ink she simply doesn't like his use of colors. Under these circumstances, Countess Nevermind is not liable to Van Ink, no matter what an objective observer would think of the portrait.

14. **Contract Calling for the Satisfaction of a Designated Third Party:** In order to avoid litigation, the parties to a contract will sometimes condition the contract on a third party's satisfaction. This arises most often in the construction industry, where the property owner's duty to make payment to the builder is conditioned upon a designated architect's certification that the builder's work is in compliance with plans and specifications.

a. **Limitations on the designated third party:** Courts are clear that such a third party must function in a strictly neutral fashion, and not as the partisan of either party.

i. **"Bad faith" defined:** Any attempt by the designated third party to determine satisfaction on grounds other than those stated by the terms of the contract is bad faith. There is no need for the injured party to prove malice.

ii. **Bad faith consequences:** If the third party acts in bad faith, the condition is excused and payment is required.

EXAMPLE: Stephen enters into a construction contract with Benny's Boat Builders for a new sailboat. According to the contract, the acceptance of the new sailboat is conditioned on Silas Mariner's approval of its seaworthiness. When the sailboat is completed, Silas fails to approve the perfectly seaworthy boat because he knows Stephen is in financial trouble. This is a clear example of bad faith, and Stephen remains obligated to pay for the boat.

b. **Gross error by designated third party:** Some courts excuse performance if the designated third party acts with gross disregard for the facts committed to his or her judgment.

B. SATISFACTION, EXCUSE, AND WAIVER

1. **Two Ways:** There are two ways in which a condition precedent or concurrent can be removed as a barrier to enforcement of the contract.

    a. **Satisfaction:** When the requisite condition is satisfied, the parties may require each other to perform.

        i. **Effect of substantial performance:** If one of the parties fails to perform one of his or her duties, as long as that party substantially performs the remainder the contract, a contract between the parties still forms. However, the other party will have a cause of action for the other party's breach.

            EXAMPLE: Elsa signs a written agreement with Kelly's Contractors to build a new home. Kelly's builds the home to all of the contract specifications, except it fails to use wiring made by Wendy's Wiring Inc., which was specified in the contract. The wiring it did use was comparable to Wendy's Wiring. In this case, there is still a contract, although Elsa can sue for Kelly's breach in using the wrong wiring. However, damages are likely to be minor. *See Jacob & Youngs v. Kent, 129 N.E. 889 (N.Y. 1921).*

        ii. **The UCC position:** The doctrine of substantial performance ***does not apply*** under UCC 2-601. Under the "perfect tender" doctrine, if the goods provided by the seller fail to conform to the contract in any way, the buyer can:

            (a) reject the whole, or

            (b) accept the whole, or

            (c) accept any commercial unit or units and reject the rest.

    b. **Excuse:** Where the parties agree to excuse the conditional requirement, the contract is enforceable even if the condition does not occur, and both parties must perform.

2. **Prevention:** If one of the parties intentionally tries to frustrate the satisfaction of the condition, the condition is excused and the contract is enforceable. Basically, the party trying to frustrate the condition is not allowed to profit from his or her actions.

3. **Waiver:** Waiver is the voluntary relinquishment of a known and appreciated right. There is no such thing as an accidental or inadvertent waiver.

    EXAMPLE: Tony enters into a contract with Tricia to buy her car. According to the contract's terms, Tricia will have the car washed and detailed before turning it over to Tony. When Tony goes to pick up the car, he discovers the car is still dirty. Tricia apologizes. Tony responds, "It's OK. Don't worry about it." At this point, Tony has waived his rights under the contract to have the car washed and detailed.

a. **Consequence of waiver:** Once a contract right has been waived, it cannot be unilaterally reclaimed. It is gone forever.

b. **Application to conditions:** Waiver can modify both covenants and conditions in a bargain.

    i. If a promisee knowingly accepts a less-than-perfect perfomance, the obligation is deemed to be modified.

    ii. Waiver can also excuse conditions precedent, concurrent, and subsequent.

c. **Partial waiver:** In an installment contract, it is possible for a party to limit his or her waiver to a single installment of the other's performance.

C. ESTOPPEL AND ANTICIPATORY REPUDIATION

1. **Estoppel:** If the advantaged party lets the other party know that a condition does not need to be satisfied, and the other party relies on this representation, the advantaged party cannot then insist upon satisfaction of the condition.

2. **Anticipatory Repudiation:** If, before performance is due, one of the parties makes it clear by word or act that he or she will not perform as promised, the other party can immediately sue for breach of the contract. Any renunciation has to be definite, defiant, unequivocal, and unyielding.

   EXAMPLE: Blind Pineapple, a famous blues singer, agrees to play a show at Chelsea's Casino on July 27. On June 16, Blind Pineapple calls up the casino and tells the manager he's found religion and there is no way he will ever play in a casino again. At this point, the casino can sue for breach immediately. Importantly, it does not have to wait for Blind Pineapple to fail to play on July 27 before initiating legal action.

3. **Option to Await the Due Date of Performance:** Although the aggrieved party can sue immediately, he or she can choose to delay responding to the notice of the breach and wait to see if the repudiating party does in fact perform under the original terms of the contract.

   a. **UCC position:** Under UCC 2-611, the repudiating party may retract the repudiation at any time before his or her performance is due unless the aggrieved party has materially changed position in detrimental reliance on the repudiation or indicated that he or she accepted the repudiation as final.

   b. **Mitigation:** As in the case of any other material breach, the aggrieved party is under a general duty to mitigate his or her damages. Consequently, under UCC 2-610, the non-repudiating party can only wait for a "commercially reasonable time" before bringing a suit for damages.

4. **Failure to Give Adequate Assurance of Performance:** When reasonable grounds for insecurity arise with respect to the future performance of the other party, the concerned party can ask for an adequate assurance of performance. If the other party fails to give the requested assurance within a reasonable time, such a failure is considered a repudiation, and the concerned party can cancel the contract. Reasonable grounds include falling behind in installment payments or defective deliveries made to other customers.

5. **UCC Position:** Under UCC 2-609, if one of the parties has reasonable grounds for insecurity, he or she can make a written demand for adequate assurance of performance. Until the insecure party receives such assurance, he or she may, if commercially reasonable, suspend any performance for which he or she has not already received the agreed return.

IV. THIRD-PARTY BENEFICIARIES

A. THE STATUS AND RIGHTS OF AN INTENDED THIRD-PARTY BENEFICIARY

1. **Timing:** A third-party beneficiary promise arises during formation of the contract.

2. **Intent: The Parties Must Intend to Benefit the Third-party Beneficiary.**

    a. **Designation by name or legal description:** While most intended beneficiaries are identified by name, a legal description that is later proven to identify a specific individual is sufficient.

    b. **Motives irrelevant:** It is sufficient that the parties intend to benefit the third-party beneficiary. Why they chose to do so is irrelevant.

       EXAMPLE: When Rich's only daughter, Madison, goes off to State U., Rich hires Domino Designs to repaint and furnish Madison's dorm room. Madison is an intended third-party beneficiary of the contract between Rich and Domino.

3. **Legal Consequence of Intended Third-party Beneficiary Status:** If the designated third party is able to prove he or she is an intended third-party beneficiary under the contract, he or she can sue to enforce it.

B. VESTING OF RIGHTS: Once the rights of an intended third-party beneficiary have vested, the parties may no longer modify or rescind the contract.

1. **How Accomplished:** There are three ways to vest the rights of an intended third-party beneficiary.

    a. The third party detrimentally relies on the promise,

    b. The third party sues one of the party's for failure to perform as promised, or

c. The third party expresses consent to receive the performance (when that consent has been requested by either of the parties and not merely volunteered).

2. **Non-vested Third-party Beneficiary:** Until a third-party beneficiary's rights vest, the parties to the contract may rescind or modify their bargain.

3. **Intended Third-party Beneficiary with Vested Rights:** Once the rights of the beneficiary have vested, the parties may no longer rescind or modify the contract.

4. **The Intended Third-party Beneficiary's Cause of Action:** If the promisor does not completely perform, the intended third party beneficiary may sue in law or equity.

   a. **Defenses:** The contracting parties may contest that the plaintiff is in fact an intended third-party beneficiary, or, admit it, and then raise any of the standard contract defenses to show that the contract is not enforceable (or was never formed in the first place).

      i. **Effect of conditions:** Just as in a regular contract, any conditions must have been either satisfied or excused before the parties are legally obligated to perform.

V. THE ASSIGNMENT OF CONTRACT RIGHTS

A. **ASSIGNMENT DEFINED:** The transfer of a contractual right to a another party. In contracts, while "assignment" is sometimes used to refer to a transfer of both the rights and duties under a contract, a more specific definition of assignment often refers to the right to be paid under the contract. In general, rights are freely assignable.

EXAMPLE: Tommy buys a new house and gets a mortgage from Westerberg Bank to do so. Westerberg immediately assigns its right to be paid to Stinson Bank. Westerberg is freely able to do so, as the only likely "damage" to Tommy is that he has to write a different name on his monthly check.

1. **Terminology:** The assignor is also known as the obligee under the contract. The non-assigning party is known as the obligor under the contract.

2. **The Intent to Make a Present Assignment:** A present assignment may occur through words, deeds, or a combination thereof.

   a. **All to assignee:** The assignor must intend to act in the present and to transfer all right, title, and interest in the particular contractual right immediately and exclusively to the designated assignee. The assignor cannot retain any control or power to revoke over the transferred right.

   b. **Acts of present assignment:** The assignor must clearly identify the subject matter and the designated assignee, and take such steps as are necessary to transfer the legal interest in the subject matter without any further action.

c. **No writing is required:** An oral assignment, if it expresses the requisite intention of the assignor to act in the present, is effective.

3. **Partial Assignment Permissible:** An assignoer may assign his or her rights to several non-competing assignees, or retain a portion of the subject matter while assigning the balance.

4. **Present Subject Matter:** The assignor's intent and actions must relate to a suitable present subject matter.

5. **Future Rights Under an Existing Contract:** The assignor may presently assign future rights under an existing contract. However, in doing so, the assignor warrants that he or she will undertake to fulfill the contract in good faith.

EXAMPLE: Pete Professor, who is in need of some fast cash, makes an agreement with Antigone. Antigone agrees to give him $800 now. In exchange, Pete assigns over his right to be paid $1,000 for an upcoming lecture. By making this assignment, Pete warrants that he will in fact give the lecture.

a. **Conditions:** If rights are conditional, being dependent upon the satisfaction or excuse of conditions precedent or concurrent, the assignee takes them subject to those same conditions.

B. **COMMON LAW RESTRAINTS ON THE FREEDOM OF ASSIGNMENT:** An assignment that would materially alter the nature of the non-assigning party's contract duties or materially expand his or her risk is not enforceable.

1. **Varying of Contract Duties:** Assignments that would materially vary the contract duties of the non-assigning party are not operative.

2. **Personal Service Contract:** The right to receive the personal services of another under an existing contract is a material alteration.

EXAMPLE: The Inn at Red Mountain, a famous restaurant, contracts to have Kristin's Kakes make custom desserts for the upcoming holiday season. Kristin's agrees to less than half of what it would normally charge because of the prestige of working for the Inn. But before Kristin's starts work, the Inn assigns its rights under the contract to Dirty John's Diner, an eatery mainly known for health code violations. Under these circumstances, a court may hold that the assignment is void.

3. **Requirement and Output Contracts:** Requirements and output contracts are not assignable under the common law, but may be assignable under the UCC.

a. **Common law view:** No two buyers are likely to generate identical requirements, nor are two manufacturing sellers likely to produce identical output.

b. **UCC position:** The treatment of output and requirements contracts under UCC 2-306(1) requires good-faith dealing and makes unenforceable a tender of output or demand for performance "unreasonably disproportionate to any stated estimate or in the absence of a stated estimate to any normal or otherwise comparable prior output or requirements."

    i. **Reasonable fluctuation:** Since the UCC assumes that reasonable fluctuations in output or demand are to be tolerated, an assignment that threatens no unreasonable fluctuation would not violate the non-assigning party's rights.

    ii. **Benchmarks:** Stated estimates or prior history provide an objective test for reasonable fluctuation.

4. **Expansion of Risk:** Assignments that do not threaten material alteration of the non-assigning party's duties, but which do materially expand the risk that he or she had assumed in forming the contract, are also void. Three types of risk must be considered:

a. **Alteration of risk of performance:** If performance is subject to a condition, an assignment that would increase the chance of satisfying that condition is void because it would materially increase the risk of having to perform. Common examples include insurance agreements or convenants not to compete.

b. **Alteration of risk of not receiving the same performance from the assignor:** The most common example is an assignment of a right to receive payment for the rendition of yet-to-be performed personal services.

    EXAMPLE: Using the example above, assume Pete Professor is much less likely to take his lecture seriously now that he has assigned it. In this case, the non-assigning party can challenge the assignment.

c. **Alteration of the risk inherent in attempting performance:** If the assignment would require the non-assigning party to perform at a different time or in a different place, it would be void.

C. CONTRACT PROVISIONS PURPORTING TO FORBID OR RESTRICT THE RIGHT TO CREATE AN ASSIGNMENT

1. **Presumption:** There is a presumption that a contract clause prohibiting or restricting a right to assign "the contract" is intended only to preclude the delegation of contract duties, not the assignment of rights by an assignor who retains the burden of performing his or her own duties.

2. **Plain Language Necessary:** Only the plainest possible language can compel a court to the conclusion that a clause prohibiting assignment means more than a prohibition on delegation. This is especially true when the subject matter of the assignment is merely the payment of money by the non-assigning party, since this is unlikely to be a significant burden.

    a. **Status of innocent assignee:** If the purported assignee does not know or should not know that the assignment is in violation of a contract term, and he or she has paid value for the assignment, he or she will hold a valid assignment.

    b. **Rights and duties of the non-assigning party:** The non-assigning party must perform or be in breach, although he or she will have a cause of action against the assignor for breach of the covenant not to assign.

D. STATUTORY POLICY: Some restraints on assignment are void under statutory policy. For instance:

  1. **Damages:** Under UCC 2-210(2), a right to damages for breach of a contract for the sale of goods may be assigned even if there is an express term in the contract precluding such assignment.

  2. **Right to Receive Payment of Money Assignable:** UCC 9-318(4) broadly invalidates an express term of a contract that purports to restrict the assignment of the right to receive payment of monies due.

E. THE STATUS OF AN ASSIGNEE: Assuming that he or she can prove the elements of a present assignment, all right, title, and interest in the subject matter of the assignment will now be exclusively vested in the assignee.

  1. **Non-assigning Party's Performance:** The non-assigning party must tender performance of the assigned duties to the assignee at peril of material breach.

    a. An attempt by the non-assigning party to ignore the status of the assignee and tender performance to the assignor is totally ineffective in discharging his or her contract duties.

F. REVOCATION: Under certain circumstances, an assignment may be revoked by the assignor.

  1. **Revocable Assignments:** If the assignment was both oral in form and gratuitous in nature, the assignor has a right to revoke the assignment. He or she may revoke in two ways:

    a. By giving notice to the gratuitous assignee or the non-assigning party, or

    b. By creating a subsequent, conflicting assignment to a second assignee.

  2. **Irrevocable Assignments:** A gratuitous assignment becomes irrevocable under any of the following circumstances See Restatement (Second) Sec. 332:

    a. **Writing:** If the assignment is in writing and is delivered to the assignee, it becomes irrevocable.

b. **Symbolic document:** If the contract right is commonly symbolized by a particular document, delivery of the document to the assignee with the understanding that the assignor is assigning his or her rights makes the assignment irrevocable. Common examples are savings account passbooks and stock certificates.

c. **Estoppel:** If the gratuitous assignee changes position in detrimental reliance upon the oral assignment, the assignor will be estopped to revoke it.

d. **Performance:** If the gratuitous assignee obtains performance from the non-assigning party, it is too late for the assignor to revoke.

3. **Assignments Made For Consideration are Irrevocable:** Both oral and written assignments are irrevocable if the assignee has paid value (incurred bargained-for legal detriment) for the assignment.

G. **PRIORITY AMONG CONFLICTING ASSIGNEES:** Partial assignments do not present this problem, for the claims of the assignees do not conflict. Each is entitled to a clearly defined portion of the non-assigning party's performance. However, if the assignor has purported to assign the same subject matter to more than one assignee, courts determine the owner of the assignment by considering the following rules:

1. **Gratuitous Assignees:** Gratuitous assignees lose out to assignees who gave consideration.

2. **Conflicting Common Law Positions Where Rivals have Equivalent Equities:** Three competing common law positions have emerged over time in the United States to resolve the priority as among rival assignees with equivalent equities.

a. **The New York or "American" Rule:** The assignee first in time is first in right. The rationale is that once an irrevocable assignment has been made, the assignor was left with nothing to assign.

b. **The English or California Rule:** The first assignee who gives notice to the non-assigning party prevails. However, that assignee must have paid value for the assignment and had no notice of any prior assignment.

c. **The Restatement or Massachusetts Rule Restatement (Second) Sec. 342(b):** If the prior assignment is revocable, any subsequent assignment revokes it, and the subsequent assignee holds the assignment. However, if the prior assignment is not revocable, the holder of the prior assignment retains the assignment unless the subsequent assignee, in good faith and for value, obtains:

   i. Performance from the non-assigning party,

   ii. Judgment against the non-assigning party for breach of the assigned duty,

    iii. A tangible symbol from the assignor representing the claim, or

    iv. A novation from the non-assigning party. See Delegation of Duties below.

H. THE ASSIGNEE'S CLAIM IN LITIGATION: If the non-assigning party fails, refuses, or defectively performs the duty that had been assigned to the assignee, the assignee has the right to sue the non-assigning party.

1. **No Claim Against the Assignor:** The assignor is not liable for the non-assigning party's breach unless:

    a. The assignor is guilty of interfering with the assignee's quiet enjoyment of the contract right by attempting a wrongful revocation, or

    b. The assignor's own material breach has discharged the non-assigning party on a theory of failure of consideration.

2. **Implied Warranties:** Breach by the non-assigning party is not a violation of the implied warranties that the assignor has both the right and power to make a present, operative assignment, and that the assignor will do nothing to interfere with the assignee's quiet enjoyment of the assigned contractual right.

    a. This warranty does not cover breach by the non-assigning party for which the assignee is not responsible.

3. **Defenses Available to Non-assigning Party:** The common law holds that the assignee "stands in the shoes of the assignor." In other words, the assignment can never create rights or status in the assignee that exceed those of the assignor.

VI. THE DELEGATION OF CONTRACT DUTIES

A. DEFINITION: Where one of the contracting parties wants another person to perform his or her duties under the contract.

Terminology: The person who delegates his or her contractual duty is the delegator of the duty and the obligor under the contract. The person who agrees to do the duty is the delegate. The other party to the original contract is the obligee.

B. THE MECHANICS OF DELEGATION: The requirements for an effective delegation are quite simple.

1. **If No Assumption of the Duty on the Part of the Delegate Is Desired:** A delegator need only:

    a. Clearly identify the intended delegate, and

    b. Express consent to the delegate that the delegate perform certain or all of the contract duties owed by the delegator to the other party under the existing contract.

2. **If an Assumption of Duty by the Delegate Is Desired:** If the delegator wishes to create a legal responsibility in the delegate to assume primary responsibility for the performance of duties owed to the other party, he or she must:

   a. Bargain for a promise from the delegate, and

   b. Support that promise with valuable consideration.

3. **Terms Explicit:** Usually the promise by the delegate to assume primary legal responsibility for the contract duties of the delegator will be explicit.

4. **Assumption Implied from Overall Transaction:** Both the UCC and the Restatement recognize that general language such as "I hereby assign my contract" creates an assignment of rights and delegation of duties.

   a. If the delegate accepts this arrangement without protest, he or she will be deemed to have implicitly promised to assume legal liability for the duties of the delegator.

C. **RESTRAINTS ON DELEGATION:** Like assignment, the power to delegate is a unilateral legal privilege that does not depend upon the prior, contemporaneous, or subsequent consent of the other party.

1. However, it has long been clear that delegation represents a far more direct threat to the other party than the mere assignment of the right to receive that party's performance.

2. Therefore, the terms of the bargain, or the nature of the contract duties, may render the attempted delegation "ineffective" given the impact upon the other party. Consequently:

   a. Contract terms prohibiting or restraining delegation will always be enforced.

   b. If the delegation has taken place in the context of a contract for the sale of goods, then UCC 2-210(5) expressly provides that the non-delegating party may treat it as creating reasonable grounds for insecurity. Such insecurity then triggers the provisions of UCC 2-609.

      i. The insecure party may make written demand upon the delegate for adequate assurance of performance.

      ii. A failure on the part of the delegate to provide adequate assurances of both a willingness and capacity to perform the delegated duties of the delegator is, itself, a material breach of the contract.

      iii. If the non-delegating party has not taken the precaution of inserting contract restraints or prohibitions respecting delegation, whether the delegation is effective will depend on the nature of the duties and the impact upon the reasonable expectations of the non-delegating party.

D. CONTRACT DUTIES OF A "PERSONAL CHARACTER" MAY NOT BE EFFECTIVELY DELEGATED WITHOUT THE CONSENT OF THE OBLIGEE: If the commercially reasonable expectations of the non-delegating party include not only what is to be performed, but who is to perform it, those duties are "personal."

1. **Criteria:** The question revolves around whether the personal reputation, skill, taste, or discretion of the delegator formed a material part of the benefit of the non-delegating party's bargain.

   EXAMPLE: Hank Homer, the star shortstop of the Boston Beanies, realizes he has a wedding to go to the weekend of the big game. Since he doesn't want to miss a paycheck, he delegates his duty to play to Wilbur Wizened, his 93-year-old neighbor. Such an attempt at delegation would be ineffective.

2. **Waiver by Non-delegating Party of Right to Object Renders Delegation Effective:** If the non-delegating party accepts an installment performance that might well have been personal in quality, such acceptance without complaint constitutes a "waiver" of the right to decline further performance by the delegate of the same quality as that previously accepted.

E. THE CONSEQUENCES OF AN EFFECTIVE DELEGATION: The non-delegating party must cooperate in the delegate's attempt to discharge the duties of the delegator.

1. Failure to cooperate in the face of an effective delegation is a repudiation of the contract by the non-delegating party.

2. If the delegate successfully performs, performance by the delegate discharges the duties of the delegator.

3. However, the delegator remains secondarily liable under the original contract unless there is a "novation." If the non-delegating party to the original contract agrees to relieve the delegator of all liability under the contract and accepts the delegate in place of the delegator, there is a novation. In such a case, the delegate must consent as well.

F. REMEDIES OPEN TO NON-DELEGATING PARTY: If the delegate fails, refuses, or defectively carries out the delegated duty, the delegator will be in material breach of the contract.

1. **Rights as Against the Delegator:** In the event of such material breach, the non-delegating party may sue the delegator for money damages or equitable relief.

2. **Rights as Against the Delegate:** Whether the non-delegating party can sue the delegate depends upon whether there has been an assumption by the delegate of the delegator's duty. See comments on novation above.

a. If the delegate has not assumed the delegator's contract duties, he or she is not liable to the aggrieved non-delegating party.

b. If there had been a contract of delegation between the delagator and delegate, the non-delegating party is an intended third-party beneficiary of that contract and may sue the delegate in that capacity.

    i. Faced with such an action, the delegate may raise any real or personal defense arising out of the contract of delegation.

    ii. The delegate may also assert any counterclaim arising from a breach by the delegator of the contract of delegation.

    iii. The aggrieved non-delegating party can elect to recover against the delegator or the delegate. However, there can be only one full recovery.

    iv. A delegator who is forced to perform the contract duties assumed by a delegate, pay damages to the non-delegating party, or make a contract with a new delegate to secure the delegated performance can recover for any loss sustained from the defaulting delegate.

VII. EXCUSABLE NONPERFORMANCE

A. COMMON LAW

1. **Impossibility—definition:** Impossibility means that the promised performance cannot be done, such as when physical barriers arise that make performance impossible. Impossibility is hard to claim successfully under the common law.

    a. **Elements of impossibility:** To excuse performance, the party seeking excuse must demonstrate that, subsequent to formation, factors neither foreseen by the parties nor reasonably foreseeable have rendered performance of the promised task objectively impossible.

    EXAMPLE: Sarah hires Mike's Music Hall to have her wedding in. Three weeks before the wedding, the music hall burns to the ground. Since the actual existence of the music hall was a basic part of the contract, the destruction of the hall excuses performance under the contract.

    b. **Subjective impossibility is not an excuse:** If it is only personally impossible for the party to accomplish performance, there is no excuse.

    EXAMPLE: Because of a particularly snowy winter, Chillin's Snow Removal signs dozens of extra contracts to clear driveways. The town is hit by another blizzard, and, because of the large number of jobs it has agreed to undertake, Chillin's finds it impossible to clear Declan's driveway. Under these circumstances, Chillin's duty to clear Declan's driveway is not excused.

c. **Objective impossibility is an excuse:** If the unforeseen and unforeseeable barriers would preclude any person from performing, the specific promisor is excused.

EXAMPLE: Telly's Painting contracts to paint Taryn's house. A week before the scheduled performance, the house is blown away by a tornado.

2. **Impracticability—definition:** A party can be excused from performance if an unforeseen event arises after the formation of the contract that defeats a basic assumption of the bargain. Importantly, such an event cannot be caused by the party seeking to be excused, and the event must create a significant burden on the party's ability to fulfill his or her duty under the contract. For example, if the unforeseen event causes the cost of performing the contract to grossly exceed the cost that was assumed by the parties during contract formation. Restatement (Second) Sec. 261.

   a. The elements of impracticability are as follows:

      i. An unexpected contingency must have arisen subsequent to formation of the contract.

      ii. The risk of the unexpected occurrence must not have been allocated to the party seeking excuse either by the terms of the bargain or by custom in the marketplace.

      iii. The consequence of this unexpected and unallocated contingency must have rendered performance commercially impracticable.

   b. **Objective test:** The test is "objective" in the sense that the cost must have become so distorted that no party could reasonably be expected to perform.

      i. Proof that the added costs were onerous given the circumstances of the particular party seeking to be excused, without proof that they would have been regarded as onerous by others in the marketplace, would be "subjective impracticability" and no excuse.

   c. **Failure to utilize insurance:** A court will consider the potential availability of general or specific insurance. If the party seeking excuse could have protected itself in this manner and failed to do so, the party seeking to be excused will be held to the contract.

   d. **Rights of the parties in the wake of excuse:** If impracticability is established, the non-completed duties of the parties are excused and the contract is discharged.

      i. **Quasi-contractual adjustments:** A party who has rendered performance prior to the discharge may not recover on the contract but may obtain the market value of such performance on a theory of quasi-contract. The restitution interests of the parties are thus fully protected.

    ii. **No protection of the reliance interest:** Any expenses incurred by either party in preparing for performance may not be recovered. Each party bears his or her own loss.

3. **Frustration of Purpose—definition:** When an unforeseen event has completely or almost completely defeated the entire reason one of the parties entered into the contract. In such a case, most courts will excuse that party's performance. Restatement (Second) Sec. 265.

   EXAMPLE: Corissa agrees to rent a room from Royal in order to have a good place to watch the crowning of the new King of Blueland. Because of the coronation, Royal charges twice the normal rental rate. Two days before the planned coronation, the new king gets a cold and the coronation is called off. While Corissa could still stay in the room, her performance is excused because the entire point of the rental has been defeated. See *Krell v. Henry,* 2 K.B. 740 (1903).

   a. **Elements of a frustration case:** A party seeking excuse from the obligation to perform must establish two elements:

      i. That subsequent to formation some event or contingency neither foreseen nor reasonably foreseeable has occurred, and

      ii. That the consequence of this after-arising development is that the value of the other party's performance has been totally or nearly totally destroyed.

   b. **The role of foreseeability:** As noted, a party seeking to establish frustration must allege and prove that the after-arising event was neither foreseen (subjective concept) nor reasonably foreseeable (objective concept) at the formation stage.

      i. **Risk foreseen:** If it was foreseen, the failure of the party to guard against the risk by an appropriate condition is fatal.

      ii. **Risk foreseeable:** If the after-arising circumstances could have been foreseen through the exercise of reasonable contracting skills, the same result follows, but for the policy reason of holding parties to objective standards of reasonableness.

   c. **Consequences of frustration:** A party able to establish the two elements of frustration of purpose is excused from all outstanding contractual duties. Neither party may recover any expectation interest from the other.

      i. **Restitution for any performance to date:** The majority rule is that a party who has partially performed at the point of frustration may not recover on the contract but may claim in quasi-contract for the reasonable value of any performance bestowed upon the other party.

   ii. **Reliance interest not protected:** Any expenses that either of the parties had incurred in preparing to perform but which had not been bestowed upon the other party are lost and may not be recovered.

4. **Excusable Nonperformance Under the UCC:** There are three situations under the UCC in which a seller may seek to excuse performance.

   a. **Casualty to goods:** The destruction of particular, identified goods.

   b. **After-arising conditions:** The second addresses after-arising conditions that do not affect the goods, but substantially prejudice the manner or mode seller had intended to employ to deliver the goods, or the means by which he or she expected the buyer to pay for them.

   c. **Common law distinction:** Finally, the UCC recognizes of the common law concept of commercial impracticability, but refers to it as an "excuse by failure of presupposed conditions."

5. **Terminology:** The UCC does not employ the terms "impossibility" or "frustration," electing to include them within a broadened meaning of "impracticability." See UCC 2-615.

6. **Casualty to Identified Goods:** A contract for the sale of goods usually has as its subject matter something that is "fungible," meaning that any unit of the goods can serve as a replacement for any other. For example, if Farmer Jane contracts to buy 50 bales of hay, any 50 bales will satisfy the contract. As an another example, money is "fungible" because whether one is paid with one particular dollar bill over another usually makes no difference—a dollar bill is a dollar bill.

   a. **Identification:** However, if a particular good has been identified, the contract requires that that particular good be delivered. For example, the sale of a particular painting involves a particular, unique, and identified good. The seller cannot uphold his or her side of the bargain by simply delivering any painting he or she has.

   b. **The techniques for identification of specific goods:** UCC 2-501(1) declares that identification can be accomplished "… at any time and in any manner explicitly agreed to by the parties." In the absence of such explicit agreement, identification occurs:

      i. When the contract is made, if it is for the sale of goods already existing and designated by the parties as the subject matter;

      ii. If the contract is for the sale of future goods, when the goods are shipped, marked, or otherwise designated by the seller as goods to which such contract refers; or

> iii. When the crops are planted or the young animals are conceived if the contract is for the sale of crops or the young of animals.

c. **Excusable nonperformance or modification predicated upon casualty to identified goods:** Where the contract requires for its performance goods identified when the contract is made, the destruction of the goods without fault of either party before the risk of loss has passed to the buyer leaves the issue of discharge or modification up to the buyer.

d. **Fault:** Under UCC 2-613, neither party must have been "at fault" in the case of identified goods. If one of the parties is guilty of negligent or willful misconduct that caused the destruction of the goods, the obligations of that party are not excused.

7. **Consequences of Casualty Without Fault:**

a. If the loss is total, the contract is avoided and the rights of the buyer to the goods and the seller to payment are both discharged.

b. If the loss is partial or the goods have deteriorated so as to no longer conform to contract specifications of quality, the buyer has an election to inspect them and an option to treat the contract as discharged or to accept the goods "as is" with due allowance from the contract price.

8. **Substituted Performance:** Substituted performance may be appropriate where destruction is not to the goods, but to the manner or mode of delivery or type of payment.

a. "Avoidance" of the affected contract is a last resort.

b. If a commercially acceptable substitute remains both available and practicable, it must be tendered and accepted. UCC 2-614.

EXAMPLE: A contract between Yeats and Bellow requires that the goods be delivered at Seaside Port. A hurricane sweeps in and destroys Seaside before the goods are delivered. Yeats proposes that he deliver the goods to Beachside Port, 10 miles away from Seaside. Under these circumstances, Bellow has to accept this substituted performance.

VIII. THE PERFECT TENDER DOCTRINE

A. **SELLER'S TENDER OF DELIVERY:** Under the perfect tender doctrine, a seller is required to deliver exactly the goods contracted for. Any difference between the goods and what was contracted for results in a breach.

1. Under UCC 2-503(1) that effort is referred to as a "tender."

2. The seller is required to put and hold goods conforming to the contract description at the buyer's disposition and give the buyer any notice reasonably necessary to enable the buyer to take delivery.

3. **Terms of Delivery:** The tender must be at a reasonable hour, and the goods must be available to the buyer for a period reasonably necessary to permit the buyer to take delivery.

4. **Receiving Goods:** Unless otherwise agreed, it is the buyer who must furnish any facilities reasonably necessary for receipt of the goods.

5. **Legal Effect of Seller's Tender:** Under UCC 2-507, if the seller has made a tender in compliance with UCC 2-503, the seller is entitled to buyer's acceptance of the goods and payment of.

   EXAMPLE: Seller agrees to sell Buyer 500 blue and white birdhouses. At the time of delivery, Seller delivers 499 blue and white birdhouses, and 1 blue and pink one. Under these circumstances, Seller has failed to deliver perfect tender.

B. **BUYER'S RIGHT TO INSPECTION OF THE GOODS:** In order to protect the buyer's interest, the buyer has an absolute right to inspect the goods before payment can be demanded or an acceptance decision required.

   1. If this inspection reveals that either the goods or the tender is "nonconforming" in any respect, the buyer may, under the terms of UCC 2-601:

      a. Reject the whole, or

      b. Accept the whole, or

      c. Accept any commercial unit or units and reject the balance.

   2. An acceptance in whole or in part of nonconforming goods by the buyer does not preclude the buyer's right to assert a claim for damages for any difference between the market value of the goods accepted and the contract price of conforming goods.

C. **MANNER AND CONSEQUENCES OF RIGHTFUL REJECTION:** A buyer determined to exercise rights under the perfect tender doctrine must reject any nonconformity within a commercially reasonable time following the seller's tender.

   1. **Manner of Rejection—Seasonable and Specific Notice to the Seller of any Claimed Nonconformity:** Under UCC 2-602, the buyer's rejection is ineffective unless, within a commercially reasonable time following the tender, the buyer gives the seller specific notice of any claimed nonconformity.

   2. **Non-seasonable Notice of Rejection:** Failure on the part of the buyer to act swiftly in providing notice of the claimed nonconformity to the seller is treated as an acceptance of the goods UCC Sec. 2-606.

a. In this case, the buyer is obligated to pay the contract price for the goods.

3. **Non-specific Seasonable Notice:** A seasonable notice that is not specific in informing the seller of nonconformity ascertainable by reasonable inspection is treated as a waiver of that nonconformity under UCC 2-605(1).

   a. The buyer is also precluded from using the non-specified ground to justify rejection, if the defect was one that the seller could have cured if given specific notice.

      i. **The meaning of "seasonable":** An action is taken "seasonably" when it is taken at or within a time agreed or, if no time is agreed, within a reasonable time.

D. **THE SELLER'S RIGHT TO CURE A NONCONFORMING TENDER:** The third affirmative obligation of the buyer is to cooperate with the seller in any cure effort.

1. **Cure as a Matter of Right:** Under UCC 2-508(1) a seller who has received notice of nonconformity has a right to correct the defect if time for the seller's performance has yet to expire.

   a. In order to perfect this right to cure, the seller must give seasonable notice to the buyer of the intention to make a conforming delivery.

      EXAMPLE: Sam agrees to deliver 1,000 Acme brand hammers to Dave on April 21. On April 1, Sam delivers 1,000 Smashy Brand Hammers. If Dave rejects the hammers as nonconforming, Sam has the right to notify Dave of his intention to cure the defect and deliver the Acme hammers by April 21.

2. **Effect of a Successful Cure:** If the seller succeeds in making a conforming replacement tender under the terms of UCC 2-508, it is an academic question whether the earlier nonconforming tender represented a breach.

   a. Receipt of conforming goods within the time allowed by the contract, or within an extended period that was not injurious to the commercial interests of the buyer, would leave the buyer without any real damages and thus no motive to litigate the earlier tender.

E. **DISPOSITION OF NONCONFORMING GOODS IN A MERCHANT BUYER'S POSSESSION:** If the buyer is a merchant, further provisions of the UCC address the buyer's responsibility with respect to rightfully rejected goods.

1. **Merchant Buyer's Duty to Follow Seller's Instructions:** Under UCC 2-603(1), a buyer in possession or control of rightfully rejected goods must follow any reasonable instructions from the seller with respect to their disposition.

2. **Merchant Buyer's Duty to Act on Own Initiative:** If the goods are perishable or are threatened with a rapid deterioration in value, the merchant buyer must make reasonable efforts to sell them for the defaulting seller's account when the seller does not provide instructions. (*e.g.*, if the contract involves food or ice).

3. **General Buyer's Privilege to Act in the Absence of Seller's Instructions:** UCC 2-603 addresses the rights of both merchant and non-merchant buyers to dispose of nonconforming goods that are not threatened with imminent destruction or deterioration. The buyer may store them for the seller's account, ship them back to the seller, or re-sell them for the seller's account (in the last case, keeping a commission of up to 10%).

F. **REVOCATION OF ACCEPTANCE IN WHOLE OR IN PART:** UCC 2-608 provides two circumstances in which it is proper for a buyer to revoke acceptance.

1. Where the nonconformity in the goods escaped detection, despite the fact the buyer made a reasonable pre-acceptance inspection.

   a. Revocation of acceptance must occur within a reasonable time after the buyer discovers or should have discovered the nonconformity.

   b. The buyer's revocation must also take place before any substantial change in the condition of the goods that is not caused by the previously undetected defects.

2. If the buyer accepted what were known to be nonconforming goods in reliance upon the seller's express assurance that the defect would be cured, a failure of the seller to cure within a seasonable time entitles the buyer to revoke the acceptance.

3. **Means of Revocation:** In either instance, the buyer who revokes acceptance must give notice to the seller.

4. **Affirmative Duties of the Revoking Buyer:** A buyer who revokes has the same duties as if the goods had been rejected in the first place.

5. In all circumstances, these duties would include acting in a commercially reasonable manner to preserve the economic value of the seller's tender and mitigate any loss that could be avoided by a timely cover.

6. If the revocation is occasioned by a discovery of a hidden nonconformity, the affirmative duties of the buyer may extend to cooperating in the seller's effort to cure the defect.

IX. CONSEQUENCES OF BREACH

A. **BREACH OF CONTRACT DEFINED:** If a contract promise is unconditional or all conditions have been either satisfied or excused, and no doctrine of excusable non-performance can be claimed, the promisor's failure to perform, refusal to perform, or rendering of a defective performance constitutes a "breach."

1. **Material or "Total" Breach:** If a defect in the breaching party's performance substantially affects the reasonable expectations of the non-breaching party, the breach is "material" or "total."

     a. The breach may occur with respect to quality, quantity, or timing of the performance.

  2. **Question of Fact:** Whether or not the defect in the breaching party's attempted performance has seriously disappointed the reasonable expectations of the non-breaching party is an issue of fact. Consequently, he non-breaching party bears the burden of proving a material breach.

B. **CONSEQUENCES OF A MATERIAL, TOTAL BREACH:** A non-breaching party faced with a material breach may elect to treat it as totally destructive of the contractual relationship.

  1. **Outstanding Duties of the Non-breaching Party Are Discharged:** Any contract performance owed by the non-breaching party on the date he or she suffers the material breach is discharged on a theory of failure of consideration.

  2. **Duty to Mitigate:** While abandoning all efforts to carry out the terms of the contract, the non-breaching party will still be required to take reasonable self-help steps designed to minimize the damages caused by the material breach.

     a. **Litigation to secure the expectation interest of the non-breaching party:** If the non-breaching party sues for the breach, he or she is seeking money damages equal to the "loss of bargain" caused by the breach.

       i. If an adequate remedy at law cannot be obtained, the non-breaching party may sue for an equitable remedy, such as a specific performance decree or injunctive relief.

       EXAMPLE: Kendra contracts to buy Whiteacre, a 100-acre farm on the ocean, from Sheldon. Sheldon fails to deliver the deed. Since land is unique, and no amount of money would be the same as Kendra receiving Whiteacre, Kendra can sue for specific performance.

C. **MINOR OR "PARTIAL" BREACH:** A minor breach is any default or defect in the breaching party's performance that does not seriously disappoint the reasonable expectations of the non-breaching party.

  1. **Consequences of a Minor or Partial Breach:** The contractual relationship is not destroyed by a minor breach.

  2. **Relationship to the Doctrine of Substantial Performance:** If the defect in the breaching party's performance attempt is only minor, then there has been substantial performance of that contract duty. See Substantial Performance above.

  3. **Effect of Minor Breach:** The contract duties of the non-breaching party are not discharged, and the non-breaching party must still perform his or her own matured duties or commit a material breach of the contract.

4. **Right of Non-breaching Party to Suspend Counterperformance:** In an effort to furnish the non-breaching party with a self-help remedy, some courts have concluded that a partial breach may justify a suspension of counterperformance by the non-breaching party in an effort to force the breaching party to correct the defect.

5. **Role of the Damage Remedy:** The aggrieved party, having performed her own contract duties, may now sue for the difference between the value of the contract performance and the actual performance. See Restatement (Second) Sec. 236(2).

D. **INSTALLMENT CONTRACTS:** It often happens that the contract calls for the seller to deliver the goods or for the buyer to make payments in installments.

1. **Test for Determining Material Impact Upon the Entire Contract:** In order to show material breach, the non-breaching party must be prepared to demonstrate that the consequences of failure, refusal, or defective performance of an installment obligation has defeated his or her expectations with respect to the entire bargain, or severely hampered his or her ability to carry out his or her own contract obligations.

2. **Isolation of the Breach:** The law will usually isolate the breach to the single installment rather than finding a material breach of the whole contract. Unless the court finds a total breach of the entire contract, the non-breaching party will recover damages for the failed installment only, while the balance of the contract between the two parties will remain in effect.

3. **Installment Contracts Under the UCC:** The UCC and the common law both prefer to keep installment contracts alive.

   a. UCC 2-612 takes a functional attitude toward recognition that a contract is of an installment nature.

   b. Such attitudes are to prevail over any uncommercial and legalistic interpretation of the agreement.

   c. **Installment contract defined:** An installment contract is one that expressly or by commercial understanding requires or authorizes delivery of goods in separate lots to be separately accepted by the buyer.

   d. **Consequence of nonconformity of one or more installments:** Under UCC 2-612(2), the rights of the aggrieved buyer are presumptively limited to the defective installment or installments, not the entire contract.

   e. **Right to reject a nonconforming installment:** The buyer may reject any installment that is nonconforming with respect to quality, quantity, or time if the nonconformity substantially impairs the value of that installment and cannot be cured.

f. **Effect of the seller's cure or assurance of cure as precluding rejection of that installment:** If the seller gives adequate assurances that the nonconformity will be cured within a reasonable time, the buyer must accept that installment.

g. **Right to terminate the entire contract:** UCC 2-612(3) declares that whenever nonconformity with respect to one or more installments substantially impairs the value of the whole contract, there is a breach of the entire contract.

h. **Right to demand adequate assurances:** If a party has been rendered insecure by the nonconformity in an installment (whether with respect to the other party's ability or willingness to avoid nonconformity in future installments), he or she may:

  i. Make a written demand upon the other party under the terms of UCC 2-609, seeking assurance of due performance with respect to future installments.

    (a) A party who has made such a written demand may, if it is commercially reasonable, suspend any further performance of his or her own pending receipt of adequate assurances.

  ii. If the other party does not provide adequate assurances within a reasonable time (not exceeding 30 days) following receipt of a justified written demand, the entire contract is repudiated, and the bargain is terminated for all purposes. The non-breaching party may then sue for a remedy adequate to protect his or her expectation interest. UCC 2-609(4).

E. **AFFIRMATIVE OBLIGATIONS OF THE NONBREACHING PARTY:** Usually, the affirmative obligation of a party faced with a breach of contract is a simple one of taking reasonable steps to minimize the resulting harm.

  1. **Recent Common Law and UCC Trends:** These impose upon the non-breaching party a duty to cooperate with the other party in "curing" (correcting) the breach.

  2. **Common-sense Steps Under the UCC:** In the sale of goods, a buyer is required to take several common-sense steps to preserve the economic value of any non-conforming goods tendered by the seller.

    a. **The duty to mitigate:** The buyer must use reasonable efforts to avoid loss or injury flowing from the contract breach.

      i. **The duty in general:** This obligation precludes the recovery of damages which, through the exercise of due diligence, the buyer could have avoided.

3. **Employee's Duty to Mitigate in the Face of a Breach of a Contract for Personal services:** If an employer breaches a personal services contract, the employee must mitigate damages by seeking out other substantially similar employment.

   a. **Same type of work:** There is no affirmative duty to seek out, or to accept if it is offered, a replacement contract involving work of a different nature than covered by the breached contract.

   b. **Same level of pay:** The duty to mitigate does not embrace work of the same nature if it is offered at a substantially inferior grade of pay.

   c. **Relocation:** Finally, an employee does not have to accept comparable work that would involve relocation to a different locale.

   d. **Burden of proof:** The employer has the duty to prove that the replacement opportunities were available and that the employee ignored them.

4. **The Duty to Mitigate Under the UCC:** In general, the non-breaching party has a duty to "cover" his or her losses.

   a. **The buyer's duty to mitigate in the event of the seller's breach:** If the seller breaches, the buyer's first remedy provided under the UCC is to cover by obtaining conforming goods from a substitute seller, and then recovering, as consequential damages, any difference between the contract price and the cost of the cover contract.

      i. UCC 2-712(1) defines a cover as a purchase or contract to purchase substitute goods undertaken by the buyer, in good faith and without unreasonable delay, following the seller's breach of the whole contract.

      ii. If the buyer has made such a cover, he or she can recover the difference, if any, between the cost of the cover and the terms of the materially breached contract.

      iii. Any reasonable cover will be respected in computing the damages of the buyer.

         (a) The test of proper cover is whether the buyer acted in good faith and in a reasonable manner.

         (b) It is immaterial that hindsight may later prove that the method of cover used was not the cheapest or most effective.

      iv. The privilege of resorting to a cover contract is not limited to merchant parties, but may be used by consumers to gain the object of their bargain (the desired goods) while fixing the size of their consequential (loss of bargain) damages.

b. **The non-breaching seller's duty to mitigate:** If the buyer wrongfully refuses to accept a tender or properly pay for it, a seller who is still in possession of the goods or who is able to regain possession is free to resell them in the marketplace.

    i. **Effect of a resale contract:** If the seller uses the self-help remedy of resale, he or she immediately accomplishes the objective of the breached contract by converting the goods into a purchase price. However, the resale must be made in good faith and in a commercially reasonable manner.

        (a) He or she also sets the size of his or her consequential damages as the difference, if any, between the price term of the breached contract and the amount realized in the resale.

X. DAMAGES FOR BREACH OF CONTRACT

A. **GENERAL:** Whenever a party suffers a material breach of contract, at least three interests are immediately threatened.

1. **The Restitution Interest:** If, on the date of the breach, the non-breaching party has already wholly or partially performed his or her own contract obligations, a material breach on the part of the other party leaves the breaching party unjustly enriched by the value of that performance, and the non-breaching party unjustly impoverished by its cost.

2. **The Reliance Test:** If, on the date of the breach, the non-breaching party has not yet performed his or her own contract obligations, but has incurred expenses or foregone other opportunities in reliance upon the expectation that the other party would perform, the breaching party is not unjustly enriched, but the out-of-pocket loss to the non-breaching party represents present unjust impoverishment.

3. **The Expectation Interest:** If, on the date of the breach, the non-breaching party has neither performed his or her own contract obligations nor changed position in detrimental reliance on the promise of the breaching party to perform, there is neither unjust present enrichment of the breaching party nor unjust present impoverishment of the non-breaching party. There is, however, a disappointment of expectations of future wealth or future advantage that would have been gained had the breaching party performed.

B. **PUNITIVE OR EXEMPLARY DAMAGES NOT RECOVERABLE:** The goal of the damage remedy at law is to compensate the non-breaching party, not to inflict a punishment upon the party in breach. This is true regardless of the moral blame incurred by the breaching party in breaching the contract.

C. **THE LOSS-OF-BARGAIN MEASURE OF MONEY DAMAGES:** Damages are computed to place the non-breaching party in the position that he or she would have occupied had there been full and timely performance.

1. **Presumptive Measure of Award:** In the absence of special circumstances, the loss of bargain is measured as the difference, if any, between the contract price and market value of the breached performance at the time and place when, under the terms of the contract, it should have been performed.

   a. **Consequential:** In order to be compensable at law, damages must be a consequence of the breach.

      i. Unless the damages are caused by the breach, they are beyond the realm of a loss of bargain recovery.

2. **Formation Expenses Disallowed:** The non-breaching party will be unlikely to recover for any expenses incurred in the actual formation of the contract.

D. **FORESEEABLE:** In order to be compensable at law, damages caused by the breach must have been either generally or specially foreseeable at the formation stage.

1. **The Limitation Is Objective:** It is no defense that the particular party did not foresee the particular injury.

2. **Generally Foreseeable Elements of Loss:** To test whether a particular loss or injury was generally foreseeable, the question is posed in the following way: "Would a reasonable person, standing in the shoes of the party on the date of formation, and knowing only the terms of the contract, have, had he or she paused to consider the question, foreseen this injury as a probable consequence of breach?"

   EXAMPLE: One day, the main drive shaft of the Funzo Toy Factory cracks, halting production of all toys. The factory owners deliver the broken shaft to Labrador Express, which agrees to carry the shaft to Rob's Repair Shop. The owners do not tell Labrador that this shaft is the only one they have. After a delay in shipment, the owners sue Labrador for damages caused by the factory remaining idle. Since Labrador had no way of knowing that a delay in delivery would shut down the entire factory, Labrador is not liable for these damages. *See Hadley v. Baxendale, 156 Eng. Rep. 145 (Exchequer 1864).*

3. **Specially Foreseeable Losses:** The magnitude of potentially recoverable losses may be dramatically increased if the special needs or circumstances of the promisee are revealed to the potential promisor prior to the formation of the bargain.

   EXAMPLE: In the example above, it might have made a difference if the owners told Labrador about the importance of the shaft.

   a. In order to set the stage for the recovery of special elements of damage, the communication by the promisee to the promisor prior to formation of the bargain must have been such as to alert a reasonable person to both the nature of the added risk and its likely dimension.

b. Assuming that there was adequate notice, the test as to whether a specific element of the non-breaching party's loss was specially foreseeable is formulated as follows: "Would a reasonable person, standing in the shoes of the breaching party on the day the bargain was formed, and aware not only of the terms of that contract but also of the disclosed special needs or circumstances of the non-breaching party have, had he or she stopped to think about it, foreseen this injury as a probable consequence of breach?"

c. Damages are not rendered non-foreseeable merely because the particular breaching party did not stop to contemplate their potential occurrence. Nor must the non-breaching party prove that a reasonable person would have actually foreseen them. It is sufficient that had the reasonable person paused to consider the matter, the losses would have been foreseeable.

d. Of those losses in fact caused by the breach and either generally or specially foreseeable at the formation of the contract, the non-breaching party may recover for only those elements of injury that proved **unavoidable** given an expenditure of reasonable efforts to mitigate damages.

4. **Certain in Dollar Amount:** Finally, of those losses in fact caused by the breach and either generally or specially foreseeable at the formation of the contract and unavoidable given reasonable efforts to mitigate by the non-breaching party, only those damages that can be proved to a specific dollar amount may be compensated at law.

a. If the marketplace is a ready source of substitution for the breached subject matter, certainty will pose little problem.

b. If the buyer formed a cover contract, his or her certain damages are the difference, if any, between the cost of the cover contract and the terms of the breached contract.

c. If the non-breaching party is the seller, his or her damages are the difference, if any, between the fruits of the resale and the price the breaching buyer was to have paid under the terms of the contract.

d. If the non-breaching party fails to make a substitute contract, consequential damages may still be established with the requisite certainty by measuring the difference between the terms of the breached contract and the market price of the subject matter at the time and place performance should have been rendered.

e. The modern trend is to hold the non-breaching party to proof of consequential damages only to a "reasonable certainty."

f. **UCC position:** The UCC specifically states that damages do not have to be calculable to an absolute mathematical certainty.

5. **The Potential for Equitable Intervention:** Inadequacy of the damage remedy is a pre-requisite to sue in equity. The term "remedy at law" refers to money damages.

   a. When a market exists offering a replacement opportunity to the non-breaching party, the remedy at law is presumptively adequate. Damages can be measured as the difference between the contract terms and the market price for the subject matter of the breached bargain. However, any presumption of adequacy is rebuttable.

   b. Where no market exists, or the subject matter is unique, the presumption is reversed, and inadequacy of the legal remedy is assumed. As stated above, the major beneficiaries of this presumption are buyers of real estate.

   c. **The UCC view:** UCC 2-716(1) declares that "[s]pecific performance may be decreed where the goods are unique or in other proper circumstances." If there is no ready market to which the aggrieved party may turn, specific performance is an appropriate remedy.

6. **Nature of Equitable Relief:** If an equity court does decide to accept jurisdiction and to intervene on behalf of the complaining party, it has many remedial powers.

   a. **Decree of specific performance:** The breaching party will be ordered to literally carry out the terms of the broken bargain.

   b. **Injunctive relief:** If enforcement difficulties dissuade the court from granting the specific performance decree, an effective substitute may be to enjoin the breaching party from disposing of the subject matter in any manner other than in compliance with the terms of his or her contract. The economic needs of the breaching party then become the source of his or her compulsion to fulfill the terms of the contract.

   c. **Restitution and reliance recoveries:** A non-breaching party unable to obtain a loss of bargain recovery at law and refused equitable relief has failed to protect his or her expectation interest. At this point, his or her only recourse is to return to the common law and seek sufficient damages to restore him or her to his or her position before the the agreement was made.

      i. **Recovery in restitution:** A party who has conferred his or her own performance on the other party before that party breaches the contract has, at a minimum, a restitution claim.

      ii. **Recission:** As an alternative response to seeking to vindicate his or her expectation interest at law or in equity, the non-breaching party may treat the material breach as an occasion to rescind the contract. Any performance that the non-breaching party had rendered to the breaching party may then be recovered in quasi-contract.

d. If the breaching party can restore performance in the form received (e.g., return the goods or reconvey the real estate), literal restitution may be achieved.

e. If the breaching party cannot restore the non-breaching party's performance as received (because it has been consumed, conveyed to an innocent third person, or deteriorated), there will be liability for the "value" of the non-breaching party's performance. In these cases, the determination of "value" can be difficult.

f. **Measure is not the non-breaching party's cost:** Although a restitution claim features unjust present impoverishment of the non-breaching party and unjust present enrichment of the breaching party, the measure of damages is the enrichment of the breaching party, not the cost to the non-breaching party.

g. If the breaching party is able to prove that the "value to him" is actually less than the market value of the performance, courts are divided on the proper measure of damages. The Restatement (Second) Sec. 371, simply declares that "as justice may require," a court may choose between the general market value of the non-breaching party's performance and the actual value as experienced by the breaching party.

7. **Claimant in Breach:** Under the common law, a party who has breached after first rendering part performance may offset, as against the non-breaching party's claim for loss of bargain, the value of any part performance that the breaching party has rendered and that the non-breaching party has consumed or retained.

8. **Stipulated Remedies Provisions:** The parties can agree within the terms of the contract to a correct measure of damages.

    a. **Liquidated damages clause vs. penalty:** The inherent suspicion of common law courts toward stipulated remedies clauses has resulted in their classification under two labels:

        i. **Liquidated damages clauses respected:** If the provision is a "liquidated damages clause," it is valid and will be respected as the measure of damages without any judicial inquiry into actual damages.

        ii. **Penalty clause void:** By contrast, if the provision is deemed a "penalty clause," it is unconscionable as an affront to public (legal) policy. Importantly, courts will not enforce a clause that is so onerous that it inhibits "efficient" or commercially beneficial breaches.

    b. **Criteria for making the distinction:** Two criteria must be satisfied before a stipulated remedies provision will be deemed a "liquidated damages clause."

i. At the formation stage, both parties must have come to the reasonable conclusion that, in the event of breach, the loss of bargain remedy would not be available.

(a) If the loss of bargain remedy was likely to have been available, the parties had no business attempting to contest its application by stipulating a different remedy.

(b) The provision must seek fairly to compensate the non-breaching party, not to penalize the other for failing or refusing to perform.

(c) **Abatement:** In a contract for real estate, if the breaching party owns less than that conveyed, the non-breaching party can reduce his or her payment by an amount that reflects this breach.

(d) **"Time is of the essence":** Parties can specifically include a clause in the contract stating that "time is of the essence." If such a clause is included, the parties' contractual duties must be completed by the specific date stated in the contract.

(e) **Covenant not to compete:** An employment contract can include a clause restricting a former employee's right to compete against a former employer, but such a clause must be reasonable as to time, industry, and geography.

EXAMPLE: As part of her employment contract with a realty company, Rosemary Realtor agrees that "in the event of the termination of her employment, Realtor agrees not to engage in any business related to real estate for 10 years." A court is unlikely to enforce this agreement because 10 years is too long, "any business related to real estate" could include almost any business at all, and any competition by Realtor outside of the company's geographic area is unlikely to damage the company.

TRUE-FALSE QUESTION
TOPIC LIST

After you have familiarized yourself with the black letter law by studying and memorizing the outline, test your knowledge using the following true-false questions. Keep track of the answers you get wrong, but read the answer explanations to all of the questions. You may get some answers right by luck, or for the wrong reasons.

While you may feel you "know" something by reading, studying, and memorizing, you won't actually be sure until you test yourself and see the legal concepts in the form of a question.

1. Contract formation

2. Implied-in-fact contracts

3. Quasi-contracts

4. Essential terms of a contract

5. Contract formation

6. Gap fillers

7. Requirements and output contracts

8. Price terms in contracts

9. Knowledge of an offer/acceptance

10. Timing of acceptance

11. Acceptance and revocation

12. Option contracts

13. Means of acceptance

14. Unilateral and bilateral contracts

15. Mailbox rule

16. Means of acceptance

17. Acceptance by silence

18. Crossed communications

19. Rejections

20. Gift promises/consideration

21. Past consideration

TRUE-FALSE QUESTIONS

For each question below, circle "T" (true) or "F" (false).

1. **T F** There must be a writing for there to be a contract.

2. **T F** Words are necessary to create a contract.

3. **T F** Quasi-contracts are also called "implied-in-law" contracts.

4. **T F** If an offer does not set out essential terms, it cannot be accepted.

5. **T F** Contracts between merchants for the sale of goods must be in writing.

6. **T F** If a term in a contract is missing or unclear, the contract will fail.

7. **T F** Contracts that have no specific quantity, but ask for everything a seller can produce or anything a buyer may require, are valid.

8. **T F** A contract must contain a price term, or it will fail for indefiniteness.

9. **T F** An offeree can accept an offer that he or she does not know about.

10. **T F** The offeror has the power to limit the offer to a set time, after which it cannot be accepted to create a contract.

11. **T F** The offeror is free to revoke the offer at any time prior to the offeree's acceptance.

12. **T F** Under the Uniform Commercial Code (UCC), no consideration is required to create an option contract.

13. **T F** The UCC requires that an acceptance have the exact same terms as the offer.

14. **T F** A bilateral contract is an agreement for an act.

15. **T F** Under the mailbox rule, the offeror does not have to actually receive the acceptance before a contract is formed.

16. **T F** If an offeror sends out an offer by email, the offeree can only accept that offer through email.

17. **T F** An offeree may accept an offer through silence.

18. **T F** If an offeree mails his or her acceptance before receiving notice the offer has been revoked a contract is formed.

19. **T F** A rejection must be communicated to the offeror to be effective.

20. **T F** A gift can constitute consideration for a promise.

21. **T F** A service or benefit conferred in the past can serve as consideration for a contract.

22. **T F** Under the UCC, the terms of a contract may be modified without any new consideration.

23. **T F** A minor's contract obligations are voidable.

24. **T F** Conditional promises are valid contractual provisions.

25. **T F** A party must have a real and valid claim before an agreement not to sue can act as consideration to support a contract.

26. **T F** A contract between two parties can be created by promissory estoppel.

27. **T F** A mutual mistake regarding any term of a contract will excuse both parties' performances.

28. **T F** In general, courts will not enforce penalty clauses in contracts.

29. **T F** A court will find economic duress and invalidate a contract whenever a party takes advantage of the other's economic needs.

30. **T F** If one party tells the other he or she won't be performing the contract, the other party may sue immediately for breach.

31. **T F** The only way a third party can have rights in a contract is if the original parties specifically acknowledge those rights.

32. **T F** One party cannot assign his or her rights under a contract without the written permission of the other party.

33. **T F** The doctrine of impossibility will excuse a party from the contract if he or she can't perform his or her duties because of work and family conflicts.

34. **T F** A material breach can concern quantity, quality, or timing of performance.

35. **T F** Even if it is only a minor breach, the non-breaching party can sue for total breach of the contract.

36. **T F** If a buyer receives nonconforming goods, the UCC requires the buyer to reject them.

37. **T F** Under the UCC, a buyer may reject goods at any time.

38. **T F** To recover damages, a non-breaching party must prove that the damages arise out of the contract and are causally connected to other party's breach.

39. **T F** Courts rarely award equitable relief.

40. **T F** Specific performance is the most likely remedy for breach of an employment contract.

ANSWERS TO TRUE-FALSE QUESTIONS

1. **False.** Although there are certain exceptions under the Statute of Frauds, an oral agreement can be a contract.

2. **False.** Even if the parties use no words in their communications, an implied-in-fact contract can be formed if the parties' conduct implies that a contract has been formed.

3. **True.** Quasi-contracts are not actually contracts. Where one party would be unjustly enriched by receiving the valuable goods or services of another party, the "law" will "imply" that a contract existed between the parties.

4. **True.** An offer must articulate the essential terms of the proposed bargain because: (1) otherwise the offeree would have no idea what to accept, and (2) a reviewing court would be unable to fashion an appropriate remedy in the event of breach. The essential terms can be communicated to the offeree either expressly or by clear implication either by express consent or clear implication.

5. **False.** Under the UCC, a contract between merchants for the sale of goods can be formed "in any manner sufficient to show agreement, including conduct by both parties which recognizes the existence of such a contract."

6. **False.** Even if a contract term is missing or unclear, modern courts try to uphold bargains when that appears to have been the mutual objective of the parties. To do so, courts use "gap-fillers"—reasonable terms that are either consistent with the past dealings of the parties or with business customs or practices that each party would be fairly expected to know.

7. **True.** These contracts are called "requirements" contracts or "output contracts," and are routinely upheld under modern law. In a requirements contract, the quantity is the amount of goods that a buyer may require in the good faith course of business. In an output contract, the seller does not guarantee a minimum quantity of goods; the seller promises to sell the buyer every good the seller is able to produce in the good faith course of business. The amount of goods that a buyer may require in the good faith course of business. In an output contract, the seller does not guarantee a minimum quantity of goods; the seller promises to sell the buyer every good the seller is able to produce in the good faith course of business.

8. **False.** While the common law required a price term, most modern courts will attempt to uphold the bargain by supplying a reasonable price term.

9. **False.** Absent communication and knowledge of the offer, the offeree is without power to accept it to form a contract.

10. **True.** Furthermore, if the offeror does not set a time limit for his or her offer, it is open for acceptance for a *reasonable* time only.

11. **True.** Once the offeree accepts, however, the offeror may no longer revoke.

12. True. The UCC does not require consideration to create an option contract. However, under UCC 2-205, the "firm offer rule," such an offer must be made in a signed writing. Unlike the UCC, the common law requires consideration to create an option contract.

13. False. UCC 2-207 does not require a "mirror image" acceptance, but only "definite and seasonable expression of acceptance."

14. False. A bilateral contract is a promise in exchange for a promise. However, a unilateral contract, is a promise in exchange for an act. Consequently, while the offer is a promise, the offeree can only accept the offer by completely performing the act.

15. True. Under the mailbox rule, an acceptance is effective upon dispatch, whether or not the offeror has received it. However, If the offeror specifies that he or she requires actual notifice, the offeror must actually receive notice of the acceptance before a contract is formed.

16. False. Because so many means of communication exist today, an offeree is impliedly authorized to use any reasonable channel for communicating his or her acceptance.

17. False. Except in an implied-in-fact contract, neither the UCC nor the common law allow acceptance by silence.

18. True. The mailbox rule does not apply to revocations, which must be communicated to be effective. Therefore, when an acceptance is dispatched before communication of a revocation, the acceptance controls.

19. True. The mailbox rule does not apply to rejections.

20. False. Because the bargain element is missing, a gift cannot count as consideration.

21. False. The bargain element requires a conscious exchange *at the time* the promise is given. A past service or benefit cannot be consideration for a contract.

22. True. Under UCC 2-209(1), parties to an existing contract are free to modify or change its terms, and such modifications or changes do not require any further consideration to be binding. Note, however, that the common law requires new consideration to modify a contract.

23. True. Contracts with minors are voidable at the option of the minor. However, under quasi-contract, a minor's parents are responsible for paying the reasonable cost of necessaries for their children.

24. True. Conditional promises are valid if the promisor lacks the power to prevent the satisfaction of the condition.

25. False. The promise to forbear or abandon the prosecution of a legal claim is valuable consideration, even if it is uncertain, as long as the party making the promise has a good faith belief in the claim's merit.

26. **False.** If there is no contract between the parties, promissory estoppel action is another way to enforce the agreement. Promissory estoppel claims are based on detrimental reliance.

27. **False.** Mutual mistake must go to the "very heart of the exchange." If it does, each party may invoke it as a basis for avoiding the obligations of the bargain.

28. **True.** Court will not enforce penalty clauses importantly, contract law only compensates for economic losses, not "emotional," "moral," or "ethical" ones because they go beyond compensating for losses and seek to punish or deter even efficient breaches of the contract.

29. **False.** A court will only find economic duress when there is an illegitimate or illegal threat to another party's economic interests. Mere economic necessity and hard bargaining are not enough.

30. **True.** In the case of an anticipatory repudiation, the non-repudiating party can sue immediately for material breach of the contract, or can affirm the contract and await the due date of performance.

31. **False.** A third-party beneficiary's rights may vest in three different situations: (1) the third party detrimentally relies on the promise, (2) the third party sues the promisor for failure to perform as promised, or (3) the third party expresses consent to receive the performance of the promisor (when that consent has been requested by one of the contracting parties and is not merely volunteered).

32. **False.** In general, a contract's rights (namely, the right to be paid) are freely assignable, even if the contract specifically states otherwise.

33. **False.** *Subjective impossibility is not an excuse.* If it is only *personally* impossible for the promisor to accomplish performance, there is no excuse. However, *objective impossibility is an excuse.* Objective impossibility means no one could accomplish performance.

34. **True.** If a defect in the promisor's performance substantially affects the reasonable expectations of the aggrieved promisee, the breach is "material," or, as the Restatement (Second) terms it, "total."

35. **False.** A minor breach is any default or defect in the promisor's performance that does not seriously disappoint the reasonable expectations of the promisee. The contractual relationship is not destroyed by a minor breach.

36. **False.** Under UCC 2-601, there are three options available to a buyer who receives nonconforming goods. The buyer may (1) reject the whole, (2) accept the whole, or (3) accept any commercial unit or units and reject the balance.

37. **False.** Under UCC 2-602, the buyer's cannot reject nonconforming goods unless the buyer gives the seller specific notice of any nonconformity within a commercially

reasonable amount of time. Failure on the part of the buyer to provide such notice is treated as an acceptance of the goods, and the buyer is obligated to pay the full contract price. Providing such notice is treated as an acceptance of the goods, and the buyer is obligated to pay the full contract price.

38. **True.** In order to be compensable at law, damages must be a consequence of the breach.

39. **True.** Equitable relief is only available if a party can show that money damages (or "remedies at law") will *not* suffice, in whole or in part.

40. **False.** A court will never specifically enforce an employment contract because the Constitution prohibits involuntary servitude and it would be next to impossible for a court to monitor the employment agreement.

MULTIPLE CHOICE QUESTION
TOPIC LIST

Now that you have used the T/F questions to reinforce your basic knowledge of the black letter law, work through the multiple choice questions to test your ability to recognize how these rules work in hypothetical scenarios similar to the ones you may see on your exam.

1. UCC 2-207; additional terms that materially alter the contract

2. Incidental third-party beneficiary

3. Bilateral executory accord

4. Statute of frauds writing requirements (UCC 2-201)

5. UCC 2-207: materially altering terms of original offer

6. Damages recoverable by buyer under the UCC (UCC 2-713)

7. Unilateral mistake

8. Statute of frauds

9. Contract modification without consideration

10. Offer—advertisement

11. Unilateral contract

12. Bilateral contract

13. Pre-existing duty rule

14. Delegator/assignor

15. Debt barred by statute of limitations

16. Breach of contract action—damages recoverable

17. Subcontractor bids—failure to perform

18. Rejection of nonconforming goods (UCC 2-601)

19. Nonconforming goods—seller's assurance to cure (UCC 2-508)

20. Unilateral offer—revocation

21. Unilateral offer—revocation

22. Part performance—implied promise to complete

23. Revocation of offer

24. Promise to pay indebtedness discharged in bankruptcy

25. Liquidated damage clause

26. Parol evidence rule

27. Constructive conditions precedent

28. Remedies—damages

29. Contract formation—mutuality of assent requirement

30. Contract interpretation

31. Failure to perform—breach

32. Acceptance—unilateral contract

33. Resale of goods (UCC 2-706)

34. Damages

35. Impossibility

36. Breach of contract

37. Rightfully rejected goods (UCC 2-603)

38. Acceptance of nonconforming goods

39. Counteroffer operates as a rejection

40. Revocation

41. Offer—acceptance

42. Rejection

43. Option contract—supported by consideration

44. Acceptance of option contract within option period

45. Unilateral mistake—knowledge of offeree

46. Mistake in transmission—knowledge of offeree

47. Unilateral contract

48. Reward offer

49. Lack of consideration

50. Promissory estoppel

51. Auction "without reserve"

52. Minor breach of contract

53. Non-performance

54. Parol evidence rule

55. Consideration—bargained-for exchange

56. Consideration—forbearance

57. Statute of Frauds—voidable promise

58. Consideration—distinguishing a condition

59. Assignment—rights of assignee

60. Subsequent promise by debtor to pay debt discharged in bankruptcy

61. Subjective impossibility

62. Assignment—material change of obligor's duty

63. Delegation—personal services contract

64. Unjust enrichment

65. Assignment of rights

66. Subsequent agreements not covered by parol evidence rule

67. Parol evidence rule

68. Pre-existing duty rule

69. Breach of contract—damages

70. Failure to cooperate as breach of condition

71. Firm Offer Rule (UCC 2-205)

72. Acceptance containing additional terms (UCC 2-207)

73. Distinction between condition precedent and parol evidence

74. Third-party donee beneficiary—vesting of rights

75. Intended third-party donee beneficiary

76. Pre-existing duty rule/modification (UCC 2-209)

77. Illusory promise

78. Divisible contract

79. Consideration—contract formation

80. Intended third-party beneficiary

81. Distinction between unilateral and bilateral contracts

82. Breach/damages

83. Option contract

84. Revocation

85. Unilateral mistake

86. Prior assignment—rights of subsequent assignee

87. Adequate assurances of performance (UCC 2-609)

88. Contract provision requiring modifications to be in writing (UCC 2-209)

89. Impracticability of performance

90. Express condition precedent

91. Constructive condition precedent

92. Condition of satisfaction

93. Personal services contract

94. Statute of frauds

95. Breach of contract/recovery for personal injuries

96. Rights of an incidental beneficiary

97. Parol evidence rule

98. Trade custom and usage

99. Consideration (pre-existing duty rule)

100. Promissory estoppel

101. Pre-existing duty rule

102. Unilateral contract

103. Discharge of contract

104. Breach of contract—measure of damages

105. Unilateral contract—acceptance by performance (UCC 2-206)

106. Delivery of nonconforming goods—remedies (UCC 2-608)

107. Architect's certificate of completion

108. Breach of implied promise

109. Breach of contract

110. Third-party donee beneficiary (vesting of rights)

111. Moral obligation—insufficient past consideration

112. Oral modifications

113. Statute of frauds—voidable promise

114. Suretyship agreement

115. Surety promise

116. Contract provision—F.O.B. seller's place of business

117. F.O.B. seller's place of business—risk of loss on buyer

118. "Requirements-output" contracts (UCC 2-306)

119. Parol evidence rule (UCC 2-202)

120. Open price term (UCC 2-305)

121. Modification (UCC 2-209)

122. Impossibility—supervening illegality

123. Parol evidence rule

124. Accord and satisfaction

125. Constructive condition precedent

126. Assignment—personal services contracts

127. Material breach—partial failure of performance

128. Specific performance—land sale contract

129. Impossibility—supervening illegality

130. Condition precedent

131. Assignment of future rights

132. Assignment of future rights

133. Defective assignment—creditor's rights

134. Duties of performance

135. Restrictive covenant—"not to compete"

136. Penalty or forfeiture clause

137. Gratuitous assignment of future rights

138. Condition precedent

139. Anticipatory repudiation—remedies available under the Restatement

140. Impossibility of performance/frustration of purpose

141. Waiver of condition

142. Installment contract (UCC 2-612)

143. Installment contract (UCC 2-612)

144. Material breach—substantial nonconformity

145. Temporary impossibility

146. Gratuitous assignment

147. Impossibility of performance—conditions in a contract

148. Bilateral contract

149. Doctrine of subjective impossibility

150. Risk of loss

MULTIPLE CHOICE QUESTIONS

Questions 1–2 are based on the following fact situation.

Kinky Friedman owned Friedman's Men's Haberdashery in Dallas. To accommodate his customer, Elton Hightower, Friedman ordered by telephone from Englishware Ltd., a wholesale supplier of cashmere and wool clothing, a "triple-dozen purple cashmere socks, size 10-13 at current resale price." Englishware's sales agent, Cass Wooley, orally accepted the order at the agreed price of $250 per dozen. In accordance with Englishware's customary business practice, Cass then mailed the following confirmation letter, which he signed and dated:

> "As per your telephone order, this letter serves to confirm the purchase of 36 dozen cashmere socks, color purple, size 10-13, at the agreed price of $250 per dozen. Total sales price: $9,000."

This letter was received by Kinky, who briefly glanced at it but failed to notice the "36 dozen" wording or the total price. Kinky placed the letter in his files and did not respond to it. Three weeks later, Englishware tendered 36 dozen purple cashmere socks, which Kinky rejected on the ground that he had ordered only three dozen.

1. Assume for the purposes of this question only that Englishware resold the same purple cashmere socks to another buyer for a total price of $8,000. Englishware now sues Friedman for the $1,000 difference. If Friedman pleads the statute of frauds as a defense, will such a defense be successful?

(A) Yes, because the statute was not satisfied by Englishware's tender of the goods that were rejected by Friedman, and Englishware did not rely on the oral agreement other than by attempting delivery.

(B) Yes, because the agreed price for three dozen socks was over $500, and Englishware's written memo incorrectly stated the quantity of goods ordered.

(C) No, because Englishware's written memo was sufficient to satisfy the statute as against Englishware, and Friedman, having reason to know of the memo's contents, failed to give notice of objection within ten days of receipt.

(D) No, because Englishware's written memo operated as an acceptance, with proposals for additional terms that became part of the contract after Friedman failed to object to such additional terms within a reasonable time.

2. For the purposes of this question only, you are to make the following assumptions: Englishware refused to supply Friedman with the purple cashmere socks in any quantity less than 36 dozen for the agreed price of $250 per dozen. In refusing to tender Friedman's order for 3 dozen socks: Englishware has thus committed an actionable breach of contract. Without having brought any action against Englishware, Friedman died and his haberdashery went out of business. In the event that Elton Hightower could not obtain the desired cashmere socks elsewhere, is it likely that he could prevail in a contract action against Englishware?

(A) Yes, because by operation of law, Hightower is an equitable assignee of Friedman's claim against Englishware for breach of contract.
(B) Yes, but only if Hightower had initially entered into an enforceable contract with Friedman for the purchase of the three dozen cashmere socks.
(C) No, because privity of contract does not exist between Hightower and Englishware.
(D) No, because Hightower is only an incidental beneficiary of the Friedman-Englishware wholesale contract.

Question 3 is based on the following fact situation.

Crednix loaned his friend Debtnor $15,000 to help pay Debtnor's daughter, Daphne's, college tuition. Six months later, Debtnor lost his job and was unable to repay the loan to Crednix. After learning of Debtnor's situation, Crednix sent Debtnor the following letter on June 1:

> "I promise to discharge the $15,000 debt that you owe me if you deliver your Ty Cobb autographed baseball bat to me by August 1st."

After receiving this letter, Debtnor telephoned Crednix and promised to accept the offer.

3. Debtnor's verbal acceptance of Crednix's offer most likely effectuated

(A) an executory accord.
(B) an accord and satisfaction.
(C) a substituted compromise agreement.
(D) a novation.

Questions 4–6 are based on the following fact situation.

Harry Hillcrest was the owner of the newly constructed Hillcrest Hotel in the city of Hillsdale. On March 15, 2008, Harry received a telephone call from Butch Burns, a distributor of hotel equipment, who offered to sell him 1,000 fire extinguishers for his hotel. Butch told Harry that the cost of the fire extinguishers would be $35,000 (or $35 apiece), payable 90 days after delivery. Butch promised to have the fire extinguishers installed no later than April 15, 2008.

On March 16, 2008, Harry telephoned Butch and accepted the offer. The following day, Harry mailed the following memo to Butch: "Please be advised that I shall take a 15% discount for cash payment 7 days after installation." Butch received Harry's correspondence on March 20, but he didn't respond until April 1, at which time, Butch sent a telegram to Harry stating: "It's apparent we don't have an enforceable contract in effect. I will not be delivering the fire extinguishers on April 15 or any other time."

4. Suppose Harry brings suit against Butch for breach of contract. Butch claims the statute of frauds as a defense. Which of the following is the most accurate statement regarding Butch's defenses?

   (A) His defense is valid because Harry's memo was not sufficient to indicate that a contract was formed.
   (B) His defense is valid because Harry's memo was inconsistent with the terms of Butch's oral offer.
   (C) His defense is not valid because Butch failed to respond to Harry's memo within a reasonable period of time.
   (D) His defense is not valid because, under the UCC, the statute of frauds is not applicable in agreements between merchants.

5. Assume for the purposes of this question only that Butch admits making a contract for the sale of the fire extinguishers, but argues there was never any agreement as to a cash discount. Harry insists on the price of $29,750 ($35,000 less 15%) with cash payment within 7 days after installation. Which of the following accurately states the legal rights of the parties?

   (A) The contract price is $29,750 for cash payment because Harry's March 17 memo was integrated into the agreement.
   (B) The contract price is $29,750 for cash payment because Butch did not object to the 15% discount stipulated by Harry in his March 17 memo within a reasonable amount of time.
   (C) The contract price is $35,000 because the discount terms in Harry's March 17 memo materially altered the terms of Butch's offer.
   (D) The contract price is $35,000 even though Butch's offer did not expressly limit acceptance to the terms contained therein.

6. Assume for the purposes of this question only that after Harry received Butch's April 1 telegram, he (Harry) filed suit against Butch for breach of contract on April 15. At trial, the court rules in Harry's favor. Under the UCC, which of the following would be used as the market price of the fire extinguishers for purposes of computing damages?

   (A) The market price on March 16.
   (B) The market price on April 1.
   (C) The market price on April 15.
   (D) The average market price between April 1 and April 15.

Questions 7–9 are based on the following fact situation.

Cheryl Miller, a purchasing agent for Strawbridge & Clothier (hereafter referred to as Strawbridge), negotiated a contract with Indian Khaki Co. (hereafter referred to as Khaki) to purchase a specified quantity of khaki garments at a price of $75,000. During negotiations, Khaki said, "Because of our long-term relationship, you're entitled to a $15,000 discount from the normal price of $90,000." In fact, Strawbridge and Khaki had never dealt with each other before. When the president of Strawbridge learned of the deal, he told Cheryl he would promote her to manager of Strawbridge's Philadelphia store.

One week later on December 3, 2008, Cheryl received a telephone call from Robert Leighton, vice-president of Khaki, who informed her that Khaki's sales representative had made an error in calculating the contract price. As a result, Leighton said that unless Strawbridge agreed to pay an additional $15,000, Khaki would not deliver the said garments. The president of Strawbridge telephones Khaki and agrees to pay the additional $15,000.

7. Suppose for the purposes of this question only that Cheryl knew that Khaki thought it was making a deal with a different customer. Which of the following is the most accurate statement?

(A) There was an enforceable contract at the original price because the mistake resulted from an error in computation, not in judgment.
(B) There was a contract at the original price because the mistake was unilateral.
(C) There was no contract at the original price because Khaki thought it was making a deal with a different customer.
(D) There was no contract because Cheryl was aware of Khaki's error.

8. Assume for the purposes of this question only that Cheryl neither knew nor had reason to know of Khaki's mistake. Consequently, the modification wherein Strawbridge agreed to pay the additional $15,000 is

(A) enforceable, even though it was not supported by any new consideration.
(B) enforceable, under the principle of promissory estoppel.
(C) unenforceable, because it is violative of the Statute of Frauds.
(D) unenforceable, because the error resulted from Khaki's computational error.

9. Which of the following is the legal effect of Strawbridge promise to promote Cheryl?

(A) It is enforceable because Cheryl conferred a material benefit on behalf of Strawbridge.
(B) It is enforceable because Strawbridge was morally obligated to make the promotion.
(C) It is unenforceable because Cheryl was not an intended third-party beneficiary to the agreement between Strawbridge and Khaki.
(D) It is unenforceable as a gift promise.

Questions 10–11 are based on the following fact situation.

Thompson's Dry Goods Store published the following advertisement in the *Silver City Morning News* on Monday, March 12, 2008:

> "8 Brand New STETSON COWBOY HATS Beaver Felt, selling for $72.50 ... out they go ... Sat. March 17, Each ... $5.00
>
> 1 Navajo Turquoise Necklace ... worth $125.00, now selling for $40.00 ...
>
> "FIRST COME, FIRST SERVED"

On the following Saturday, Roy was the first person to arrive at the store and demanded the necklace. The store clerk refused to sell it to him because it was a "house rule" that the sale was intended for women only.

10. If Roy brings suit against Thompson's Dry Goods for its refusal to sell him the necklace, Roy will

    (A) lose, since the advertisement was only intended as an invitation to make an offer.
    (B) lose, since Roy did not notify the Store in writing that he intended to accept the offer.
    (C) win, because the advertisement should be construed as a binding offer.
    (D) win, even if Roy was not the first customer to appear at the store to purchase the necklace.

11. In evaluating the relationship between Roy and the Dry Goods Store, the court would most likely find that

    (A) Roy's acceptance created a bilateral contract.
    (B) Roy's acceptance created a unilateral contract.
    (C) under the resulting contract, both parties had a right and a duty of performance.
    (D) the "house rule" of selling to women only would preclude Roy from becoming a party to a contract with the store.

Questions 12–14 are based on the following fact situation.

On the morning of Wednesday, January 9, the following conversation took place:

Tony: "My stereo speakers haven't been sounding well lately. The owner of Stereo Sound promised to give me $15.00 for them, and I think I'll take him up on the offer."

Ruben: "Don't do that, Tony. In my spare time, I repair stereo speakers. If you promise to pay me $20.00, I promise to repair them by next Tuesday and they'll be in tip-top condition."

Tony: "Super! It's a deal."

The following Wednesday, this conversation took place:

Tony: "Have you repaired my speakers yet?"

Ruben: "No. I've decided to leave tomorrow for a month's vacation in Bermuda, and I won't have time to fix the speakers."

Tony: "Look, I realize that $20.00 was a low price for the work that's needed. If you can fix them by tomorrow, I'll pay you an additional $20.00. Also, I won't file the small claims suit against you that I was planning to initiate today."

Ruben: "Okay. Hold off on the suit and give me $20.00 more tomorrow when I return the repaired speakers."

The next day, Ruben gave Tony the speakers, repaired to tip-top condition. Tony refused to give Ruben the additional $20.00.

12. The conversation that took place on January 9 resulted in

(A) a contract for the sale of services governed by the Uniform Commercial Code.
(B) a unilateral contract.
(C) a bilateral contract.
(D) an unconscionable contract.

13. In a suit by Ruben in small claims court to recover the additional $20.00 promised by Tony, Ruben will

(A) win, because he performed his part of the bargain.
(B) win, because the second contract for $40.00 superseded the original $20.00 contract.
(C) lose, because the $40.00 contract did not supersede the $20.00 contract.
(D) lose, because Ruben had a pre-existing duty to repair the stereo speakers for $20.00.

14. Assume that on January 10, Ruben gave the stereo speakers to Pancho, who entered into a valid contract with Ruben to restore the speakers to tip-top condition. Pancho was under the legitimate impression that the speakers actually belonged to Ruben. If Pancho fails to repair the speakers

(A) Tony has a cause of action against Pancho only.
(B) Tony has a cause of action against Ruben only.
(C) Tony has a cause of action against Ruben and Pancho.
(D) Tony has no cause of action against Ruben or Pancho.

Question 15 is based on the following fact situation.

Debtrix owed Creditor $750 on an old debt. On July 1 the debt was barred by the statute of limitations. On August 1 Debtrix ran into Creditor at a party and overheard him telling mutual friends that "Debtrix is a deadbeat." Feeling pangs of guilt, Debtrix approached Creditor and orally agreed to pay him the $750 debt on September 1.

15. Assume that Debtrix refuses to pay Creditor the $750 as promised on September 1. If Creditor sues Debtrix to recover the $750 debt, which would provide the strongest grounds that Debtrix's oral promise was unenforceable?

(A) It was not supported by new consideration.
(B) It was violative of the statute of frauds.
(C) The debt was already barred by the statute of limitations.
(D) There was no mutuality of obigation.

Questions 16–17 are based on the following fact situation.

Ohner wanted to have a security system installed in his home. He contacted several companies and asked them to submit bids for the installation work. One of them, Alarmco, in turn, requested bids from several wholesalers for the burglar alarms it planned to use if it was awarded the job. Supplier submitted a bid to Alarmco that the latter used in computing the bid that it was preparing for Ohner.

On September 1, Alarmco sent Ohner its bid proposing to install the security system for $12,000. On September 9, Supplier notified Alarmco that it would be unable to supply any burglar alarms to it. On September 11, Ohner sent the following telegram to Alarmco, "I hereby accept your offer to install the security system for $12,000."

Alarmco had to pay another wholesaler $3,000 above the price quoted by Supplier for the burglar alarms. As a result, Alarmco advised Ohner that the total price for the job would have to be increased to $15,000. Ohner replied that he would hold Alarmco to the original price of $12,000. Alarmco installed the security system, but Ohner has not yet paid it anything.

16. In an action by Alarmco against Ohner for services rendered, Alarmco will be able to recover

   (A) $12,000, because that was the contract price.
   (B) $15,000, because there was an unanticipated change of circumstances after the parties entered into their contract.
   (C) only in quantum meruit, because of the doctrine of commercial frustration.
   (D) only in quantum meruit, because, by demanding $15,000 Alarmco repudiated its original contract with Ohner.

17. Which of the following arguments best supports the claim for $3,000 by Alarmco against Supplier?

   (A) Alarmco made an offer to Supplier that Supplier accepted when Alarmco submitted its bid.
   (B) A contract was created between Supplier and Ohner when Alarmco used Supplier's bid.
   (C) Supplier's bid was an offer that it was obligated to hold open for a reasonable amount of time because both Supplier and Alarmco were merchants.
   (D) An option contract was created because Alarmco used Supplier's bid in the bid it submitted to Ohner and notified Supplier of that fact.

Questions 18–19 are based on the following fact situation.

On February 15, 2008, The Alumalloy Co. (Alumalloy), a manufacturer of metal sidings for home exteriors, received the following order from Westside Construction Co. (Westside): "Please ship 300 sheets of 1/4″ refabricated aluminum siding. Delivery by April 1, 2008."

On March 8, 2008 Alumalloy shipped 300 sheets of 1/2″ refabricated aluminum siding to Westside. The following day, Dave Shell, owner of Westside, emailed Timothy Trister, Alumalloy's president, "Be advised that your shipment is rejected. Order stipulated 1/4″ sheets." This email was received by Trister on March 13, 2008. Westside, however, did not ship the nonconforming aluminum sheets back to Alumalloy.

On March 14, 2008, Trister sent the following email to Shell: "Will ship conforming 1/4″ aluminum sheets before April 1, 2008." This email was received by Shell on March 15, 2008, but he did not respond to it. On March 27, 2008, Alumalloy tendered 300 sheets of 1/4″ refabricated aluminum siding to Westside, which the latter refused to accept.

18. Did Westside properly reject the first shipment delivered on March 10, 2008?

    (A) Yes, because the aluminum sheets were nonconforming goods.
    (B) Yes, because Alumalloy did not notify Westside that the 1/2″ sheets were for accommodation only.
    (C) No, because Westside waived its right to reject the nonconforming goods by not returning them immediately to Alumalloy.
    (D) No, because Alumalloy could accept Westside's offer by prompt shipment of any goods, whether conforming or nonconforming, so long as the goods were similar to those ordered by Westside.

19. Did Westside properly reject the aluminum sheets delivered on March 27, 2008?

    (A) No, because Alumalloy effectively modified the contract.
    (B) No, because Alumalloy cured the March 8th defective shipment by its tender of conforming goods on March 27th.
    (C) Yes, because Alumalloy's shipping of the 1/2″ sheets on March 8 constituted an anticipatory breach.
    (D) Yes, because Alumalloy's shipping of the 1/2″ sheets on March 8 constituted a present breach of contract.

Questions 20–22 are based on the following fact situation.

On Friday, February 13, Orlando dispatched the following letter to Juan:

"Dear Juan,

My Volvo hasn't been running very well lately. I'll pay you $275 if you will change the oil, replace the oil filter, and adjust the carburetors.

/s/ Orlando"

Juan received Orlando's letter on Monday, February 16. That same day, he telephoned Pep Boy's Auto Supply Co. and ordered the necessary materials to perform the repair work. Two days later, however, Orlando met Juan at a party and this conversation took place:

Orlando: "Disregard the letter that I sent you last week."

Juan: "No way, man, I ordered the materials on Monday from Pep Boys."

Orlando: "Sorry, man, but I sold the Volvo yesterday to Leon, so forget the repair work."

20. If Juan initiates suit for breach of contract, which of the following is Orlando's strongest argument that no enforceable contract was formed between him and Juan?

    (A) Juan had not completed performance before Orlando revoked his offer.
    (B) Orlando's offer could only be accepted by a return promise.
    (C) Since Orlando made his offer by letter, Juan could accept only in the same manner.
    (D) Although Juan was preparing to perform the repair work, he had not begun the requested acts of acceptance when Orlando revoked his offer.

21. If Juan initiates suit for breach of contract, which of the following is his strongest argument that an enforceable contract was formed between him and Orlando?

    (A) Since Juan had a reasonable time in which to accept the offer, Orlando's wrongful revocation would be ineffective.
    (B) Since Juan was a merchant, Orlando's written offer was irrevocable for a period not exceeding three months.
    (C) Because Orlando's offer invited a return promise as acceptance, Juan manifested his intent to perform by ordering the materials.
    (D) After Juan obtained the materials for the repair work, he went over to Orlando's and changed the oil on the Volvo.

22. Suppose for the purposes of this question only that Orlando did not sell his Volvo and he did not attempt to revoke his offer. Instead, he gave his car to Juan, who proceeded to perform the necessary repair work. However, after Juan replaced the oil filter and changed the oil in the Volvo, he telephoned Orlando and told him that he was leaving the next day for a month's vacation in Maui. As a result, Juan told Orlando that he wouldn't be able to make the necessary carburetor adjustment until he returned home. If Orlando brings suit against Juan for breach of contract, judgment for whom?

    (A) Juan, because he has substantially performed by completing two-thirds of the job.
    (B) Juan, because the contract was divisible and he could elect to perform part of the services requested by Orlando's offer.
    (C) Orlando, because Juan's part performance necessarily implied an acceptance and a promise that he would render complete performance.
    (D) Orlando, because under the doctrine of equitable estoppel, Juan's part performance was evidence of his intent to honor the entire contract.

Questions 23–24 are based on the following fact situation.

Wyeth, an art collector, by letter dated March 15, 2008, offered to sell Warhol a painting by Pyle for $10,000. The letter stated that the offer would remain open for 30 days from the date of the letter, with delivery of the painting within ten days of acceptance. On March 25, Wyeth wrote Warhol that the offer of March 15 was withdrawn. Warhol received the March 25 letter on March 26. On March 27, Warhol wrote Wyeth the following letter: "Please be advised that I hereby accept your offer of March 15, 2008." Wyeth received this letter on March 28.

Thereafter, Wyeth and Warhol engaged in several telephone discussions. On April 10, Warhol, in a telephone conversation, told Wyeth that he would pay $15,000 if the Pyle painting was delivered on or before April 15; Wyeth agreed to deliver the painting for $15,000.

Wyeth owed Dixon $15,000 on a debt that had been discharged by Wyeth's bankruptcy a year previously. On April 12, Wyeth wrote Dixon a letter stating that he would pay Dixon $10,000 from the proceeds of the sale of the Pyle painting in payment of the discharged debt. Warhol knew nothing of the arrangement between Wyeth and Dixon.

On April 15, 2008, Wyeth tendered the painting, but Warhol refused to pay more than $10,000.

23. If Wyeth asserts a claim against Warhol for breach of contract, which of the following is the most accurate statement?

    (A) Wyeth is obligated to sell Warhol the painting for $10,000 because Warhol, as offeree, had the right to accept Wyeth's offer within the option period.

    (B) Since Wyeth, as offeror, had the power to revoke the original offer before acceptance, Warhol is obligated under the terms of their April 10 agreement.

    (C) Since the parties entered into a subsequent modification of the original contract, Warhol is obligated to pay Wyeth $15,000 for the painting.

    (D) An enforceable contract does not exist between the parties because of mutual mistake of fact.

24. Assume for the purposes of this question only that Wyeth now refuses to pay Dixon anything. If Dixon brings suit against Wyeth for breach of contract, he should be entitled to recover

    (A) nothing.

    (B) $10,000.

    (C) $10,000, only if Warhol purchased the painting from Wyeth.

    (D) $15,000.

Question 25 is based on the following fact situation.

Charlene was hired by Bob's Big Boy Restaurant (Bob's) as a cashier under an employment-at-will contract. On Charlene's first day at work, she noticed a sign in the kitchen area that read:

"IMPORTANT NOTICE TO ALL EMPLOYEES

Employees are not permitted to smoke during working hours. Any employee who is found to be in violation of this policy will be fined $50 for the first offense; $100 for the second offense; and fired for the third violation."

Charlene, who was a smoker, read the notice but did not object or make any comment regarding the restaurant's non-smoking policy. For six months, Charlene worked at Bob's and never smoked during business hours. One afternoon Charlene was working when an armed robber stormed into the restaurant. He pointed a pistol at Charlene and demanded all the money from the cash register. Frightened and panic-stricken, Charlene handed over the money and then collapsed. Moments later, she regained consciousness and then smoked a cigarette while she regained her composure. Thereafter, Charlene resumed her duties for the rest of the day. The next week, however, when Charlene received her pay-check, she noticed that Bob's had deducted $50. A note was attached indicating that Charlene was being fined for smoking during business hours. Although Charlene protested, Bob's refused to make any waiver and stood by its policy.

25. In an action by Charlene against Bob's to recover the $50, which of the following is the best argument in Charlene's favor?

    (A) Bob's non-smoking policy concerned a collateral matter that was not incorporated within the terms of their employment contract.
    (B) Bob's impliedly waived the non-smoking provision by permitting Charlene to continue working for the rest of the day.
    (C) The non-smoking provision constituted a constructive condition subsequent that was excused due to temporary impracticability.
    (D) The non-smoking provision concerning disciplinary action is unenforceable because it attempts to impose a penalty instead of reasonably liquidating the damages, if any, sustained by Bob's.

Questions 26–28 are based on the following fact situation.

Morgana, a 25-year-old concert pianist, lived in a small studio apartment on West 52nd Street in New York City. Morgana couldn't keep a piano in her apartment because of its small dimensions. In order to practice each day, she had to travel to the Julliard School of Performing Arts to use their musical facilities. Finally, Morgana decided to move out of her apartment and buy a more spacious home where she could have her own piano. As she was house hunting, Morgana found a quaint Cape Cod-style home in Westchester that she wanted. She put a bid down on the home with the seller's broker. She was informed that the owner was in Europe on a business trip and would not be entertaining any offers until he returned.

While she was awaiting word on the Westchester property, Morgana's friend, Tito, orally agreed to sell his Baldwin Baby Grand to her for $8,000. Morgana explained that she wanted the piano only if she should succeed in her efforts to buy the Westchester home. For this reason, the parties agreed that the piano sale would not take effect "unless Morgana buys the Westchester home." The next day, the parties reduced their oral agreement to a signed writing, but the writing did not mention that the sale would not take effect unless Morgana bought the home in Westchester. Two weeks later, the owner of the Westchester property returned from Europe and rejected Morgana's offer.

26. Tito now brings an action against Morgana for breach of contract to buy the Baldwin piano. How should the court rule on Morgana's offer to prove, over Tito's objection, that she has not been able to buy the Cape Cod home in Westchester?

    (A) The evidence is admissible in order to show that the written agreement was not a correct statement of the parties' intentions.
    (B) The evidence is admissible to show frustration of the purpose of the contract.
    (C) The evidence is barred because the oral agreement is within the statute of frauds.
    (D) The evidence is barred by the parol evidence rule.

27. Assume for the purposes of this question only that Tito and Morgana had incorporated in their written agreement a provision wherein the sale would not take effect "unless Morgana is successful in her bid to buy the Cape Cod home in Westchester." Subsequently, the owner of the property made a reasonable offer to sell the house to Morgana. She, however, had reservations about moving out of the city and decided that she would rather remain in New York City because of job commitments. Which of the following would be Tito's strongest argument in support of an action against Morgana for breach of contract?

(A) The purchase of the Westchester home was not worded specifically as a "condition" to Morgana's duty to buy the piano.

(B) Although the purchase of the Westchester home was a condition to Morgana's duty to buy the piano, the condition should be excused because its non-occurrence would cause a forfeiture to Tito.

(C) Although the purchase of the Westchester home was a condition to Morgana's duty to buy the piano, it should be stricken from the contract because it is an unconscionable term.

(D) Morgana breached an implied promise to make a reasonable effort to purchase the Westchester home.

28. Assume for the purposes of this question only that Morgana did, in fact, purchase the Cape Cod home in Westchester. Thereupon, she tendered a $8,000 cashier's check to Tito for the Baldwin piano. Tito rejected the tender and refused to deliver the piano to Morgana. If Morgana brings an action for breach of contract against Tito, Morgana is entitled to which of the following remedies?

(A) Specific performance.

(B) Specific performance or the difference between the market price of the piano and the contract price, at Morgana's election.

(C) Specific performance or the contract price for the piano, at Morgana's election.

(D) None of the above.

Questions 29–30 are based on the following fact situation.

Andy Toney, a third-year student at Delaware Law School, was the captain of the law school rugby club. One evening, Toney and a few of his rugby teammates were drinking beer at Pete's Pub, a favorite Delaware Law School hangout. They were worried that the rugby club, know as the "Leatherballs," would be forced to disband because the law school had withdrawn its sponsorship. While Andy was discussing the problem with his teammates, Pete Maravich, the owner of the tavern, approached the players. He indicated that he was interested in sponsoring the rugby club because he felt it would help business at the pub. During their ensuing discussion, Pete agreed to sponsor the rugby club. The parties then orally agreed that Pete "would pay for all the usual sponsoring fees" incurred by the club.

Pete had understood the agreement to mean that he would pay for the rugby shirts and supply the keg of beer following each "home" game that the "Leatherballs" played. Conversely, Andy thought that Pete would be reimbursing the team for (a) the shirts, (b) the keg of beer (following "home" games), as well as (c) transportation expenses for "away" games and (d) equipment expenses.

29. Assume for the purposes of this question only that it was the customary practice of the rugby teams in the community to have the sponsors pay for (a) the shirts and (b) the beer. Before the "Leatherballs" were to play their first game under Pete's sponsorship, which of the following is the most accurate statement regarding the legal relationship between the parties?

    (A) A contract exists on the terms understood by Pete.
    (B) A contract exists on the terms understood by Andy.
    (C) A contract exists on the terms that are customary for the other teams in the community.
    (D) No contract exists.

30. Assume for the purposes of this question only that Pete and Andy entered into an enforceable contract. Which of the ollowing, if true, would establish that the contract was made using Pete's terms?

    I. The customary practice of the other rugby clubs in the community is the same as Pete's understanding that the sponsor be responsible for paying for (a) the shirts and (b) the beer.
    II. A reasonably objective individual would have attached the same meaning to the negotiations between the parties.

III. At the time the agreement was entered into, Andy had reason to know Pete's understanding of the contract.

    (A) I and II.
    (B) I and III.
    (C) II and III.
    (D) I, II and III.

Question 31 is based on the following fact situation.

M, a manufacturer of widgets, entered into a written agreement to deliver 500 widgets to B. The contract provided that the widgets would be shipped C.O.D. M subsequently delivered 490 widgets, which were accepted and paid for by B.

31. If B brings suit for breach of contract against M, plaintiff will most likely

    (A) not recover, because under the circumstances, M substantially performed.
    (B) not recover, because B accepted delivery of the 490 widgets.
    (C) recover, because M failed to perform his contractual obligation.
    (D) recover, only if M's failure to deliver the additional widgets resulted in a material or "total" breach.

Questions 32–34 are based on the following fact situation.

National Widget Company, whose principal business office is located in Ft. Worth, Texas, is engaged in the retail sale of widgets throughout the United States. McCormick Equipment Corporation is the nation's largest manufacturer and wholesaler of widgets. McCormick's corporate headquarters are located in Nashville, Tennessee. On March 7, 2008, Johnny Lee, President of National, sent McCormick the following purchase order:

> "Promptly ship 1,000 widgets, catalogue #B4-IEU, at the current wholesale price to our Ft. Worth office. Thank you for your attention to this matter.
>
> s/J. Lee"

This order was received by McCormick on March 9. The next day, McCormick replied by telegram:

> "Your order has been received. Shipment date will be March 12. Price $50 for each widget delivered. Be advised that these are the last widgets under catalogue #B4-IEU we can deliver since this variety is no longer being manufactured."

This telegram was received by Lee on March 11. He immediately telegraphed McCormick:

> "Cancel our previous order for 1,000 widgets under catalogue #B4-IEU. Price too high."

McCormick received this telegram on March 11. On March 13, McCormick sold the 1,000 widgets, catalogue #B4-IEU, to Western Widgetry, another retail widget company in Dallas, for $50 each, which was the current wholesale market price.

32. Was an enforceable contract in effect between National and McCormick?

(A) No, because National's order was too indefinite to constitute an offer since it didn't contain a price term.
(B) No, because even if National's order was a valid offer, it was effectively revoked prior to acceptance.
(C) Yes, because National's order created a valid option contract.
(D) Yes, because McCormick's telegram of March 10 constituted an acceptance of National's offer.

33. Assume for the purposes of this question only that a contract was in fact formed between National and McCormick. On receipt of National's telegram on March 11, McCormick would be legally justified in pursuing which of the following courses?

(A) Shipping the widgets to National.
(B) Selling the widgets to another buyer by means of a public sale.
(C) Selling the widgets to another buyer by means of either a public or private sale.
(D) Selling the widgets to another buyer, but only if McCormick is successful in whatever claims it has against National.

34. Assume for the purposes of this question only that a contract was in fact formed between National and McCormick. In an action for breach of contract by McCormick against National, what is the maximum amount of damages that McCormick should be entitled to recover?

   (A) Nothing.
   (B) Only incidental damages, if any, that McCormick has incurred in preparing the widgets for shipment to National before receiving National's telegram of March 11.
   (C) $50,000, or the price of $50 per widget as ordered.
   (D) Consequential damages since these widgets were unique due to the fact that they were the last of their kind to be manufactured.

Questions 35–36 are based on the following fact situation.

As a 25th anniversary present, Mr. and Mrs. Claus, of Montreal, decided to spend their Christmas and New Year's holidays at the La Valencia Hotel in the country of Erewhon to see the coronation of the island's new queen, Mary. Because the coronation was such a special occasion, the Clauses decided to splurge and stay in the Presidential Suite, the hotel's most luxurious room accommodations. On September 1, Mr. and Mrs. Claus mailed a letter to the La Valencia reserving the Presidential Suite for the period from December 24 to January 1. The La Valencia then sent back a confirmation notice stating that it was reserving the Presidential Suite for the Clauses from December 24 to January 1 "for the weekly rental of $10,000." A week before the coronation, Mary changed her name to Killer and announced she was forming a punk rock band and renouncing her royal rights. Consequently, there would be no coronation. Even so, the Clauses decided they might as well go and enjoy staying in a nice hotel.

On December 23, a blizzard struck Montreal, blanketing the city with five feet of snow. As a result of the storm, the Montreal Airport was shut down. The Clauses immediately telephoned Mr. Martinez, the manager of the La Valencia, and explained their predicament. When Mr. Martinez requested assurance that the Clauses would still be making the trip, Mr. Claus responded, "The airport is scheduled to re-open tomorrow…if it does we hope to make the trip." The next morning, Mr. Martinez sent an email to Mr. and Mrs. Claus advising them that the Presidential Suite had been rented to another couple for the period from December 24 to January 1.

35. If Mr. and Mrs. Claus bring suit against the La Valencia for breach of contract, which of the following will provide the hotel with its best defense?

   (A) La Valencia's duty to hold the Presidential Suite for the Clauses' arrival was excused by the apparent impossibility on December 23 of their timely performance.
   (B) La Valencia acted in good faith when it attempted to cover its potential losses by renting the room to another couple.
   (C) La Valencia's duty to hold the Presidential Suite for the Clauses' arrival was excused by frustration of purpose.
   (D) The Clauses' apparent inability on December 23 to make the trip constituted a material breach that excused La Valencia of any obligation to hold the Presidential Suite for their arrival.

36. Assume for the purposes of this question only that the Clauses did arrive at the La Valencia on December 24 and tendered the agreed rental of $10,000 for the Presidential Suite. Without legal excuse, the hotel had rented the Presidential Suite to former President Reagan and his wife Nancy, who were vacationing in Erehwon for the holidays. Quite apologetic, Mr. Martinez offered the Clauses the hotel's next best accommodation, the Del Mar Suite, at a weekly rental of $9,500. Mr. Martinez informed the Clauses that the Del Mar Suite was beautifully furnished "but not quite as luxurious as the Presidential Suite." Visibly upset, the Clauses rejected Mr. Martinez's offer and traveled eighty miles to the another hotel, where they rented its Presidential Suite for the weekly rental of $10,000. If the Clauses now sue the La Valencia for breach of contract, they will most likely

(A) prevail, because the La Valencia did not act in good faith.

(B) prevail, because the substitute accommodations offered by the hotel were not comparable to the Presidential Suite and therefore not an effective cure for La Valencia's breach.

(C) not prevail, because the La Valencia did offer substitute accommodations at a $500 savings.

(D) not prevail, because the Clauses sustained no legal damages in renting a comparable suite at another hotel for the same rental.

Questions 37–38 are based on the following fact situation.

Christie's Fine Art Emporium contracted in writing to sell a rare 16th century tapestry to Feingold's Home Furnishings for $100,000. The contract stipulated that delivery would be "F.O.B. at point of destination," with payment to be made one week after tender.

When Feingold received the tapestry, Art Feingold, Feingold's CEO, noticed that it had been damaged in transit. Feingold immediately contacted Christie's and notified it that he was rejecting the tapestry because it had ripped apart and was becoming unwoven. Christie's told Feingold that it would get back to him with regard to re-shipping instructions. Christie's did not make any further contact with Feingold. Finally, Feingold kept the tapestry for four weeks and then sold it to Getty for $120,000.

37. Assume for the purposes of this question only that there was no acceptance of the tapestry. If Christie's sues Feingold's for damages, Christie's should recover

(A) $120,000, for conversion.

(B) At most, $108,000, since Feingold's is entitled to a reasonable sum not exceeding 10% on the resale.

(C) $100,000.

(D) $20,000, which covers the difference between the contract price and the sale price.

38. Assume for the purposes of this question that the tapestry was damaged in transit. Nonetheless, Feingold's accepted delivery and notified Christie's of the damaged quality. Feingold's kept the tapestry for four weeks when it sold it to Getty for $120,000. Feingold's has refused to pay anything to Christie's. Christie's brought a breach of contract action against Feingold's who, in turn, has filed a counterclaim against Christie's. Judgment should be rendered as follows:

    (A) Feingold's is entitled to nominal damages, because the tapestry was received in a damaged condition.
    (B) Neither party, because the risk of loss was on Christie's but Feingold's did not incur any loss since it sold the tapestry for a profit.
    (C) Christie's is entitled to $100,000, because Feingold's accepted delivery of the tapestry.
    (D) Christie's is entitled to $120,000, because Feingold's resale constituted a conversion.

Questions 39–40 are based on the following fact situation.

Yardley mailed Stokes a letter promising to sell his motorcycle for $1,000. After receiving Yardley's letter, Stokes sent Yardley a fax which stated, "The price is a little high, I'll give you $800." Yardley responded and told Stokes, "I will not accept $800." The next day, Stokes telephoned Yardley and said, "I changed my mind, I will pay $1,000 for the motorcycle." At this point, Yardley told Stokes he was a jerk and refused to sell Stokes his motorcycle.

39. If Stokes sues Yardley for breach of contract, which of the following defenses would best serve Yardley?

    (A) Since Stokes's purported acceptance was oral, it constituted a different mode of communication from the written offer.
    (B) The contract was unenforceable under the statute of frauds because Stokes's purported acceptance was oral.
    (C) Stokes's counteroffer terminated his power of acceptance.
    (D) Yardley's rejection of Stokes's counter offer terminated the counteroffer.

40. Assume for the purposes of this question only that Yardley did not sell the motorcycle to Stokes. Instead, Yardley offered to sell the motorcycle to Dugan for $1,000. After receiving Yardley's offer, Dugan responded, "Let me think it over." Yardley then said, "If you say so." The next day, Yardley sold the motorcycle to Elgin for $1,000. Thereafter, Dugan sought to accept Yardley's offer, but learned that the motorcycle had been sold to Elgin. If Dugan sues Yardley for breach of contract, judgment for

    (A) Yardley, because the offer to Dugan terminated when he learned of the sale to Elgin.
    (B) Yardley, because he acted in good faith when he sold the motorcycle to Elgin.
    (C) Dugan, because the offer became irrevocable for a reasonable time when Yardley allowed Dugan to "think it over."
    (D) Dugan, if, but only if, he is a merchant.

Questions 41–44 are based on the following fact situation.

Hymie Hendrix owned Meadowlands, a sixty-acre tract located just outside West Grove in Oxford County. Meadowlands included a large family home which was a restored antebellum mansion, complete with tennis court, stables, and a small carriage-house. Hendrix rented the carriage-house to Janet Jopland for $250 per month. On September 3, Hendrix mailed the following letter to Jopland:

"September 2

Dear Ms. Jopland:

In consideration of one dollar, receipt of which is acknowledged, I hereby give you an option for 20 days from the above date to sign a two-year lease at $225 per month, provided you pay two months rent in advance.

/s/ Hymie Hendrix"

Jopland received Hendrix's letter of September 4, but did not read it until September 5. On September 13, Jopland met with Carla Cass, an adjoining landowner, and inquired about renting a cottage on her property. No agreement was reached between Jopland and Cass. On September 18, however, Hendrix was informed by Greta Gossip that Jopland was interested in renting a cottage from Cass.

On September 23, Jopland telephoned Hendrix and said, "I want to give you the $450 and sign the two-year lease as soon as possible." Hendrix replied, "Get stuffed, I heard about your conversation with Cass." Hendrix then abruptly hung up the telephone. On the morning of September 25, Jopland went to Hendrix's home and told him that she wanted to accept his offer and sign the two-year lease. Hendrix responded, "The option's expired. Moreover, I want you to vacate the carriage-house immediately." At no time after receiving Hendrix's letter on September 4 did Jopland pay him the one-dollar consideration.

41. Did Hendrix's letter constitute an effective offer for a two-year lease?

(A) Yes, because it manifested a willingness to enter into a specific bargain.

(B) Yes, because consideration for the option can be inferred from the previous month-to-month lease.

(C) No, unless Jopland paid or tendered to Hendrix the one-dollar consideration.

(D) No, because the letter contained a condition precedent to execution of the proposed lease.

42. Assume for the purposes of this question only that Hendrix's letter created in Jopland a valid power of acceptance. Was that power terminated when Hendrix learned from Gossip of Jopland's conversation with Cass?

(A) Yes, if Gossip gave factually accurate information to Hendrix.

(B) Yes, because it gave Hendrix reasonable grounds to believe that Jopland had rejected his offer.

(C) No, because the indirect communication to Hendrix was oral.

(D) No, because Jopland's conversation with Cass did not constitute a rejection.

43. Assume for the purposes of this question only that Hendrix's letter created in Jopland a valid power of acceptance. Was that power terminated by lapse of time before Jopland came to Hendrix's home on September 25?

    (A) Yes, because the letter was mailed on September 3.
    (B) Yes, because the letter was dated September 2.
    (C) No, because Jopland received the letter on September 4.
    (D) No, because Jopland did not read the letter until September 5.

44. Assume for the purposes of this question only that Hendrix's letter expressly gave Jopland an "option" until September 26, and Jopland's statement on September 23, "I want to give you the $450 and sign the two-year lease," did not constitute a valid acceptance. Consequently, when Hendrix told Jopland, "Get stuffed...," was Jopland's power of acceptance thereby terminated?

    (A) Yes, because Jopland's communication of assent was not by the same medium (letter) used by Hendrix in making his offer.
    (B) Yes, because Hendrix's statement was unequivocal notice that he no longer wished to contract with Jopland.
    (C) No, because Hendrix's letter recited the receipt of one dollar as consideration for the option.
    (D) No, because an offer in a signed writing that by its terms gives assurance that it will be held open is not revocable for lack of consideration during the time stated.

Questions 45–46 are based on the following fact situation.

Kirby Construction Co., in preparing its bid for the construction of a new hospital, received a quote of $120,000 from Kat's Interior Inc to do the kitchen work in the new hospital. This bid was $30,000 lower than Kirby's next lowest bid for the kitchen work. As a result, Kirby used Kat's bid and lowered its bid by $20,000 before submitting it to the hospital board. After Kirby was awarded the construction bid, Kat's president discovered that in his preparation of the quote, he had overlooked some subsidiary kitchen installments required by the plans.

45. Immediately thereafter, Kat's Interiors brings suit for rescission of the contract. It should

    (A) succeed, because of Kat's unilateral mistake.
    (B) not succeed, unless Kirby knew or should have known of Kat's error.
    (C) succeed, because the mistake was an essential element of the bargain.
    (D) not succeed, since the computation mistake was antecedent to acceptance of the bid.

46. Assume that Kat's sent their bid of $120,000 by email to Kirby. However, the email incorrectly listed the bid as $20,000, making it $130,000 lower than the next lowest bid. Kirby, in turn, utilizes this figure in preparing its bid for the hospital construction. Kirby is awarded the contract, but Kat's refuses to perform. Kat's best defense in an action for breach of contract by Kirby would be:

(A) that Kirby should have been aware of the mistake because of the disparity between Kat's bid and the next lowest one.
(B) that the Internet service provider should be liable as an independent contractor for facilitating the mistaken transmission.
(C) that Kirby was under an affirmative duty to investigate all submitted bids.
(D) that the mistake made the contract unconscionable.

Questions 47–48 are based on the following fact situation.

After the murder of his brother, Marvin Fish published the following notice in the *Vicksburg Courier* on June 7, 2008:

"REWARD

Any person who supplies information leading to the arrest and conviction of the murderer of Melvin Fish will be paid $5,000."

Don Archer, an amateur detective, without knowledge of the reward notice, began investigating the matter as a result of his own curiosity kindled by the sensationalism surrounding Melvin's murder. On November 6, 2008, Archer secured information that led to the arrest and conviction of the murderer. After the trial, Archer found out about the reward and demanded the $5,000 from Marvin Fish.

47. A court will likely find that the June 7, 2008, reward notice in the *Vicksburg Courier* proposed a

(A) unilateral contract only.
(B) bilateral contract only.
(C) unilateral contract or bilateral contract, at the offeree's option.
(D) unilateral contract that ripened into a bilateral contract when Archer supplied the information leading to the murderer's conviction.

48. In an action by Archer to recover the $5,000 reward, he will

(A) succeed, because his apprehension of the murderer created a contract implied in law.
(B) succeed, even though he was unaware of the offer.
(C) not succeed, because he did not know about the reward.
(D) not succeed, because his investigation was not a bargained-for exchange.

Questions 49–50 are based on the following fact situation.

Linda Law, a recent graduate of UCLA Law School, was hired by Bar Review of California (hereafter referred to as BRC) under an oral agreement as an editorial consultant. Her job responsibilities included preparing new course outlines, proofreading, and grading student homework assignments. BRC agreed to pay Linda a starting salary of $2,500 a month.

Three months later, Linda was approached by Emanuel Josephs, BRC's West Coast Regional Director, who handed her a newly published 60-page booklet entitled "BRC Employer's Manual." He instructed Linda to read the manual and indicated that it contained important information concerning company policy considerations and employee benefits.

When Linda returned home that evening, she started to read the manual. The first few pages described the history of BRC and provided a personal biography of its president, Michael Finzer. On page 20, the manual stated that BRC treats its employees "as family" and that employees will be discharged "only with good cause." After reading about 30 pages, Linda became tired and went to sleep. She never got around to reading the rest of the manual.

After she worked at BRC for six months, Linda received a termination notice from Emanuel. In his letter, he indicated that Linda was being fired for insubordination because she complained about the poor quality of BRC's course materials and refused to work overtime grading papers. Following her dismissal, Linda now brings suit against BRC for breach of contract.

49. Which of the following, if true and provable, would furnish BRC with its best defense?

(A) All other BRC employees worked overtime whenever requested to do so.

(B) When Linda accepted employment with BRC, the company never made any promises regarding job security or duration of employment.

(C) BRC's course materials had recently been reviewed by the American Bar Association's Committee on Legal Education and they received "high acclaim."

(D) The second page of the BRC manual contained a paragraph stating that all policies, guidelines, and employee benefits are "purely gratuitous and not intended to create any contractual obligation."

50. Assume for the purposes of this question only that Linda seeks to recover on grounds of promissory estoppel. Which of the following facts, if true and provable, would be most helpful for her cause of action?

(A) At the time when Josephs hired Linda, he subjectively intended that Linda be given job security.

(B) Linda interpreted the clause in the manual stating that BRC employees would be treated "as family" to mean that she would have job security and could only be fired for good cause.

(C) Just prior to receiving the manual, Linda seriously considered quitting but continued to work for BRC in reliance on the provisions contained on page 20 of the manual.

(D) Linda's complaints regarding the poor quality of BRC's course materials were factually true and justifiable.

Question 51 is based on the following fact situation.

Adler placed the following advertisement in his local newspaper:

"Public Auction Sale ... without reserve
December 7 10:00 A.M.
110 Walnut St., Ely, Nevada
Entire furnishings of home must go:
antiques, piano, pool table, appliances, tables, stereo system, etc."

On the morning of December 7, a group of approximately 20 people showed up at Adler's home. The first item which Adler put up for bids was an antique Baldwin grand piano. Adler announced that the bidding would be "without reserve" and said, "How much am I bid for this beautiful Baldwin grand piano?" Butler opened the bidding with $100.00. Adler then commented, "This piano is worth at least $5,000. What other bids am I offered?" When Adler did not receive any other bids, he informed Butler that he would not accept $100.00 and was removing the piano from sale.

51. If Butler asserts an action against Adler for breach of contract, Butler will most likely

   (A) prevail, since goods put up at an auction "without reserve" may not be withdrawn.
   (B) prevail, since whether or not the auction is "without reserve" goods cannot be withdrawn after the auctioneer calls for bids.
   (C) not prevail, since at an auction "without reserve," the auctioneer may withdraw goods until he announces completion of the sale.
   (D) not prevail, since at an auction "without reserve," the auctioneer invites offers which he may accept or reject.

Questions 52–53 are based on the following fact situation.

Amish was a mushroom farmer in Kennett Square, Pennsylvania. On January 2, Amish agreed in a signed writing to deliver to Mennonite on March 1 a specified quantity of mushrooms at a specified price. The mushrooms on Amish's farm were usually picked and packaged by Amish's three sons, Ezekiel, Hyman, and Olaf. On February 27, Ezekiel and Hyman were injured in a farming accident and hospitalized. As a result, Amish encountered a manpower shortage and couldn't process all of the mushrooms for Mennonite's order.

On February 28, Amish telephoned Mennonite and said, "Because my two sons, Ezekiel and Hyman, were injured yesterday, I won't be able to deliver your mushrooms on March 1. However, I am trying to hire some other farm hands to help process your order. Although I can't promise it, I should be able to deliver the mushrooms by the end of the week." Mennonite, who knew that Amish's sons were responsible for the mushroom farming, said, "No problem. I think I'll be able to get by without them for a few days. However, be advised that I will hold you liable for any loss I sustain as a result of your failure to deliver the mushrooms on March 1." When Mennonite failed to receive the mushrooms on March 5, he sent the following email to Amish, "I must have the mushrooms no later than March 9." This email was received and read by Amish on March 6.

52. Suppose that Amish does deliver the mushrooms to Mennonite on March 9 and Mennonite accepts them. If Mennonite thereafter brings a contract action against Amish to recover damages resulting from the delay in delivery, judgment for whom?

   (A) Amish, because temporary impracticability excused his duty to deliver the mushrooms on March 1.
   (B) Amish, because Mennonite's statements and acceptance of the mushrooms constituted a waiver of the condition of timely delivery.
   (C) Mennonite, because his statements to Amish did not constitute a promise to forgo any cause of action he then had or might later acquire.
   (D) Mennonite, because there was no consideration to support his waiver, if any, of timely delivery.

53. Suppose that Amish fails to deliver the mushrooms to Mennonite on March 9. Will Mennonite be entitled to cancel the contract?

(A) Yes, provided both parties are merchants.
(B) Yes, provided a three-day notice afforded Amish a reasonable time in which to perform.
(C) No, because Mennonite's February 28 statement effectuated a waiver of any condition of timely delivery.
(D) No, because Amish, by his February 28 statement, did not promise to deliver the mushrooms by the end of the week.

Question 54 is based on the following fact situation.

Toshi is the owner of Hama, a sushi restaurant in Venice. Toshi contracted in writing with Fishco, a fish distributor, to buy 50 pounds of toro (which is a yellow fin tuna). At the time the contract was signed, Toshi orally said to Fishco, "We do have an understanding that Kifune, our chef, must approve the quality of the fish before I will pay you." Fishco acknowledged Toshi's request and responded, "If you say so."

Thereafter, Fishco delivered the yellow fin tuna to Toshi. After inspecting the fish, Kifune refused to give his approval because the toro was spotted instead of its customary shiny skin. As a result, Toshi refused to accept and pay for the fish.

54. Fishco brought a breach of contract action against Toshi because he refused to pay for the fish delivery. How should the court rule on Toshi's offer to prove, over Fishco's objection, that Kifune refused to approve the toro that was delivered?

(A) The evidence is admissible to show frustration of purpose.
(B) The evidence is admissible to show that the written agreement was subject to an oral condition precedent.
(C) The evidence is barred because the written contract appears to be a complete and total integration of the parties' agreement.
(D) The evidence is barred because the oral agreement is within the statute of frauds.

Questions 55–57 are based on the following fact situation.

Marty Golby was accepted by Nixon School of Law for the fall term of 2008. Several generations of Marty's family had attended the prestigious law school. On August 14, at a party to celebrate Marty's acceptance, his father, former United States Attorney General Dick Golby, announced to Marty, in the presence of the partygoers, "Son, it's your obligation to uphold the family tradition for excellence at Nixon. In this regard, if you promise to study a minimum of five hours a day, then I shall pay you $1,000 for each 'A' you achieve during your first year; $2,500 for each 'A' you achieve during your second year; and $5,000 for each 'A' you achieve during your third year. Moreover, I will buy you a baby blue Eldorado at the end of the first semester if you promise me not to smoke marijuana" Marty replied, "Dad, not only shall I study five hours a day, but you can order the Eldorado right away. I promise not to smoke marijuana as you requested."

After the first semester, Marty returned home on December 24 and showed his father his grade report, which indicated that Marty received "A's" in Contracts, Torts, and Property. His father then wrote Marty a check for $3,000. He then asked Marty, in the presence of Marty's Uncle Homer, "Did you abide by your promise not to smoke marijuana?" Marty replied, "Yes, Father." Marty's father then told him that he had already ordered the car and that it would be available for delivery within one month. Uncle Homer, also an old Nixon grad, made the following statement: "Marty, I want you to know that if anything ever happens to your father, that I'll continue to pay you, as per your father's promise, for your 'A's' at Nixon."

When Marty returned to Nixon the following week, he received the tragic news that his father had died suddenly. At the funeral, the executor of his estate told Marty that he did not feel compelled to give Marty the newly arrived Eldorado. Furthermore, Uncle Homer approached Marty and told him that he did not believe that he was obligated to pay Marty for any "A's" that he might receive in the future.

55. The most accurate statement concerning his late father's promise to reward Marty for achieving "A's" at law school would be that

(A) the promise constituted an unenforceable conditional gift.
(B) the promise would not be legally binding, since it was nondetrimental.
(C) the promise would be enforceable if a bargained for exchange was so intended.
(D) the promise constituted a voidable proposal.

56. In a suit against the executor of his late father's estate to recover the Eldorado, Marty will

(A) succeed, since Marty was under no legal obligation to refrain from smoking marijuana.
(B) not succeed, since his father's promise was not reduced to writing in compliance with the Statute of Frauds.
(C) not succeed, since his father's promise was only a conditional gift.
(D) not succeed, since Marty's promise was void.

57. Uncle Homer's December 24 promise to Marty with respect to achieving "A's" at Nixon would constitute

(A) an enforceable promise, binding Uncle Homer as a surety.
(B) an unenforceable promise, because Marty's father had the duty to pay Marty.
(C) a voidable promise as violative of the Statute of Frauds.
(D) a void promise at the time of inception.

Questions 58–59 are based on the following fact situation.

Lyle is the owner of Foggy Bottom, a 30-acre tract of rural farmland. On December 1, Lyle and Yellin each signed the following written instrument: "In consideration of one dollar, receipt of which is acknowledged, Lyle hereby offers to sell Foggy Bottom to Yellin for the purchase price of $30,000. This offer shall remain open until 4:00 p.m. December 30." Thirty thousand dollars was the fair market value of the property.

Yellin failed to pay Lyle the one dollar consideration as recited in their written instrument. On December 15, Lyle sent Yellin a letter in which she stated, "Please be advised that I am hereby withdrawing my offer to sell Foggy Bottom." This letter was received and read by Yellin on December 16. The next day, Yellin tendered a cashier's check to Lyle in the amount of $30,001 (the $30,000 purchase price plus the $1 consideration). Lyle refused to accept Yellin's cashier's check. Yellin has now brought suit against Lyle for specific performance.

58. At trial, Lyle seeks to testify that Yellin did not in fact pay him the $1 consideration as recited in their written instrument. Yellin objects to Lyle's proposed testimony. Should the judge sustaining Yellin's objection?

(A) No, because even if the written instrument is a complete integration, parol evidence is permissible to contradict a recital of fact in the agreement.

(B) No, because the parol evidence rule does not operate to exclude evidence of contemporaneous or subsequent oral modification of the written terms.

(C) Yes, because the written instrument appears to be a complete integration of the parties' agreement.

(D) Yes, because the doctrine of promissory estoppel will prevent Lyle's denial of his signed acknowledgment that he received the $1.

59. Assume for the purposes of this question only that in his pleadings Yellin admits that the recited $1 was not in fact paid to Lyle when their written agreement was executed. As a result, which of the following is Yellin's best argument that such failure of payment does not bar his claim to specific performance?

(A) The recited consideration was only a sham pretense of bargained-for consideration, and was therefore de minimis and of no legal significance.

(B) Yellin's inclusion of the $1 in his tendered check on December 17 was a timely cure of an immaterial breach of a bilateral real estate option contract.

(C) Whether the $1 was paid or not, courts will not inquire into the sufficiency of the consideration.

(D) The written instrument embodied a proposal for a fair exchange within a reasonable time period and was therefore an enforceable option contract, regardless of whether the nominal consideration recited was bargained for or paid.

Question 60 is based on the following fact situation.

Debtor owed Creditor $12,000 under a promissory note due on June 10, 1997. The statute of limitations for such debt obligations in writing is 10 years. On June 1, 2008, Creditor received a letter from Debtor stating, "I shall pay you $5,000 on July 1, 2008, in full satisfaction of what I owe you."

60. If Debtor asserts the statute of limitations as an affirmative defense and refuses to pay Creditor anything, which of the following accurately states Creditor's legal rights against Debtor?

    (A) On June 1, 2008, Creditor will be entitled to a judgment against Debtor for $5,000 only.
    (B) On July 1, 2008, not June 1, 2008, Creditor will be entitled to a judgment against Debtor for $5,000 only.
    (C) On July 1, 2008, not June 1, 2008, Creditor will be entitled to a judgment against Debtor for $12,000.
    (D) Creditor is not entitled to anything since the original debt was barred by the statute of limitations.

Questions 61–62 are based on the following fact situation.

Rufus Ruffino was 16 years old and a junior at Woodrow Wilson High School in Ft. Lauderdale. After Rufus's sixteenth birthday, he decided to purchase a new Corvette from Morrisey Motors for the sales price of $36,000. Rufus thereafter entered into a written contract with Morrisey, which provided that Rufus would make monthly payments of $1,000 for three years. During the first year of the contract, Rufus made 12 monthly payments totaling $12,000. However, Rufus failed to make any payments during the second year of the contract.

Morrisey repeatedly threatened to sue Rufus for the remaining balance that it claimed was due under the contract. Finally, in order to avoid litigation, Rufus sent Morrisey the following letter:

"The car I purchased from you is a real lemon. I have spent a considerable sum of money during the last two years in repair work. I don't believe that the car is worth $36,000, but I am willing to pay you $10,000 if my financial position improves."

Rufus had just turned 18 when he sent this letter to Morrisey. Two weeks after mailing this letter, Rufus was involved in an automobile accident and the Corvette was totally demolished. Following the accident, Rufus has refused to make any payments to Morrisey. At the time of the accident, the Corvette was worth $18,000. In this jurisdiction, the age of majority is 18 years of age.

61. If Morrisey brings suit against Rufus for breach of contract, what, if any, is the plaintiff's proper recovery?

    (A) Nothing.
    (B) $10,000.
    (C) $18,000.
    (D) $24,000.

62. Assume for the purposes of this question only that Morrisey brings suit to recover damages from Rufus. Which of the following would provide Morrisey with his best argument for recovery?

    (A) The automobile was demolished in the accident.
    (B) Morrisey was unaware that Rufus was a minor at the time the contract was entered into.
    (C) Rufus' financial position has improved to the extent that he is able to pay the $10,000 which he promised.
    (D) The automobile that Rufus purchased is viewed as a necessity.

Questions 63–65 are based on the following fact situation.

On February 1, 2008, Winston and Mildred Grimsby entered into a contract with Antoine LeVey, a famous landscape architect, to landscape their five-acre estate. They were pleased with the work he had done on their neighbor's gardens, so they hired LeVey, who promised to complete the job before May 30, the date of their annual garden party. On March 1, the Grimsbys left for a month's vacation on their yacht. Unknown to them, LeVey, because of previous commitments, assigned the contract to Herman. After Herman had completed 60% of the work, the Grimsbys returned and were displeased with the landscaping already completed. They contacted LeVey, who informed them of the assignment to Herman and told them he was no longer obligated under their original contract. Disgruntled, the Grimsbys fired Herman.

63. If the Grimsbys assert a claim against LeVey based on breach of contract, the fact that LeVey assigned the work to Herman will

   (A) relieve LeVey of liability, because the contract was assignable.
   (B) relieve LeVey of liability, because Herman's work was the cause of the Grimsbys' dissatisfaction.
   (C) not relieve LeVey of liability, because a personal service contract of this nature is non-delegable.
   (D) not relieve LeVey of liability, unless there was an express contractual provision against assignments.

64. After the Grimsbys refusal to pay Herman for the work he had completed, if Herman brings an action against the Grimsbys, he will most probably:

   (A) recover for unjust enrichment.
   (B) recover under the doctrine of substantial performance.
   (C) recover for loss of profits.
   (D) not recover, since there was no contract between him and the Grimsbys.

65. For this question only, assume that the landscaping job for the Grimsbys was assignable. On March 1, LeVey assigned the contract to Herman. In turn, Herman assigned the contract to Green, who performed the landscaping work. The Grimsbys return from their vacation and LeVey tells them that he assigned the contract to Herman, whom they promptly pay. Now, if Green seeks to recover for services he performed, he will

   (A) recover against LeVey only.
   (B) recover against Herman only.
   (C) recover against either Herman or LeVey.
   (D) recover against the Grimsbys only.

Questions 66–68 are based on the following fact situation.

Zelda Zellman went to Dr. Dreck, a dermatologist, for treatment of an abnormal growth on the back of her right shoulder. Under a written contract, Dr. Dreck agreed to surgically remove the growth for $750. As Zelda subsequently recalled, the parties orally agreed that if any additional medical procedures were required during surgery, they would be included in the $750 fee. Dr. Dreck, however, has no recollection of any such oral agreement.

As agreed, the surgery was performed on an out-patient basis at Dr. Dreck's office. He applied a localized anesthesia that enabled Zelda to remain conscious during surgery. While the operation was being performed, Dr. Dreck noticed a brown mole on Zelda's back. As Dr. Dreck subsequently recalled, he informed Zelda about the mole and asked whether she wanted it removed as well. According to Dr. Dreck's account, Zelda orally agreed to have the mole removed for an additional $150. Zelda has no recollection of any such oral agreement.

Dr. Dreck performed both removal procedures satisfactorily. Following the surgery, Zelda paid Dr. Dreck $750, but refused to pay any additional money for the mole removal. After unsuccessfully attempting to collect the $150, Dr. Dreck brought suit against Zelda to recover the additional fee. At trial, Dr. Dreck objects to the introduction of testimony regarding any oral agreement made before the written contract was signed. By the same token, Zelda objects to the introduction of testimony concerning any oral agreement made during surgery.

66. Which of the following considerations is most important to a judicial ruling on Zelda's objection?

(A) Dr. Dreck's removal of the mole conferred a clear benefit on Zelda.

(B) The proffered oral agreement regarding payment of the additional $150 occurred after the written agreement had been signed.

(C) The written agreement was for services rather than the sale of goods.

(D) The proffered oral agreement regarding payment of the additional $150 concerned a new medical procedure that was unrelated to the subject matter of the prior written contract.

67. Assume for the purposes of this question only that the court sustains Dr. Dreck's objection. Which of the following would constitute the probable grounds for such a ruling?

(A) The writing was construed as a complete integration of the parties' agreement.

(B) The writing was construed as a partial integration of the parties' agreement.

(C) An implied-in-law contract was created at the moment Dr. Dreck performed the removal procedure for the mole.

(D) The parties entered into a collateral oral agreement for free medical services that was excludable from the integrated writing.

68. Under the majority view, will Dr. Dreck be entitled to recover the additional $150 if both offerings of parol evidence are admitted and believed?

(A) No, because the oral agreements contradicted each other, and neither would be enforceable under the so-called knock-out rule of the UCC.

(B) No, because in removing the growth from Zelda's shoulder, Dr. Dreck performed a legal duty already owed her that was neither doubtful nor the subject of an honest dispute.

(C) Yes, because the oral modification of the prior writing was fair and equitable in view of circumstances not anticipated by the parties when the writing was executed.

(D) Yes, because Zelda would be unjustly enriched by not paying the additional $150, and injustice can be avoided only by enforcement of her oral promise.

Questions 69–70 are based on the following fact situation.

In 2007, J. Theisman, Jr. owned Redland Pines, a 70-acre tract in St. Georges County, Maryland. The estate had been owned by the Theisman family for many generations. It consisted of farm lands, a fine manor house with a driveway lined with magnificent pine trees, and a second smaller house that was occupied by the tenant who farmed the land.

On November 19, 2007, Theisman entered into a valid written brokerage agreement with Crosby, a real estate broker. According to terms of the agreement, Crosby promised to undertake best efforts to sell Redland Pines for a purchase price of not less than $1,250,000. The contract also provided that Crosby was to be paid a commission of 6.5% on the gross sale price following the consummation of the sale and transfer of title. The brokerage agreement was effective for a period of two months, with an expiration date of January 19, 2008.

After diligently attempting to find a suitable buyer, Crosby finally struck pay dirt. On January 3, 2008, Crosby notified Theisman that she had found a wealthy playboy named Riggins who wanted to purchase the property for $1,500,000. That same day, Crosby handed Theisman a real estate sales contract, signed by Riggins, in which he agreed to pay $1,500,000 for the purchase of Redland Pines.

69. Assume for the purposes of this question only that Theisman knew that Riggins was financially able and willing to complete the purchase of Redland Pines. However, on January 3, Theisman changed his mind and decided not to sell the property. After being presented with the real estate sales contract executed by Riggins, Theisman told Crosby that he would not sign the agreement. In addition, Theisman told Crosby that he was canceling their brokerage agreement because he was withdrawing Redland Pines from the market. Theisman also refused to pay Crosby any commission. If Crosby now sues Theisman for breach of contract, which of the following, if anything, is Crosby's proper measure of recovery?

(A) Nothing, since a condition precedent, namely, the consummation of the sale and transfer of title, has failed to occur.

(B) Quantum meruit for the reasonable value for services rendered in obtaining a buyer for the property.

(C) $97,500, or the commission equivalent of 6.5% on the sale of the property for $1,500,000, since all conditions precedent to Theisman's duty to pay the commission were fulfilled when Crosby produced a buyer who was ready, willing, and able to perform.

(D) $97,500, or the commission equivalent of 6.5% on the sale of the property for $1,500,000, since the consummation condition to Theisman's duty to pay the commission was excused by Theisman's refusal without cause to accept Riggins's offer and perform the land sale contract.

70. Assume for the purposes of this question only that on January 3 Crosby presented Theisman a real estate sales agreement, executed and signed by Riggins, for the purchase of Redland Pines for the price of $1,500,000. Theisman then signed the agreement himself. On January 17, before consummation of the sale and transfer of title, Riggins without cause repudiated the contract. Despite Crosby's insistence, Theisman refused to either sue Riggins to enforce the land sale contract or pay Crosby her commission. If Crosby sues Theisman for breach of the brokerage agreement, which of the following, if anything, is Crosby's proper measure of recovery?

   (A) Nothing, because as a third-party beneficiary of the Theisman-Riggins land sale contract, Crosby can enforce the contract only against Riggins but not against Theisman.
   (B) Nothing, because the consummation condition has not been fulfilled, and Theisman's refusal to sue Riggins will not excuse that condition.
   (C) $97,500, or the commission equivalent of 6.5% on the sale of the property for $1,500,000, because fulfillment of the consummation condition was prevented by an event beyond Crosby's control.
   (D) $97,500, or the commission equivalent of 6.5% on the sale of the property for $1,500,000, because all conditions precedent to Theisman's duty to pay the commission were substantially fulfilled when Theisman and Riggins entered into the land sale contract.

Questions 71–72 are based on the following fact situation.

On September 1, 2008, Stolper Products, a manufacturer of portable drinking fountains, mailed to Sparklets, a drinking fountain retailer, a signed offer: "Have 200 water bubblers (drinking fountains) available at $100 each for October delivery. Be advised that this offer will remain open until October 1, 2008." On September 30, 2008, Sparklets mailed the following letter, which was received by Stolper on October 1, 2008: "Your offer is hereby accepted, but request delivery of 100 water bubblers in October and 100 water bubblers in November."

71. Assume for the purposes of this question only that Stolper sent an email to Sparklets on September 29, 2008, revoking its offer. This revocation is

   (A) valid, unless Sparklets had changed its position in reliance on the offer.
   (B) valid, because there was no consideration to support an option contract.
   (C) not valid, because Sparklets had 90 days in which to accept.
   (D) not valid, because Stolper gave assurance that the offer would remain open until October 1.

72. Which of the following is the most accurate statement regarding the legal effect of Sparklets's September 30 letter?

   (A) It constitutes a counteroffer because it contains different terms than those contained in the original offer.
   (B) It constitutes a rejection because the offer impliedly limited acceptance to the terms contained therein.
   (C) It creates an enforceable contract with delivery of 100 water bubblers in October and delivery of 100 water bubblers in November.
   (D) It creates a reformation integrating the terms of both writings.

Questions 73–74 are based on the following fact situation.

On March 1, Homeowner and Painter entered into a written contract wherein Painter promised to paint the exterior of Homeowner's house and Homeowner promised to pay Painter the sum of $3,000. According to their agreement, Homeowner was to pay the money to Graduate, Painter's son. Painter intended the $3,000 to be a law school graduation present.

Prior to the signing of the contract, Homeowner and Painter orally agreed that their agreement would be null and void unless Homeowner was able to obtain a $3,000 loan from National Bank before April 1. Graduate was not informed about the agreement between his father and Homeowner. On March 31, Homeowner was informed by the National Bank that his loan application had been rejected. The next day, Homeowner telephoned Painter and informed him that the deal was off.

73. If Painter brings an action for breach of contract against Homeowner, would the latter's inability to secure the loan provide him with a valid defense?

(A) No, because Homeowner is estopped to deny the validity of the written contract.
(B) No, because the agreement regarding the loan varied the express terms of the writing.
(C) Yes, because the agreement regarding the loan constituted a valid modification of the writing.
(D) Yes, because the loan agreement was a condition precedent to the existence of the contract.

74. Assume for the purposes of this question only that Homeowner was successful in obtaining the loan from the National Bank. After Painter completed the job on April 15, he requested that Homeowner pay him the $3,000 instead of his son. The next day, Homeowner went ahead and paid Painter. On April 20, Graduate learned of the contract between Painter and Homeowner, as well as the payment to his father. In an action by Graduate against Homeowner, for $3,000, the plaintiff will likely

(A) prevail, because the written contract between Homeowner and Painter operated as a valid assignment to Graduate.
(B) prevail, because Graduate was the intended beneficiary under the terms of written contract between Homeowner and Painter.
(C) not prevail, because Homeowner and Painter effectively modified their agreement, thereby depriving Graduate of any rights he may have had.
(D) not prevail, because Graduate did not give any consideration.

Questions 75–78 are based on the following fact situation.

On December 16, 2004, Franco, owner and operator of Pizza Palace, entered into a written contract with Mario that provided that Mario would be employed as manager of the Pizza Palace for a period of three years. The contract provided that Mario would commence working in January 2005 and that Franco was "to pay Mario a salary of $1500 per month, payable one-third to Mario, one-third to Mario's elderly mother, Mia, and one-third to the Venice National Bank (to whom Mario was indebted in the sum of $50,000, which was secured by a mortgage on Mario's oceanfront villa)." In addition, the employment contract provided that Franco would pay Mario an annual bonus "to be determined by the parties hereto within two weeks after the year's profits have been ascertained." The contract further stipulated that "the monies due hereunder shall not be assignable."

When Mia learned of this contract, she wrote a letter to Franco stating, "Kindly pay the amounts due me under your contract with my son directly to the Pine Creek Nursing Home, where I am presently a patient." During the first year of the contract, Franco paid $500 per month to Mario, $500 per month to the Pine Creek Nursing Home, and $500 per month to the Venice National Bank. At the end of 2005, Pizza Palace's net profit was $50,000. Accordingly, Mario and Franco agreed that Mario should receive a bonus of $5,000; this amount was subsequently paid to Mario.

In January, 2006, Pizza Hut, a new pizza franchise, opened a restaurant across the street from the Pizza Palace. During the next few months, business at the Pizza Palace steadily declined. As a result of the loss in business, Franco informed Mario that unless he agreed to take a cut in his salary, Mario would be fired. Reluctantly, on May 20, 2006, Mario orally consented to a salary reduction of $500 per month. By the terms of their verbal agreement, Franco promised to continue to pay $500 per month to the Venice National Bank. However, their new agreement provided that beginning June 1st, Franco would no longer be obligated to pay $500 per month to the Pine Creek Nursing Home. Thereafter, Franco discontinued his $500 per month payments to Pine Creek Nursing Home.

At the end of 2006, Pizza Palace realized a net profit of $10,000. On January 3, 2007, Franco telephoned Mario and offered him a second year bonus of $1,000. Mario refused and requested a bonus of $2,000. Moreover, Mario

stated that he would no longer be bound by the salary adjustment and demanded that Franco thereafter pay him, his mother, and Venice National Bank on the basis of $1,500 per month. Franco refused Mario's demand and immediately terminated his employment.

75. In June 2006, the Pine Creek Nursing Home brings suit against Franco for breach of contract. Judgment for

(A) Franco, since Mia's assignment to Pine Creek was void as violative of the anti-assignment clause in the Franco-Mario contract.
(B) Franco, since the May 20 agreement between Franco and Mario released Franco of any further obligations to Pine Creek.
(C) Pine Creek, since Mia's assignment would be enforceable despite the May 20 release.
(D) Pine Creek, since Mia's gratuitous assignment was irrevocable.

76. Which of the following statements regarding the May 20 agreement between Franco-Mario is most accurate?

(A) It effectuated a valid reformation of their original written contract.
(B) It effectuated a valid modification of their original written contract.
(C) It effectuated a novation of their original written contract.
(D) It did not alter the rights and obligations of the parties under the terms of their original contract.

77. Following his dismissal, Mario brings suit for breach of contract against Franco. Which of the following is (are) correct?

    I. Mario has a cause of action against Franco to recover a bonus for the year ending 2006.
    II. Mario has a cause of action against Franco for loss of wages.
    III. Neither Franco nor Mario had the power to vary Mia's rights as a third-party beneficiary under the terms of their original contract.

    (A) II only.
    (B) I and II.
    (C) II and III.
    (D) I, II, and III.

78. The December 16, 2004, agreement between Franco and Mario may best be interpreted as

    (A) an entire contract.
    (B) a divisible contract.
    (C) an installment contract.
    (D) neither divisible nor entire.

Questions 79–80 are based on the following fact situation.

Larry Browning was a highly successful basketball coach at Kansas City University. Browning's Kansas City team, nicknamed the Hucksters, won the coveted National Collegiate Athletic Association (NCAA) championship in 2007. After winning the championship, Browning announced that he would be leaving Kansas City but wanted to continue coaching at a west coast university.

After Browning's announcement was made public, University of East Los Angeles (U.E.L.A.) fired its head coach and actively sought Browning to fill the coaching vacancy. The U.E.L.A. basketball team, which had been a traditional powerhouse through the 1980s and 1990s, had fallen on bad times and experienced consecutive losing seasons in 2005 and 2006 for the first time in 50 years. Under considerable alumni pressure, Joan Wooden, the president of U.E.L.A., decided to make a concerted effort to lure Browning to U.E.L.A. She met with Browning on two occasions, but their negotiations stalled after Browning demanded more money than the university was prepared to offer.

Thereafter, Wooden met with Don Vandeway, a wealthy booster who was interested in enhancing the U.E.L.A. basketball program, to see if he could help in recruiting Browning. Vandeway then contacted Browning and told him that if he would sign a coaching contract with U.E.L.A., Vandeway would pay him $100,000 a year as an unpublished supplement to his U.E.L.A. salary. Furthermore, Vandeway promised to contribute $5,000 to the U.E.L.A. athletic fund every time the basketball team won a game under Browning's tutelage. Browning thereupon signed a three-year contract as the U.E.L.A. head basketball coach at an annual salary of $125,000.

During Browning's first year as coach, the U.E.L.A. basketball team compiled a record of 18 wins and 12 losses. Vandeway, however, refused to pay anything to either Browning or the U.E.L.A. athletic fund. Note: assume for the purpose of these questions that the Vandeway-Browning agreement does not violate any rule of the university or of any intercollegiate athletic association.

79. If Browning brings a breach of contract action against Vandeway, judgment for whom?

    (A) Browning, because his signing a contract with U.E.L.A. was legally sufficient consideration to support Vandeway's promise to pay him the $100,000 year supplement.
    (B) Browning, because Vandeway, in effect, promised to make a $100,000 annual gift for charitable purposes, and such promises are enforceable without consideration.
    (C) Vandeway, because his promise to Browning was illusory and in contravention of public policy considerations.
    (D) Vandeway, because at the moment Browning signed an employment contract with U.E.L.A., he came under a pre-existing obligation that was insufficient consideration to support Vandeway's promise.

80. Assume for the purposes of this question only that there was an enforceable contract in effect between Browning and Vandeway. After Browning's first season as U.E.L.A. coach, U.E.L.A. now brings suit against Vandeway to recover $90,000 for breach of his promise to pay $5,000 into the athletic fund for each game won by the basketball team. Is it likely that U.E.L.A. will prevail in this contract action?

    (A) Yes, because U.E.L.A. is an intended third-party beneficiary of the Browning-Vandeway contract.
    (B) Yes, because U.E.L.A. detrimentally relied on Vandeway's promise by hiring Browning.
    (C) No, because Vandeway's promise was, in essence, an illegal form of procurement and void as against public policy.
    (D) No, because Vandeway's promise was made to Browning rather than U.E.L.A. and, therefore, was not a charitable subscription.

Question 81 is based on the following fact situation.

Lorenzo owned a beautiful Spanish-style home in Rancho Cordova. The home, which was built in 1932, had a tile roof made of red slate. One day, Lorenzo said to Izod, a roofer, "My roof leaks. I think the old tiles are cracked. If you will replace them with all new tiles, I will pay you $5,000." Izod replied, "Sure, if I can see my way clear of my busy schedule." Lorenzo then remarked, "That's all right, but let me know soon." Three days later, Izod drove his pick-up truck to Lorenzo's home and unloaded the materials and equipment needed to perform the roofing job. When Lorenzo looked out his window and saw what was transpiring, he immediately ran outside and exclaimed, "Hey, dude, the deal's off. I decided to repair the roof myself."

81. In an action by Izod against Lorenzo for breach of contract, which of the following would provide Izod with his best theory of recovery?

   (A) A bilateral contract was formed when Izod unloaded the materials and equipment at Lorenzo's house.
   (B) A bilateral contract was formed when Izod said, "Sure, if I can see my way clear of my busy schedule."
   (C) Lorenzo made an offer that proposed a unilateral contract, and the offer became irrevocable when Izod purchased the materials and equipment needed for the job.
   (D) Lorenzo made an offer that proposed a unilateral contract, and Izod manifested an intent to accept the offer when he began performance by unloading the materials and equipment at Lorenzo's house.

Questions 82–83 are based on the following fact situation.

Ohner owned a large three-story office building in downtown Metropolis. She planned to renovate the building and requested several contractors to submit bids to perform the work. One of the contractors, Builder, in turn sought bids from several subcontractors to determine the overall cost of the job. Electrician submitted a bid to Builder that he used in computing the bid he sent to Ohner. Builder notified Electrician to that effect.

On November 1, Builder submitted his bid to Ohner, in which he offered to perform the renovation work for $75,000. On November 4, Electrician notified Builder that he was unable to perform the electrical work on Ohner's project. On November 5, Ohner sent Builder a signed confirmation letter wherein she stated, "I hereby accept your offer to perform the renovation work for the quoted cost of

$75,000." Thereafter, Builder hired another electrician to complete the electrical work at a cost of $5,000 above Electrician's bid. Builder explained the situation to Ohner and informed her that the overall cost of the job would have to be increased to $80,000. Ohner responded that she would hold Builder to his original bid of $75,000 and would not be responsible for any additional costs. Builder then performed the renovation work, but Ohner has not yet paid him anything.

82. In an action by Builder against Ohner for the services rendered, Builder will probably be able to recover

   (A) only in quantum meruit, because of the doctrine of commercial frustration.
   (B) only in quantum meruit, because by demanding $80,000, Builder, in effect, repudiated his contract with Ohner.
   (C) $75,000 only, because that was the contract price.
   (D) $80,000, because Builder reasonably relied to his detriment on Electrician's bid in formulating his job estimate.

83. Which of the following best supports a claim for $5,000 by Builder against Electrician?

   (A) Electrician's offer was the best one that Builder received.
   (B) Electrician's bid was a "firm offer" that was not revocable since both Electrician and Builder were merchants.
   (C) Builder made an offer to Electrician that Electrician accepted when he submitted his bid.
   (D) An option contract was created because Builder used Electrician's bid in computing the bid he submitted to Ohner and notified Electrician of that fact.

Questions 84–85 are based on the following fact situation.

Donner, an avid stamp collector for over 20 years, had amassed a large and valuable collection. Many of his stamps were extremely rare and highly coveted. On numerous occasions, Donner had rejected offers to sell his collection. Finally, on May 1, Donner sent Martin, his cousin who was also a fellow stamp collector, the following letter:

"I've decided to part with my stamp collection. Since I want to keep it in the 'family,' I'll sell you my entire collection for $75,000. You have until May 15 to make up your mind."

Donner had dictated this letter to his secretary, who mistakenly typed $75,000 instead of the $78,000 that Donner had actually specified. After typing the letter, the secretary gave it to Donner, who hastily signed it without noticing the mistaken price. Martin received this letter on May 3. Without notifying Martin, Donner went ahead and sold his stamp collection to Bigalow for $80,000 on May 10. The next day, Donner sent a letter to Martin regretfully informing him that he had sold the collection. This letter was received by Martin on May 13. However, on May 12, Martin read a local newspaper article concerning Donner's sale of his unique stamp collection to Bigalow. After reading the article, Martin immediately dispatched an email to Donner accepting his offer to buy the stamp collection. This email was received by Donner that same afternoon (i.e., May 12).

84. Was Martin's email to Donner on May 12 effective as an acceptance?

(A) Yes, because Donner's May 11 letter did not effectuate a revocation since it was not received by Martin until May 13.

(B) Yes, because consideration is not necessary under the Uniform Commercial Code for the creation of a sale-of-goods contract.

(C) No, because Donner's sale of the stamp collection to Bigalow on May 10 terminated Martin's power of acceptance.

(D) No, because Martin's reading the newspaper article on May 12 terminated Martin's power of acceptance.

85. Assume for the purposes of this question only that Martin's email of May 12 was an effective acceptance of Donner's offer. If so, which of the following correctly states the agreement's price term and its legal effect?

(A) The price term is $75,000, and it is enforceable.

(B) The price term is $78,000, and it is enforceable.

(C) The price term is $75,000, but the court will reform the price to $78,000 in order to correct a mistake in integration.

(D) The price term is $75,000, but either party can rescind the contract because there was a mutual mistake as to a basic assumption of fact.

CONTRACTS

Arnie Banks, who was an avid fan of the Chicago Cubs baseball team, lived in Elgin, Illinois. While reading the *Sporting News* magazine, Banks learned that the Cubs organization was conducting a baseball camp for fans who wanted to meet and receive instruction from the Cubs players. The cost of the two-week camp was advertised for $2,500, which included meals and housing. Banks, who was a 54-year-old salesman, forwarded the Cubs organization a $50 registration deposit, which reserved him a spot in the baseball camp.

Thereafter, Banks received a contract from the Cubs organization, which all baseball camp attendees were required to sign. The agreement provided that the $2,500 entrance fee was nonrefundable. According to the agreement, all attendees would receive group instruction during the baseball camp. Consequently, the Cubs organization's operating costs would not be reduced if one or more of the attendees failed to participate or complete the two-week program. Banks signed the contract and forwarded it with his $2,500 entrance fee to the Cubs organization. Two days before the start of the baseball camp, however, Banks died from a heart attack.

86. In a restitutionary action, can the executor of Banks's estate, a surviving brother, recover on behalf of the estate either all or part of the $2,500 paid to the Cubs organization?

(A) No, but only if the Cubs organization can show that before the start of the baseball camp that it rejected another applicant because of its commitment to Banks.
(B) No, because under the terms of the agreement, the $2,500 entrance fee was non-refundable.
(C) Yes, because the Cubs organization would otherwise be unjustly enriched at Banks's expense.
(D) Yes, under the doctrine of frustration of purpose.

Questions 87–88 are based on the following fact situation.

On February 28, Foodtown Supermarket entered into a written contract with Citrus Produce Co. to purchase oranges. The contract contained a provision wherein Foodtown promised to purchase "as many oranges as required in shipments of about 100 bushels per month, at a price of $20 per bushel, until November 1." The agreement also provided that any modifications must had to be in writing.

On March 1, Citrus shipped Foodtown 70 bushels of oranges, which were accepted and paid for. On April 1, Citrus tendered 80 bushels of oranges, which Foodtown accepted and paid for. The next month, Citrus delivered 100 bushels of oranges to Foodtown. This shipment was accepted on May 1 and also promptly paid for.

On May 2, however, Perkins, the manager of Foodtown, became concerned because a Florida drought had resulted in a sharp increase in the price of oranges. The month before, the market price for oranges had risen to $50 per bushel. Consequently, Perkins consulted Aarons, Foodtown's attorney, who advised him to demand adequate assurances that Citrus would perform its obligations under the terms of the contract. Heeding Aarons' advice, Perkins sent a letter to Citrus the next day expressing his concern and requesting an adequate assurance of due performance for the balance of the contract. This letter was received by Citrus on May 4. Twenty days have elapsed, and Citrus has not yet responded.

87. Which of the following best states Foodtown's legal rights against Citrus?

(A) Foodtown can cancel the contract on June 1, cover immediately, and then sue for damages.
(B) Foodtown can wait until the June 1st shipment; if Foodtown doesn't get the oranges, it can demand assurances again, and then sue for damages if it doesn't obtain them.
(C) Foodtown can wait until November 1, and then sue for damages.
(D) Foodtown can wait until June 4; if adequate assurances are not received, it can then cancel the contract, cover immediately, and sue for damages.

88. Assume for the purposes of this question only that on May 6, Bryant, Citrus's president, telephoned Perkins and told him that he was willing to make up for the past shortages and that all future shipments would be conforming. Realizing that the price of oranges had increased quite substantially, Perkins in return promised to pay Bryant $30 per bushel for all future deliveries (including those covering the prior deficiencies). On June 1, Citrus shipped Foodtown 150 bushels of oranges (which included the 100 bushels for the June delivery, as well as 50 bushels covering the previous shortages). After accepting this shipment, Foodtown sent a check to Citrus in the amount of $3,000. Thereafter, Citrus brought suit against Foodtown for $1,500, claiming the contract price was $30 per bushel, not $20. Will Citrus succeed in this action?

(A) Yes, because the May 6 modification was enforceable even though it was not supported by new consideration.
(B) No, because there was no consideration to support the modification.
(C) Yes, because no writing was necessary under the circumstances.
(D) No, because the modification was not in writing, and was, therefore, unenforceable under the Uniform Commercial Code.

Questions 89–93 are based on the following fact situation.

On October 15, 2008, Turquoise Starr, an aspiring young Hollywood actress, entered into a written contract with Cameron Nikkon, a famous photographer. Their contractual agreement provided that "herein it shall be agreed that Nikkon will supply Starr with twelve glossy prints designed to capture and convey Starr as a gifted dramatic actress with varied talents." Their contract further stipulated that "said twelve prints to be delivered to Starr on or before November 15, 2008; and Starr to pay $750 thirty days thereafter." Another contractual provision recited that "Nikkon guarantees that the prints will be fully satisfactory and delivered on time."

The following day, Nikkon accidentally fell down a flight of stairs, and sustained a broken leg. As a result of his injury, Nikkon was unable to photograph Starr until October 31. At that time, he informed Starr that because of the delay "I am going to need a few more days beyond November 15 to make delivery." Starr responded, "Please, hurry with the pictures because I need to submit my promotional portfolio for the leading role in an upcoming movie.

Nikkon diligently worked to speed production and delivered the prints to Starr's manager, Sapphire Scarlet, on November 18, 2008. After Sapphire looked over the photographs, she told Nikkon, "...I'm sure that Ms. Starr will find these shots to her liking." However, the following day, Nikkon received a telephone call from Starr, who said, "These prints are just awful. I'm sending them back to you and not paying anything. Besides, these prints were two days late."

89. If Starr initiates an action against Nikkon for breach of contract, which of the following would be Nikkon's best defense?

   (A) An objective person would think the photographs were satisfactory.
   (B) A reasonable person would think the photographs were satisfactory.
   (C) The photographs were not delivered on time, thereby resulting in a failure of condition precedent to Nikkon's liability.
   (D) Nikkon's injury constituted a temporary impracticability of performance, which excused his duty to perform for a reasonable period of time.

90. Which of the following is the most accurate statement regarding Starr's contractual obligation to pay Nikkon $750?

   (A) Payment of the $750 by Starr would be an express condition precedent to Nikkon's duty of performance.
   (B) Payment of the $750 by Starr would be an express condition subsequent to Nikkon's duty of performance.
   (C) Nikkon's performance under the contract would be an express condition precedent to Starr's duty of payment of the $750.
   (D) The performances of Starr and Nikkon were, in essence, concurrent conditions.

91. Suppose that the Starr-Nikkon contract did not contain any express stipulations relating to the order of the respective performances of the parties. In such an event, which of the following statements is most accurate?

(A) The performance of Nikkon would have been a constructive condition precedent to the performance by Starr.
(B) The performance by Starr would have been an implied condition subsequent to the performance by Nikkon.
(C) The performances of Starr and Nikkon would have been constructive concurrent conditions.
(D) The contract would have been unenforceable, because it is vague as to an essential term.

92. Assume for the purposes of this question only that the court ruled that a proper interpretation of the contract terms required that the photographs be personally satisfactory to Turquoise Starr. As a result, which of the following arguments would be LEAST helpful to Nikkon in his efforts to recover on a breach of contract theory?

(A) Starr's dissatisfaction with the quality of the photographs was not genuine.
(B) Starr failed to make an adequate examination of the quality of the photographs.
(C) Starr's dissatisfaction with the photographs was the result of delivery after November 15, rather than of any lack of quality in the photographs.
(D) Because of Nikkon's injury, he did not have sufficient time to produce photographs of a quality satisfactory to Starr.

93. Which of the following is the LEAST accurate statement with regard to Nikkon's taking of the photographs?

(A) By entering into the contract, Nikkon assumed the risk that Starr would fail to cooperate in arranging for the taking of the photographs.
(B) Starr was under an implied duty to act in good faith to reasonably cooperate with Nikkon in arranging for the taking of the photographs.
(C) An implied condition of Nikkon's duty of performance was that Starr reasonably cooperate in arranging for the taking of the photographs.
(D) Starr's refusal to cooperate in arranging for the taking of the photographs would excuse Nikkon from further obligation under the contract and also give Nikkon a right of action against Starr for breach of contract.

Questions 94–95 are based on the following fact situation.

Witt was the undisputed record owner of South Fork, a tract of farmland located in the State of Durango. Bordering South Fork on its northern edge was North Fork, a 20-acre dairy farm, owned and occupied by Mann. North Fork was flanked on its eastern border by the Muddy River. For many years, Witt used to make regular use of a trail across North Fork whenever he or his cattle needed to reach the Muddy River.

In 2008, Witt sold his farm to Stone, a developer who planned to convert South Fork into a residential subdivision. After Stone took possession of South Fork, he met with Mann and informed him of the proposed development plans. During their discussion, Mann expressed concern about the increased traffic and noise from the subdivision. Consequently, the parties orally agreed that Stone would contract with someone to erect a brick wall between their respective properties, and that Mann would reimburse Stone for half the expenses. Thereafter, Stone hired Mason to erect the wall for $10,000. Stone explained to Mason that the wall was being built between his property and Mann's. He further advised Mason that although he (Stone) would be paying him the $10,000, Mann had agreed to reimburse Stone for half the price.

Mason went ahead and built the wall as agreed. However, Stone refused to pay Mason anything, and Mason, in turn, did not sue Stone for the agreed price.

94. Assume for the purposes of this question only that Mason has now brought an action against Mann to recover $5,000. Which of the following is Mann's best defense?

(A) By suing Mann for half the contract price, Mason is wrongfully splitting his cause of action.
(B) Mason is not an intended beneficiary of the Stone-Mann agreement.
(C) The Stone-Mason agreement was not in writing.
(D) The Stone-Mann agreement was not in writing.

95. Assume for the purposes of this question only that Mason built the wall as agreed and Stone paid him the sum of $10,000. Two weeks later, Mann was operating his tractor near the North Fork–South Fork property line when a section of the wall suddenly cracked and fell on top of Mann, seriously injuring him. A subsequent investigation revealed that Mason did not erect the wall according to specifications. In order to increase his profit margin, Mason used a cheap collagenous compound instead of cement. Which of the following is Mason's best defense in a contract action brought against him by Mann in which the only damages alleged are those for Mann's personal injuries?

(A) Damages for personal injuries cannot be recovered in a contract action.
(B) Damages for personal injuries to Mann were not within the contemplation of Stone and Mason at the time they entered into their agreement.
(C) Mann is only an incidental beneficiary of the Stone-Mason agreement.
(D) Mann has no standing to assert such an action since he was not a party to the Stone-Mason agreement.

Question 96 is based on the following fact situation.

The First National Bank of Denver loaned the Ajax Company $1,500,000 for the manufacture of a widget control system. As a condition of the loan, Bridget Baxter, a majority shareholder in Ajax, agreed in writing to personally guarantee the loan. Thereafter, Ajax defaulted on the loan and entered into a repayment agreement with First National. This agreement provided that First National would "use maximum efforts in selling Ajax's assets at the highest possible price." First National proceeded to sell Ajax's assets, discharging the indebtedness of the widget company.

Later, it was ascertained that First National did not realize the "highest possible price" in administering the sale of Ajax's assets. Consequently, Bridget was forced into bankruptcy and lost her entire investment in the Ajax Company.

96. Bridget brings an appropriate action against First National to recover her investment in Ajax's stock. She will most likely

  (A) not prevail, because Bridget was an incidental beneficiary of the First National sale of Ajax's assets.
  (B) not prevail, because First National's sale of Ajax's assets discharged whatever contractual relationship existed between Bridget and the bank.
  (C) prevail, because First National did not realize the highest possible price from the sale of Ajax's assets.
  (D) prevail, because First National breached its fiduciary duty to Bridget under the terms of the First National-Ajax contract.

Questions 97–98 are based on the following fact situation.

Cooley Calhoun was the Republican candidate for governor in the state of Ticonderoga. Before the election, Calhoun hired Sunrise Canyon Video Co. to shoot a series of commercials that Calhoun planned to use in his campaign. The written contract entered into between Calhoun and Sunrise included a "production fee clause" that provided that Sunrise would be "paid $100,000 for the filming and editing of ten 30-second commercials" that would be suitable for Calhoun's television campaign broadcasts. The "production fee clause" also stipulated that the $100,000 would be paid to Sunrise "on condition that the filming and editing be directed under the personal supervision of Lindsey Lens, the president of Sunrise Canyon Video Co." The contract made no other reference to compensation.

Thereafter, Sunrise filmed and edited the ten campaign commercials that Calhoun approved. When the production was completed, Sunrise submitted to Calhoun an invoice statement in the amount of $150,000. Besides the $100,000 contract figure, the bill included a $50,000 charge for Lindsey Lens's full-time services in directing the filming and editing of the videos. Denying any additional liability, Calhoun sent Sunrise a check for $100,000. Sunrise then brought suit against Calhoun to recover the $50,000 to cover Lens's services.

97. Which of the following arguments would be most persuasive in Calhoun's efforts to prevent the introduction of parol evidence to show that prior to the parties' execution of the written contract they had orally agreed that Calhoun would cover Lens's salary in addition to the $100,000 production fee?

   (A) There was no latent ambiguity contained within the actual written contract.
   (B) The written "production fee clause" is clear on its face and no patent ambiguity is present in the writing.
   (C) Parol evidence of a prior oral agreement is barred if it contradicts a term of a written contract.
   (D) Since the agreement contained a compensation clause that specified a stipulated amount, the contract was fully integrated on that subject.

98. Which of the following arguments would be most persuasive to support Sunrise's contention that when the written contract was executed Calhoun agreed to pay Sunrise $50,000 for Lens's services in addition to the $100,000 production fee?

   (A) According to the customary trade practice of the video industry, a $100,000 fee for filming and editing means $100,000 in addition to the director's salary for supervisory services.
   (B) An antecedent oral agreement to that effect, if provable, would only supplement, not contradict, the "production fee clause" as written.
   (C) Under the Uniform Commercial Code, extrinsic evidence, if available, of additional terms agreed to by the parties is admissible unless such terms "would certainly vary or contradict those contained in the document."
   (D) Assuming arguendo that the written "production fee clause" was fully integrated and neither patently nor latently ambiguous, equitable considerations require admission of extrinsic evidence, if available, of the parties' intent, since Sunrise would stand to lose $50,000 on the contract.

Questions 99–100 are based on the following fact situation.

Asburn, Craig, and Thornberry were old friends who had served together in the Navy during World War II. For over forty years, they lived in the same neighborhood in the town of Metsville. While Asburn was away on a business trip to Philadelphia, someone broke into his garage and stole his golf clubs. The next week, Asburn was planning to go on vacation in Bermuda and asked Craig if he could borrow his golf clubs. Craig agreed and loaned his golf clubs to Asburn, who promised to return them after his vacation. When Asburn returned home from Bermuda, he kept Craig's golf clubs and continued to use them.

A few weeks later, Craig was having dinner with Thornberry and learned that he owed Asburn $4,000. Thornberry had just been laid off his job and didn't have the money to repay Asburn. Craig felt indebted to Thornberry ever since he saved Craig's life during the battle of Iwo Jima. As a result, Craig told Thornberry that he would contact Asburn and make arrangements to repay the loan on his behalf.

Thereupon, Asburn and Craig entered into a written agreement wherein Craig promised to pay Asburn, at a rate of $400 a month, the matured $4,000 debt that Thornberry owed Asburn. In the same written instrument, Asburn promised to return Craig's golf clubs, which he still had in his possession. Asburn, however, made no written or oral commitment to forbear to sue Thornberry to collect the $4,000 debt, and Craig made no oral or written request for any such forbearance.

After this agreement between Asburn and Craig was signed and executed, Asburn promptly returned the golf clubs to Craig. For the next six months, Craig made the $400 monthly payments as agreed. During that period, Asburn did not take any legal action against Thornberry. Craig then repudiated his agreement with Asburn, and thirty days later, Asburn filed a contract action against Craig.

99. Assume for the purposes of this question only that the applicable statute of limitations on Asburn's antecedent claim against Thornberry expired the day before Asburn filed his contract action against Craig. Which of the following is the most persuasive argument that Craig is not liable to Asburn under the terms of their written agreement?

(A) Since Asburn did not expressly promise to forbear to sue Thornberry to collect the antecedent $4,000 debt, Asburn's forbearance for six months could not constitute consideration for Craig's promise.

(B) Since the written agreement between Craig and Asburn shows a gross imbalance between the value of the promises exchanged, the consideration for Craig's promise was legally insufficient to support it.

(C) Since Thornberry, when the Craig-Asburn agreement was made, had a pre-existing duty to repay his $4,000 debt to Asburn, there was no consideration for Craig's promise to Asburn.

(D) Since Asburn had a pre-existing duty to return Craig's golf clubs to him when the Craig-Asburn agreement was made, there was no consideration for Craig's promise to Asburn.

100. Assume for the purposes of this question only that the applicable statute of limitations on Asburn's antecedent claim against Thornberry expired the day after the written agreement between Craig and Asburn was executed. Which of the following is the most persuasive argument that Craig is liable to Asburn under the terms of their agreement?

(A) Craig's promise and Asburn's reliance thereon gave rise to a valid claim by Asburn against Craig based on the doctrine of promissory estoppel.

(B) Because it was foreseeable that Craig's promise would induce Asburn to forbear taking any action against Thornberry, such forbearance was, as a matter of law, a bargained-for consideration for Craig's promise.

(C) Craig's six payments to Asburn totaling $2,400 manifested a serious intent on Craig's part to be contractually bound, and such manifestation is generally recognized as an effective substitute for consideration.

(D) By assuming the antecedent debt obligation that Thornberry owed to Asburn, Craig became a surety whose promise to Asburn was enforceable since it was in writing and supported by adequate consideration.

Question 101 is based on the following fact situation.

Daisy DuPont was a descendant of Pierre DuPont, the founder of the DuPont Chemical Company. Daisy, who was very wealthy, owned an extensive art collection that she displayed at Montepellier, her country mansion. While Daisy was away on a Mediterranean cruise, there was a burglary at Montepellier and her favorite Picasso painting, entitled *Margaux*, was stolen. Although the painting was insured for $1,000,000 by Floyd's of Flounder Insurance Company, it had a market value of over $1,500,000.

When Daisy returned from her trip, she met with Jayson Jewell, a detective employed by Floyd's of Flounder to investigate the theft. During their meeting, Daisy told Jayson that she would pay him an extra $50,000 if he recovered the painting. For the next three weeks Jayson investigated the theft as part of his job responsibilities with Floyd's. Within the course of this investigation, Jayson learned who was responsible for the burglary. As a consequence, the culprit was apprehended and the Picasso painting was recovered and returned to Daisy.

101. Jayson then requested the $50,000 that Daisy had promised to pay him. After Daisy refused to make the payment, Jayson sued Daisy for breach of contract. Judgment for

(A) Daisy, because her promise was gratuitous.

(B) Daisy, because the insurance company owed her a pre-existing duty to find the painting.

(C) Daisy, because as an intended third-party beneficiary under Floyd's employment agreement with Jayson, she did not incur any legal detriment.

(D) Jayson, because the market value of the painting exceeded its insured value, constituting sufficient consideration to support Daisy's promise.

Question 102 is based on the following fact situation.

Tex was a well-known rodeo performer who lived in Ft. Worth. One day, Barnum approached Tex and said, "If you will ride my bucking bronco for one minute, I will pay you $500." Tex then went and purchased a special saddle for the bronco ride. After saddling Barnum's bronco, Tex mounted the horse and started to ride. Barnum suddenly yelled, "I hereby revoke my offer!"

102. If Tex thereafter goes ahead and rides the bronco for one minute, will he recover the $500?

   (A) No, because Barnum's revocation was effective since Tex had not completed performance.
   (B) Yes, because there was an offer for a unilateral contract that became irrevocable prior to Barnum's attempted revocation.
   (C) Yes, under the doctrine of estoppel in pais.
   (D) Yes, under the doctrine of quasi-contract.

Questions 103–104 are based on the following fact situation.

On April 10, Gallop, owner of the Galloping Hill Golf Course in Unionville, entered into an oral agreement with Sprink. Based upon their agreement, Sprink promised to install all new sprinkler heads on the sprinkler system at the golf course. In return, Gallop promised to pay Sprink $2,400 upon completion of the job. Since the Unionville County Golf Tournament was scheduled for the weekend of April 20-21, Sprink agreed to replace all the sprinkler heads no later than April 19. Before accepting the job, Sprink inspected the golf course and determined that 240 sprinkler heads had to be replaced.

By April 14, Sprink had installed eighty new sprinkler heads on the first six holes of the golf course. That afternoon, however, Gallop learned that Sprink had been adjudicated bankrupt on April 12. Based on this information, Gallop notified Sprink to discontinue the job. The next day, Gallop hired Hand to complete the installation work at eight dollars ($8) per head. Hand installed the remaining 160 sprinkler heads and completed the work on April 19. Despite making reasonable efforts, Sprink was unable to find any gainful employment during the period that Hand completed the job. Also, Sprink's application for unemployment compensation was rejected at the same time.

103. Which of the following statements, if any, would provide Gallop with legally justifiable grounds for discharging Sprink:

   I. Sprink had been adjudicated bankrupt on April 12.
   II. Sprink had only completed 33% of the installation work when he was discharged.
   III. The Sprink-Gallop contract was not in writing.

   (A) I only.
   (B) I and II.
   (C) II and III.
   (D) Neither I, II, nor III.

104. Assume for the purposes of this question only that Gallop was legally justified in discharging Sprink. In an action by Sprink against Gallop, which of the following is Sprink's proper measure of recovery?

   (A) $640 (or the equivalent of $8 per sprinkler head installed).
   (B) $800 (or the equivalent of $10 per sprinkler head installed).
   (C) Quantum meruit for the reasonable value of his services rendered in installing the eighty sprinkler heads.
   (D) Nothing, because he has not completed performance of the entire job.

Questions 105–106 are based on the following fact situation.

On August 10th, The Clip Joint, a retail stationery store, sent the following purchase order to American Office Supply Company, a wholesaler of office supply equipment: "Please ship immediately 24 pairs (two dozen) 3-1/2 inch, right-handed scissors at your current list price of $4 per pair."

American received this purchase order on August 12. The next day, Sam Shipley, American's shipping clerk, ascertained that there were only 18 pairs of 3-1/2 inch, right-handed scissors in stock. Shipley, however, found that American had 6 pairs of 3-1/2 inch, left-handed scissors in stock. Without notifying The Clip Joint, Shipley went ahead and shipped the 18 pairs of right-handed scissors along with the 6 pairs of left-handed scissors to the stationery store. The Clip Joint was aware that the wholesale price for the left-handed scissors was $3 per pair, or $1 less than the list price for the right-handed scissors.

105. Was an enforceable contract formed when American shipped the 24 pairs of scissors to The Clip Joint?

(A) Yes, because American's shipment constituted acceptance of the offer, and there was no notification by American to The Clip Joint that the shipment was made for accommodation only.

(B) Yes, because American acted in "good faith" in making the shipment in reliance on The Clip Joint's offer.

(C) No, because American could accept The Clip Joint's offer only by a prompt promise to ship the goods ordered.

(D) No, because acceptance by performance of an offer for immediate or prompt shipment is not legally binding unless the nonconforming goods are reasonably resalable.

106. Which of the following is the most accurate statement regarding The Clip Joint's legal rights following receipt of the scissors?

(A) The Clip Joint may either accept or reject all of the scissors upon seasonable notice to American, but it cannot accept only the right-handed scissors without American's approval.

(B) The Clip Joint may either accept or reject all of the scissors, or accept any combination of right- or left-handed pairs and reject the rest, but, in either case, it must give American seasonable notice of either total or partial rejection.

(C) The Clip Joint may either accept or reject all of the scissors, or accept the right-handed pairs and reject the left-handed pairs, but it cannot accept any combination of the two pairs.

(D) The Clip Joint may either accept or reject all of the scissors, or, provided American seasonably gave notice that the shipment was made for accommodation only, The Clip Joint may accept any combination of right- and left-handed scissors and reject the rest.

Question 107 is based on the following fact situation.

107. Suppose that a construction contract contains a provision that calls for an architect's certificate of completion. In the event that the architect refuses in bad faith to execute a certificate, most courts will:

   (A) order the architect to execute the certificate.
   (B) require the contractor to proceed in equity for reformation to eliminate the clause.
   (C) award the contractor damages against the architect.
   (D) none of the above.

Questions 108–109 are based on the following fact situation.

Hoedown was the undisputed record owner of Cornish Acres, a 200-acre farmland in northern Kansas. In 2003, Hoedown entered into a three-year lease with Overalls, who planned to use Cornish Acres for the raising of cattle and hogs. The lease provided that Overalls would pay Hoedown a monthly rental of $1,500, payable on the first day of each month.

Overalls took possession of Cornish Acres on June 1, 2003. Shortly thereafter, he built thereon, at his own expense, a corn crib made of lumber which was fifteen feet wide and twenty feet long and set on loose bricks. At each corner of the corn crib, he set a wood post in the ground fifteen inches deep and nailed the corn crib to the four corner posts. In 2005, Overalls also built a hog house of brick and mortar on the premises. The hog house was constructed on a cement foundation which extended into the ground twenty-four inches. This structure was thirty feet wide by seventy feet long, and was used to keep the brood sows warm during the winter months.

These permanent improvements increased the appraised market value of Cornish Acres from $250,000 to $275,000. In May 2006, Hoedown informed Overalls that he was going to put the farm up for sale. The next month, when the Hoedown-Overalls lease expired, the parties settled a dispute over Overalls's right, if any, to compensation for the improvements by the following written agreement:

> "On the sale of Cornish Acres, Hoedown hereby agrees to pay Overalls two-thirds of any sale proceeds in excess of $250,000, provided that Overalls may remain on the farm until November, 2006, rent-free while Hoedown tries to sell it. After that time, however, Overalls may remain on the farm until closing, but at a $1,000 monthly rental."

Hoedown initially set the asking price at $300,000. After receiving scant interest, Hoedown decided to reduce the price to $260,000. This price reduction so infuriated Overalls that he thereafter made negative comments about the farm to all of the prospective buyers except Husker, who inspected Cornish Acres while Overalls was away on vacation.

On February 1, 2007, after rejecting offers for $240,000 and $250,000, Hoedown finally sold Cornish Acres to Husker for $256,000. Thereupon, Overalls, who had paid no rent since June, 2006, moved out. After closing, Hoedown refused to pay Overalls any of the sale proceeds, and Overalls brought suit to recover damages for breach of contract.

108. Which of the following is Hoedown's most persuasive argument in defense of Overalls's suit?

   (A) Overalls committed an uncured material breach of an implied promise to cooperate in Hoedown's efforts to sell the property, or at least not to hinder the proposed sale.
   (B) Overalls's negative comments about the farm to prospective buyers amounted to an anticipatory repudiation of the Hoedown-Overalls agreement.
   (C) Overalls's failure to pay any rent for the last two months of the eight-month holdover period was a material breach of contract that discharged Hoedown's remaining duties of performance.
   (D) The Hoedown-Overalls agreement was voidable because it was a restraint on alienation since it conditioned a promise to pay for a conveyance of land upon an otherwise invalid leasehold contract.

109. Which of the following statements, if true, most persuasively supports Overalls's contention that he is entitled to recover at least $2,000 from Hoedown (or the equivalent of two-thirds of the sale proceeds in excess of $250,000, minus two months unpaid rent at $1,000 per month)?

   (A) Hoedown breached an implied promise by failing to attempt to sell the property at $275,000, which was the appraised market value of Cornish Acres.
   (B) Since Overalls made no negative comments about the farm to Husker, there is no showing that Overalls' remarks to the other prospective buyers necessarily caused any loss to Hoedown (i.e., prevented him from selling the farm for more than $256,000).
   (C) The Hoedown-Overalls agreement contained only one express condition (i.e., Overalls was permitted to remain on the farm during Hoedown's efforts to sell it), and since that condition has occurred, Overalls is entitled to his share of the proceeds from the sale.
   (D) Even if Overalls's failure to pay any rent for the last two months of his holdover was a material breach of contract, Hoedown's promise to pay Overalls a share of the proceeds of the sale was an independent covenant.

Questions 110–111 are based on the following fact situation.

Peter McDermott had been employed by the Fairmont Hotel as a window cleaner for eight years when the hotel issued to him and other employees the following certificate:

"In appreciation of the faithful service hitherto rendered by you as an employee of this hotel, there will be paid in the event of your death, if still an employee of this hotel, to the party designated by you below as your beneficiary, the sum of $5,000. The issuance of this certificate is understood to be purely gratuitous.

Fairmont Hotel
(signature) Montee Hall
President"

After receiving the certificate, Peter McDermott writes the following in the spaces provided:

"I hereby accept this certificate and name my wife, Cathy Lee McDermott, as beneficiary.

(signature) Peter McDermott"

On August 15, 2005, McDermott, while washing a window on the thirteenth floor of the hotel, saw Hall sprawled on the floor of his room. Breaking the glass of the window to effect entry, McDermott discovered the gas jet of the heater in the room open and the room filled with gas. He turned off the jet, opened all windows, and applied artificial respiration to Hall, finally reviving him. In the process of breaking the window to get in, McDermott cut his arm badly. Seeing this, and grateful for his rescue, Hall said, "You'll have a job with us for life." Three months later, McDermott's injured arm had to be amputated. Although McDermott did not perform any services, he was left on the payroll at the direction of Hall. On December 31, 2007, the Fairmont Hotel mailed letters revoking the aforementioned certificate. On January 1, 2008, before receipt of this letter, McDermott died.

110. In an action by McDermott's widow, Cathy Lee, against Montee Hall and the Fairmont Hotel to recover the sum of $5,000, which of the following, if established, is the strongest argument against enforcement of the certificate agreement?

(A) Cathy was unaware of the certificate agreement until after Peter died.
(B) There was no privity of contract between Cathy and the Fairmont Hotel.
(C) The Fairmont Hotel effectively revoked its certificate offer before Peter died.
(D) Cathy was never an employee of the hotel.

111. Which of the following best characterizes the legal relationship between Montee Hall and Peter McDermott as of August 15, 2005?

(A) As per Hall's oral promise, McDermott had an enforceable lifetime contract with the hotel.
(B) Hall had a duty to pay McDermott reasonable compensation for saving his life based upon a contract implied-in-fact.
(C) McDermott's act of saving Hall's life was sufficient past consideration to render enforceable Hall's subsequent promise.
(D) Since McDermott gratuitously rendered assistance to Hall, there was insufficient consideration to support Hall's subsequent promise to provide McDermott with a lifetime contract.

Question 112 is based on the following fact situation.

Logan Industries contracted in writing to purchase 1,000 framises (which are similar to widgets, but are more popular because of their greater durability and resiliency) from Clich Company, a manufacturer, for a total contract price of $4,000. After this agreement was executed and before delivery, Logan and Clich agreed in a telephone conversation to change the quantity term from 1,000 to 800 framises.

112. This modification is probably unenforceable because

    (A) it violates the statute of frauds.
    (B) there was no consideration.
    (C) the original contract was in writing.
    (D) the parol evidence rule bars contradictory terms.

Questions 113–115 are based on the following fact situation.

Hamilton Humphrey is the father of J.P. Humphrey, vice-president of a small electronics firm known as Electro-Aeronautics, Inc. In January, 2006, the company decided to radically overhaul its manufacturing processes and borrowed $200,000 from the City National Bank for this purpose. The loan was secured by a mortgage on the plant and building site, and it would become due on February 1, 2007.

When the debt came due, Electro-Aeronautics was short of ready cash and City National threatened to foreclose. Hamilton Humphrey then intervened on behalf of the company and told the Bank officials that if they would refrain from any legal action against the company for a year (until February 1, 2008), he would personally see that the debt was paid. The bank orally agreed to Hamilton's surety arrangement. However, it was never reduced to writing.

On April 15, 2007, the Bank filed a foreclosure suit against Electro-Aeronautics. Hamilton Humphrey did not learn of the suit until a week later, but he raised no objection, since he thought the Bank was violating its agreement with him by foreclosing prior to February 1, 2008, and thus relieving him of his part of the bargain.

Two weeks later, on May 1, 2007, the Bank's loan officer called Hamilton Humphrey and said that the Bank would hold off on the foreclosure suit as per their agreement since the company had just made a new technological development that would place it in a very lucrative and competitive position.

113. The Bank's promise to Humphrey in February 2007 to refrain from foreclosing on the mortgage until February 1, 2008, would constitute

    (A) a void promise at the time of inception.
    (B) a voidable promise as violative of the Statute of Frauds.
    (C) an unenforceable promise, because Electro-Aeronautics had a pre-existing duty to pay the debt at maturity.
    (D) an enforceable promise, binding Humphrey as a surety.

114. With regard to Humphrey's obligation under his February 2007 agreement with the Bank, the court would most likely

    (A) relieve Humphrey of liability, because the Bank filed for foreclosure of the mortgage.
    (B) relieve Humphrey of liability, because Humphrey was never under a duty as a surety.
    (C) not relieve Humphrey of liability, because of the Main Purpose Exception.
    (D) not relieve Humphrey of liability, because his surety duty "sprang back" on May 1, 2007.

115. Assume for the purposes of this question only that soon after the new technological development took place, Electro-Aeronautics' business fortunes declined, which resulted in its insolvency. In an action by the Bank against the appointed receiver in bankruptcy and Hamilton Humphrey, the Bank will most likely recover for the outstanding loan from

(A) Humphrey only.
(B) receiver only.
(C) either Humphrey or receiver.
(D) both Humphrey and receiver.

Questions 116–117 are based on the following fact situation.

In a written contract, Seller agreed to deliver to Buyer 1,000 widgets at a stipulated price of $10 each FOB at Seller's place of business. The contract stipulated that "any party who wishes to assign this contract must have the written consent of the other party." On March 1, Seller placed the widgets on board a cargo vessel that was destined to transport the widgets to Buyer. On March 2, Buyer received the following telegram from Seller, "Please be advised that the widgets are in transit. In addition, I hereby assign all my rights under our contract to Creditor." Buyer did not consent to the assignment. The next day, the ship carrying the widgets sank in a violent storm, destroying its entire cargo.

116. If Creditor brings an appropriate action against Buyer, the former will most likely recover

(A) nothing, because Buyer never assented to the assignment.
(B) nothing, because Buyer never received the widgets.
(C) the contract price of $10,000.
(D) the difference between the contract price and the market value of the widgets.

117. In an action by Buyer against Seller for breach of contract, Buyer will

(A) succeed, because the risk of loss was on Seller.
(B) succeed, because the carrier was Seller's agent.
(C) not succeed, because the risk of loss was on Buyer.
(D) not succeed, because of frustration of purpose.

Questions 118–122 are based on the following fact situation.

Reynolds Manufacturing Company, an aluminum can manufacturer, entered into negotiations with White Owl, a cigar manufacturer, to supply White Owl's requirements of specially designed aluminum cigar containers for a new brand of cigars. The cigars were to be manufactured from Brazilian tobacco at White Owl's plant in Rio de Janeiro.

On June 1, Reynolds contacted Alco, a small manufacturer of aluminum sheeting and told it that Reynolds expected to have a monthly demand of 1,000 units of sheeting after it finalized its contract with White Owl. The next day, Reynolds and Alco signed the following contract:

> "Alco agrees to supply all of Reynolds requirements of aluminum sheeting for a period of two years beginning on August 1 at a price of $3.00 per unit."

On June 15, Reynolds and White Owl entered into a written contract whereby Reynolds agreed to supply White Owl with as many cigar containers as White Owl may require up to a maximum of 10,000 containers per month. However, Reynolds orally agreed to supply White Owl with an unusually large first delivery of 20,000 containers by September 15 to cover White Owl's promotional requirements.

On June 16, Reynolds notified Alco that it would need a delivery of 2,000 units by August 1 in order to accommodate White Owl's first order. Alco informed Reynolds that it did not contemplate such high requirements, since their plant's capacity was only 2,800 per month. Moreover, Alco pointed out that in order to meet Reynolds's order of 2,000 units, it would probably lose two long-time customers whose outstanding orders would have to be canceled.

After a week of negotiations, on June 23, Alco orally agreed to deliver 2,000 units of sheeting to Reynolds by August 1. The parties signed the following contract:

"Alco agrees to supply all of Reynolds's requirements of aluminum sheeting for a period of two years beginning August 1st, at a price of $3.50 per unit. Reynolds agrees that it will require a minimum of 800 units in every month of the agreement."

On June 25, Alco notified its two long-time customers that it was canceling their August orders (of 800 units), because of other contract commitments. The following day, the Brazilian government was overthrown. Then, on July 1, the United States Government announced an embargo on the importation of all Brazilian products. As a result of the embargo, White Owl contacted Reynolds on July 2, and instructed it not to make any deliveries of the cigar containers until further notice.

118. The June 2 agreement entered into between Reynolds and Alco would best be described as a (an)

(A) illusory contract.
(B) best-efforts contract.
(C) requirements and output contract.
(D) aleatory contract.

119. Reynolds's oral agreement on June 15 to supply White Owl with the 20,000 containers would most likely be held

(A) enforceable in all respects.
(B) unenforceable, since their written contract on the same date was the final integration of the terms of their agreement.
(C) unenforceable, since the agreement was violative of the Parol Evidence Rule.
(D) unenforceable, since there was inadequate consideration to support Reynolds's unilateral promise.

120. With respect to the Reynolds–White Owl written contract on June 15, which of the following statements is most accurate regarding the omittance of a fixed contract price?

(A) The contract is unenforceable as violative of the Statute of Frauds.
(B) The contract is unenforceable, because of indefiniteness.
(C) The contract may be enforceable if it is later modified to include the price term.
(D) The contract is enforceable with reasonable price being fixed at time of delivery.

121. Which of the following is the most accurate statement regarding the Reynolds-Alco agreement on June 23?

    (A) The agreement constituted a valid modification of their June 2 contract.
    (B) The agreement was unenforceable, since Alco was under a pre-existing duty to supply Reynolds with the sheeting under their June 2 contract.
    (C) The agreement constituted an enforceable reformation of their June 2 contract.
    (D) The agreement was unenforceable, since there was no new consideration.

122. What is the probable legal effect of the United States government's embargo of Brazilian imports on the Reynolds–White Owl contract?

    (A) Both parties' duties of performance would be excused by impracticability of performance.
    (B) Both parties' duties of performance would be discharged by frustration of purpose.
    (C) Both parties' duties of performance would be suspended through temporary impossibility.
    (D) The parties' duties of performance would be excused by impossibility due to a supervening illegality.

Questions 123–124 are based on the following fact situation.

In June 2007, the South Philadelphia School of Law advertised in *The National Law Journal* for a Legal Ethics and Jurisprudence professor. Among those applicants responding to the ad was Harlan Heckler, who was a practicing attorney in the nearby city of Sherman Oaks. Alfred Avis, the assistant dean at the South Philadelphia School of Law (who was in charge of interviewing all applicants), was impressed with Heckler's credentials. He immediately wrote Heckler to offer him the position and enclosed the following instrument for Heckler's signature:

"1. The South Philadelphia School of Law agrees to employ Harlan Heckler as a Legal Ethics and Jurisprudence professor during the academic year 2007-2008. Mr. Heckler's salary will be $25,000, payable in equal bi-weekly installments during the period from September 1, 2007, to June 1, 2008.

2. Mr. Heckler agrees to accept such employment and to perform his duties as law school professor diligently and competently.

3. Mr. Heckler shall be entitled to ten sick days, with full pay, for the academic year.

South Philadelphia School of Law

By/s/ _____

Alfred Avis

_____

Harlan Heckler"

After Heckler received this letter, he replied by mail, requesting a salary of $30,000 and sick leave of fifteen days. Upon receipt of Heckler's letter, Avis telephoned Heckler on June 30 and told him that the law school followed the American Bar Association guidelines with respect to salary and sick leave for its professors. Heckler acquiesced on the salary question, but insisted that his sick leave be extended to fifteen days. Avis told Heckler that the law school was bound by the ABA guidelines but said, "Let's not permit a minor issue to stand in the way of your coming to South Philadelphia. In the event you require more than ten sick days, I promise that the matter will be taken care of to your benefit." Heckler informed Avis that he would sign the contract and forward it to Avis (which he promptly did).

Heckler began teaching at South Philadelphia School of Law on September 1, 2007. Three months later, Heckler was out sick for five days with laryngitis. Heckler did not miss another school day until Monday, March 1, 2008, when he fell ill with food poisoning. This illness kept Heckler home for five additional sick days. By this time, several other professors, as well as numerous students, contracted botulism after eating in the law school cafeteria. As a consequence, Heckler telephoned Dean Avis on Monday, March 8 and said, "Dean, please be advised that I shall not be resuming my teaching duties until this botulism epidemic has safely been brought under control."

Although the law school remained open during the week of the botulism epidemic, only a few of the regularly scheduled classes were held as the majority of professors and students stayed home. By Monday, March 15, the epidemic had been safely arrested and the law school resumed normal operations. Heckler, who had fully recovered from his attack of food poisoning, also resumed his teaching duties on March 15. When Heckler received his salary check at the end of the week, his check did not include payment for the previous week (from March 8 to March 12). Accompanying the check was a statement that read:

> "Salary payment for period from Monday,
> March 1 through Friday, March 19 with
> pro rata deduction to reflect five teaching
> days missed during said period."

On the back of Heckler's check, the law school typed the following statement:

> "Endorsement of this check by payee
> constitutes surrender of all claims against
> South Philadelphia School of Law arising
> out of his/her employment contract."

When Heckler received his check, he immediately confronted Dean Avis and requested full payment for the week of March 8 through 12. Avis responded, "Harlan, I'm sorry, but there is absolutely nothing I can do about it." In need of money, Heckler endorsed the check and cashed it.

123. Suppose Heckler asserts a claim against South Philadelphia School of Law for breach of contract. Heckler offers to introduce evidence that during his telephone conversation with Avis on June 30, Avis promised, if necessary, to provide him with additional sick days. The most accurate statement concerning Avis's oral promise would be that

(A) Parol evidence is admissible to show that the parties assented to their written contract only as a partial integration of their complete contract.
(B) Parol evidence is admissible to prove a subsequent oral agreement that varies or contradicts the terms of a prior written contract.
(C) Parol evidence is admissible to show that the written contract is not enforceable because of undue influence or fraud.
(D) Parol evidence is inadmissible to prove contemporaneous oral agreements that vary or contradict the terms of a written contract.

124. What is the probable legal effect of Heckler's endorsement of the check?

(A) It constituted a discharge of a liquidated claim.
(B) It constituted an accord and satisfaction of an unliquidated claim.
(C) Part payment of a liquidated claim would not constitute a discharge of the entire amount due.
(D) Part payment of an unliquidated claim does not constitute sufficient consideration for the discharge of the entire claim.

Questions 125–127 are based on the following fact situation.

Dexter Danforth was a successful attorney who had a lucrative law practice in Century City, California. Dexter, who was an avid Los Angeles Avoiders fan, frequently wagered on baseball games with his bookie in Las Vegas. On October 4, 2008, before the start of the World Series between his beloved Avoiders and the New York Patriots, he wanted to place a "large" bet on the Avoiders. When Dexter was unable to contact his bookie, he called his law clerk, Duke Hodges, into his office. Dexter told Duke that he wanted to bet $10,000 on the Avoiders to win the World Series. Since he couldn't place the bet with his bookie, Dexter wanted Duke to travel to Las Vegas to "lay" the bet for him.

As a consequence, Dexter and Duke entered into the following written agreement:

"I. Duke shall travel to Las Vegas on October 5, 2008, and wager $10,000 (which shall be given to him by Dexter) on the L.A. Avoiders to win the World Series. The bet shall be made at The Diamond Head casino.

II. Dexter shall pay Duke $500 for placing the wager on his behalf. Moreover, if the Avoiders in fact win the World Series, then Dexter shall pay Duke an additional $500 bonus.

III. Duke shall never tell anyone about The Diamond Head wager.

IV. Duke shall be made a junior partner in Dexter's law firm at a starting salary of $20,000 after he (Duke) passes his California bar examination."

After the agreement was signed and sealed, Dexter handed Duke $10,000 and a round-trip airline ticket to Las Vegas. Dexter then told Duke that he would be paid $500 after he returned from Nevada. Duke arrived in Las Vegas the next day and immediately went to The Diamond Head casino. There, he noticed a sign in the front window that read, "Diamond Head Casino Temporarily Closed Due to Renovations." After he was unable to reach Dexter by telephone, Duke placed the bet at The Keno Palace, another gaming establishment located next door to The Diamond Head.

The following morning, Duke flew back to Century City and gave the betting receipt to Dexter. When Dexter saw that the bet had been made at The Keno Palace, rather than at The Diamond Head, he angrily told Duke, "You, dummy, I purposely directed you to wager that $10,000 at The Diamond Head. Since you failed to follow my instructions, the deal's off." As a result, Dexter refused to pay Duke the $500 and terminated his employment with the law firm.

125. If Duke initiates suit for breach of contract, the court will most likely determine that placing the $10,000 wager at The Keno Palace, rather than at The Diamond Head, constituted a

(A) breach of contract.
(B) modification.
(C) constructive condition precedent.
(D) discharge by impossibility.

126. Assume for the purposes of this question only that Duke did, in fact, place the wager at The Diamond Head casino for Dexter. In addition, Duke bet $15,000 with Mickey that the Patriots would win the World Series. After Duke lost his bet, Mickey, who was an unemployed lawyer, suggested that Duke assign to him the right to be made a partner in Dexter's law firm as payment for the outstanding debt obligation. Duke agreed and assigned "the right(s) under my contract with Dexter Danforth to be made a junior partner in his law firm at a starting salary of $20,000 to Mickey." Which of the following is the most accurate statement regarding the legal effect of this assignment?

(A) Dexter would be required to recognize the validity of the assignment and the delegation of duties under the Danforth-Hodges contract, so that Mickey would be entitled to become a junior partner in the law firm.
(B) Dexter would be required to recognize the validity of the assignment but would be entitled to demand adequate assurances of performance from the delegate, Mickey, as to the latter's willingness and professional capacity to perform satisfactory work.
(C) Dexter would not be required to recognize the validity of the assignment of rights because a contract to make a future assignment of a right is not an assignment.
(D) It would constitute a breach of contract on the part of Duke, thus giving Dexter an immediate right to rescind their agreement because neither the rights nor the duties under a personal service contract are properly assignable.

127. Assume for the purposes of this question only that when the Danforth-Hodges agreement was entered into, Duke was a first-year student at Pepperdine Law School. After the Avoiders won the World Series, Dexter refused to pay Duke the $500 bonus (although the latter had been paid $500 for placing the bet at The Keno Palace after his return from Las Vegas). In a breach of contract action, which of the following is Dexter's BEST defense against Duke if he doesn't pay the latter the $500 bonus?

(A) The contract was void ab initio because the contract could not be performed in its entirety within the span of one year.

(B) Duke's placing the $10,000 wager at The Keno Palace constituted a material breach of contract, thereby relieving Dexter of any further contractual obligations under the terms of their agreement.

(C) During one of the World Series games, Duke told his girlfriend Emily about the $10,000 which he wagered on behalf of Dexter.

(D) Since The Diamond Head casino was temporarily closed, all contractual obligations would be suspended under the doctrine of frustration of purpose.

Questions 128–130 are based on the following fact situation.

On November 15, 2005, Abdul Ahmat, agent in Gulf Shores, Alabama, of the Tehranian Realty Co. (an Iranian corporation with headquarters in Tehran) contracted on its behalf and with its authority to sell to Kent Stabler a three-acre track of vacant land in Gulf Shores, owned by Tehranian, for a price of $100,000. In accordance with the arrangement made between Ahmat and Stabler, the latter forwarded a certified check for $100,000 to the Farsi National Bank in Tehran, to be delivered by it to the Tehranian Co. in exchange for a deed to the three-acre tract, which the Farsi National Bank was then to forward to Stabler. On the same day, Ahmat and Stabler signed the following instrument:

> "In order to help Kent Stabler with his plans for development of the three-acre tract he has this day bought from the Tehranian Realty Co., I will lend him $50,000 at 10% interest provided he signs a contract with a builder for construction on this tract or on the adjoining lot now owned by him. Repayment to me at the rate of $5,000 per year to be secured by a mortgage on the three-acre tract sold by Tehranian."

Stabler did own a much smaller lot adjoining the three-acre tract that he had contracted to buy from Tehranian. On December 3, 2005, Stabler signed a contract with Jimmy Paycheck, by which Paycheck agreed for a price of $25,000 to build a structure suitable for use as a nightclub on the small lot Stabler already owned. Stabler also paid $5,000 for nightclub fixtures that cannot be resold for more than $2,500. On December 7, 2005, the Iranian government was overthrown by a military coup led by some colonels, who promptly issued a decree, reinforced by heavy penalties, forbidding any Iranian citizen or corporation from transferring any assets to a foreign national and from disposing of any assets owned in any foreign country.

It is entirely uncertain how long this decree will continue in effect. Stabler has sought unsuccessfully to reclaim his certified check and was similarly unsuccessful in his attempts to borrow money from local banks and other potential lenders in the area. He has only $5,000 in realizable assets of his own, and the corner lot on which he plans to build is already mortgaged to its full mortgage value. On December 15, Stabler told Ahmat that he had signed the contract with Paycheck and wanted the $50,000 promised on November 15. Ahmat refused to lend it, saying, "Sorry, but there never was a contract. Anyway, the deal is off."

128. In an appropriate action to secure specific performance of Ahmat's promise to lend him the $50,000, Stabler will

   (A) win, because there is a memorandum that satisfies the Statute of Frauds.
   (B) win, because parol evidence may be introduced to prove that the parties' manifestations were such that the loan agreement was part of the real-estate sales contract.
   (C) lose, because Stabler's only remedy is for damages.
   (D) lose, unless Stabler can show detrimental reliance.

129. Which of the following best states the legal relationship between Ahmat and Stabler?

   (A) Ahmat's performance was excused because of impossibility, but Stabler can recover any damages he suffered because of the supervening illegality.
   (B) Ahmat's performance was not excused due the supervening illegality and Stabler can recover damages because of the former's prospective inability to perform.
   (C) Ahmat's performance was not excused due to the supervening illegality and Stabler can recover damages because the former's repudiation amounted to an anticipatory breach of contract.
   (D) Both parties are excused from performance because of frustration and neither can recover from the other one.

130. Ahmat's promise to lend $50,000 to Stabler is

   (A) a condition precedent in form but subsequent in substance to Stabler's duty to enter into a building construction contract.
   (B) a condition subsequent in form but precedent in substance to Stabler's duty to enter into a building construction contract.
   (C) a condition subsequent to Stabler's duty to enter into a building construction contract.
   (D) not a condition, either precedent or subsequent, to Stabler's duty to enter into a building construction contract.

Questions 131–133 are based on the following fact situation.

Aaron Amesway, the noted author, was writing a screenplay, which he was adapting from his novel *Quiet Winter*. He assigned in writing 25 percent of any future royalties, when and if the screenplay was made into either a movie or a stage play, to his friend Lady Buffington, who had subsidized him during his early years as a struggling writer. Shortly after the screenplay was completed, Amesway was killed in an auto accident. Seven Brothers Studio purchased the screenplay from the executors of Amesway's estate, and filmed the movie *Quiet Winter,* which was a great success.

131. In an action against the executors of Amesway's estate to recover her percentage of the movie royalties, Lady Buffington will most likely

   (A) lose, since, under the circumstances, an assignment of future rights is unenforceable.
   (B) lose, since the attempted gift of royalties failed for nondelivery.
   (C) win, because she was an intended beneficiary.
   (D) win, because the assignment of future rights is enforceable.

132. If the court holds the aforementioned assignment unenforceable, the most applicable legal principle would be:

   (A) a purported assignment of a right expected to arise under a contract not in existence operates only as a promise to assign the right when it arises.
   (B) a contract to make a future assignment of a right is not a validly enforceable assignment.
   (C) an assignor's after-acquired property interest does not vest in the assignee after the assignor's death.
   (D) a gratuitous assignment is revocable, and the right of the assignee is terminated by the assignor's death.

133. For this question only, assume that Amesway had incurred large debts before his death. These prior creditors have now attached the proceeds from the movie royalties that have so far been paid into the estate. Lady Buffington also asserts her assigned rights to the movie royalties. In subsequent actions by the creditors and Lady Buffington, the court will most probably hold in favor of

   (A) Lady Buffington, since the rights of an assignee are superior to a lien against property of the assignor subsequently obtained by legal/equitable proceedings.
   (B) Lady Buffington, since any proceeds of the assigned right received by the assignor thereafter are held in constructive trust for the assignee.
   (C) creditors, since Amesway's assignment to Lady Buffington was unenforceable.
   (D) creditors, since the rights of creditors/lienors are superior to those of a donee beneficiary.

Question 134 is based on the following fact situation.

John and Sue Davis entered into a contract with Tri-Mutual Insurance Co. to purchase a fire insurance policy for their new home. The policy provided that Tri-Mutual promises to pay up to $50,000 if said house is destroyed by fire or fire-related explosion, while the insured promises to pay a quarterly premium of $40.

The Davises failed to make the last two quarterly payments before their house burned to the ground. Tri-Mutual refused to pay the Davises for the loss because of their failure to make the last premium payments.

134. In an action by the Davises against Tri-Mutual to recover for the loss of their house, their best theory of recovery is that:

(A) although they failed to make the last two premium payments, there was a bargained-for exchange.
(B) Tri-Mutual's duty to pay was not expressly conditioned on the Davises' duty to make the payments.
(C) Tri-Mutual was under an independent duty to pay for the loss.
(D) the Davises did not receive notice of cancellation.

Questions 135–137 are based on the following fact situation.

In 1994, Bart Reynolds started to work for the Farmingham Hardware Co., in their only store, which was located in Armourville, a town with a population of 30,000. Bart was paid a monthly salary of $300. In 2004, Mr. Farmingham appointed Bart as manager of the store and paid him an additional $400 monthly. Although all prior employment arrangements had been made orally, in February 2005, Mr. Farmingham and Reynolds both signed a written agreement drafted by Farmingham, whereby Reynolds agreed to work for a salary of $700 per month. The agreement further specified that either party had a right to terminate the contract by giving sixty days notice to the other. Moreover, the agreement stipulated that if Reynolds's employment at the hardware store should be terminated, he would not be able to engage in any aspect of the hardware business, for a period of two years, within a fifty-mile radius of Armourville. If Reynolds should violate this agreement, he will be liable to the Farmingharn Co. for $1,500.

In 2006, Farmingham made a $100 donation to the local Senior Citizen's Center. He also handed the Center's Director the following signed agreement: "If Bart Reynolds should breach his covenant with me, he will be liable to me for $1,500. I hereby assign this to the Center's trustees to use as they so desire."

In September 2007, Farmingham sold his hardware store to United Hardware Stores, Inc., a nationwide chain of hardware stores. As part of this sales agreement, Farmingham assigned all assets, claims, and contracts relating to the hardware business to United. On February 1, 2008, United notified Reynolds that his employment with the company was being terminated as of April 1, 2008. Two months later, Reynolds secured a job as manager of a small hardware store in Milltown, which was located about twenty-five miles from Armourville. Then, in November 2008, Mr. Farmingham died.

135. The written agreement of February 2005 between Mr. Farmingham and Reynolds would most likely be held

    (A) enforceable in all respects.
    (B) enforceable only with respect to the salary and termination provisions.
    (C) enforceable in all respects, except with regard to the $1,500 penalty clause.
    (D) unenforceable in all respects.

136. The contract provision making Reynolds liable for violating the covenant not to compete may best be described as a (an)

    (A) liquidated damage clause.
    (B) unliquidated damage clause.
    (C) penalty and forfeiture clause.
    (D) aleatory clause.

137. The written agreement between Farmingham and the Senior Citizen's Center may best be interpreted as a (an)

    (A) equitable lien.
    (B) conditional assignment.
    (C) irrevocable assignment.
    (D) gratuitous assignment of future rights.

Questions 138–141 are based on the following fact situation.

On October 7, 2003, Joan Fonda, who was three months pregnant, signed the following agreement with Workout Inc.:

> "I hereby enroll in Workout's Special six month PreNatal and six month Post-Natal exercise program at a total cost of $1,500. A condition of this contract is that all fees are to be paid in advance. If, however, the total enrollment fees exceed $1,250, then one-third shall be paid upon the signing of said agreement, with one-third payable three months later, and one-third six months later. Under no circumstances shall any fees be refundable."

Upon signing the contract, Joan made her first payment of $500 and started classes the next day. Joan attended classes on a regular basis for the next three months. On January 1, 2004, however, Joan was involved in an automobile accident. Although she was not seriously injured, her doctor advised Joan that she needed complete rest. Her doctor told her to avoid strenuous activity and advised her to discontinue her pre-natal exercise classes. On January 9, 2004, Joan received a billing notice from Workout indicating that her second installment payment of $500 was past due. She immediately telephoned Hayden Thomas, the manager of Workout, and informed him that she would not be attending any further classes because of her accident. Also, Joan said she didn't feel obligated to make any additional payments.

138. Which of the following most accurately describes the installment payment of $500 due on January 7, 2004? It should be construed as a

    (A) condition precedent.
    (B) condition subsequent.
    (C) concurrent condition.
    (D) constructive condition.

139. Assume for the purposes of this question only that after Joan's automobile accident, she sent the following letter to Workout:

> "Please be advised that because of injuries sustained in an automobile accident, my physician has advised me not to engage in any strenuous activities. Since I will not be attending anymore pre-natal exercise classes, no further installment payments will be forthcoming."

This letter was received by Workout January 4, 2004. Under the Restatement, which of the following accurately states the immediate legal effect of Joan's letter?

    I. Workout has the right to bar Joan from attending any further pre-natal exercise classes.
    II. Workout has the right to sue Joan immediately for breach of contract.
    III. Joan may retract her repudiation if she does so before Workout initiates legal action against her.

(A) I only.
(B) II only.
(C) I and III.
(D) I, II, and III.

140. After Workout received Joan's letter on January 4, which of the following most accurately describes Joan's duty to pay Workout the second installment fee of $500 when it becomes due on January 7?

(A) It would be excused because of impossibility of performance.
(B) It would be excused because the essential purpose of the contract was frustrated.
(C) It would not be excused because a workout is a "necessary."
(D) It would not be excused because her covenant to make the installment payment is also enforceable as a condition precedent.

141. Assume for the purposes of this question only that Joan's condition improved and she resumed her exercise classes on January 6, 2004. The next day, Hayden informed Joan that the payment of her second installment fee was due. Joan told Hayden that she was having financial difficulties and asked for an extension. Hayden agreed to permit Joan to attend classes for one week. On January 14, 2004, however, Joan received a letter from Workout informing her that she would be barred from attending any further classes unless the second installment payment was made. Is Workout justified in refusing to permit Joan from attending classes after January 14?

(A) No, because by permitting Joan to attend classes beyond January 7, Workout waived its right to have the second installment fee paid on time.

(B) No, because Workout's allowing Joan to attend classes beyond January 7 created an implied contract, thus permitting her to complete the pre-natal program without advance payment of the second installment.

(C) Yes, because Joan's failure to make the second installment payment on January 7 constituted an anticipatory breach.

(D) Yes, because there was no consideration to extinguish the payment of the second installment fee, which was a material part of the contract.

Questions 142–145 are based on the following fact situation.

Following preliminary negotiations, Timberlane Products and Redwood Fence Co. signed the following agreement on May 1, 2006: "Timberlane promises to sell and Redwood promises to buy 7,000 sections of redwood stockade fence at $30 per section. Each section is to be made of good quality split redwood poles and is to be 7 feet long and 6 feet high; 1,000 sections are to be delivered by seller on or before June 1, 2006, and 1,000 sections by the first day in each of the following six months. EACH MONTHLY DELIVERY IS A SEPARATE CONTRACT. The following conditions are to be met by this agreement: (1) Timberlane is to give the buyer advance notice of the arrival time of each shipment, (2) Redwood is to pay for the sections delivered within ten days of delivery, and (3) Timberlane is to give the buyer the right to inspect each shipment before acceptance and to report all complaints within two days."

The first shipment of 1,000 sections arrived on May 27 and Redwood sent its payment on June 5. The second shipment did not arrive until July 5. On the following day, Woody Scarlet, Redwood's president, telephoned Bob Jones, president of Timberlane, complaining about the late delivery. Woody also stated, "The next delivery better be on time, or we'll cancel the next contract." The July shipment was in conformity and Timberlane sent its payment on July 11.

Timberlane's August shipment arrived on the afternoon of August 1. After the initial inspection, the redwood poles were found to be 7 feet long and 6-1/4 feet high. However, Scarlet, away on vacation, did not complain about the deviation until August 7, when he telephoned Bob Jones. During their conversation, Jones told Woody that Timberlane could not replace the August shipment, but would allow a price adjustment. Woody refused Jones's offer. The next day, Woody sent Jones a telegram, stating that he was hereby canceling all future deliveries and returning the last shipment because of nonconformity.

142. The May 1, 2006, agreement between Timberlane and Redwood may best be interpreted as

   (A) a divisible contract.
   (B) an installment contract.
   (C) seven separate contracts.
   (D) a requirements-output contract.

143. If Timberlane sues Redwood for breach of contract, Timberlane will

   (A) succeed, since Woody failed to comply with the inspection provision of the contract.
   (B) succeed, since Jones offered to adjust the price for the August shipment.
   (C) not succeed, since Jones refused to replace the nonconforming poles.
   (D) not succeed, since the deviation impaired the value of the entire contract.

144. What is the probable legal effect of Jones's conversation with Woody with regard to the August shipment?

   (A) Woody would have the right to reject the third shipment and cancel their contract.
   (B) Woody would have the right to reject the third shipment, but would be held liable for the remaining deliveries.
   (C) Woody would not be entitled to reject Jones's offer to "cure."
   (D) Woody would have a right to "cover" by purchasing substitute poles.

145. Assume for the purposes of this question only that the June, July, and August shipments were in compliance with the contract specifications. Then, on August 16, Jones informed Redwood that Timberlane would not be able to meet the September 1 delivery date because their California lumber reserve had been destroyed by a forest fire. Jones then asked Woody to excuse Timberlane from further performance. Woody refused and demanded that the remaining shipments be delivered on time. When the September shipment failed to arrive, Redwood immediately brought suit for breach of contract. How would the court hold?

   (A) Judgment for Redwood, because Timberlane's duties of performance would not be excused.
   (B) Judgment for Redwood, because Timberlane should have foreseen such a contingency occurring.
   (C) Judgment for Timberlane, because its performance would be discharged by impossibility.
   (D) Judgment for Timberlane, because its performance would be discharged by frustration of purpose.

Questions 146–150 are based on the following fact situation.

On March 1, 2006, Paul Parsons and Otto Owens executed a contract that provided that Owens would construct a two-level "redwood deck" on each of the eight specified beach houses that Parsons owned at Hampton Beach, with all work to be completed by May 1, 2006. The contract provided the following: "The cost is $2,500 per deck, to be paid upon completion of the decks in each of the eight beach houses." The contract further stipulated, "Approval would be required by Alton Jones, the architect, that the work had been satisfactorily performed in accordance with the plans and specifications." Furthermore, the contract stated, "THIS CONTRACT IS NOT ASSIGNABLE."

On March 15, Owens assigned the "monies to become due under the contract of March 1" to the Wilmington Trust Co. as security for a debt owed by Owens's nephew to the bank. On the morning of March 25, Parsons went to one of the beach houses as Owens and his assistants were completing the work on the fourth deck. Parsons said to Owens, "I'm very pleased with your progress to date. If you are willing, I would like you to build the same kind of decks on four identical beach houses that I own at Fire Island, on the same terms and conditions as our existing contract, the work to be completed by May 20. If you can meet that deadline, I'll pay you $10,000 at that time." Owens replied, "Agreed. Let's shake hands on it." They shook hands.

On April 2, Parsons left on a month-long vacation to the Orient. The following day, Wilmington Trust Co. sent a letter to Parsons's home notifying him of Owens's assignment of March 15. Owens completed the work on the first beach houses by April 15 and immediately started the construction of the decks on the Fire Island beach houses. On April 22, Hurricane Zelda totally destroyed four of Parsons's beach

houses at Hampton Beach. In addition, the hurricane demolished a beach house at Fire Island, on which Owens had completed 85 percent of the deck work. Two of Owens's assistants were seriously injured and all of his equipment was washed away.

When Parsons returned on April 27, he found the letter from Wilmington Trust and also the following letter dated April 23 from Owens: "The hurricane destroyed my equipment worth $4,000. I am dead broke and cannot complete the work on the three remaining beach houses at Fire Island. Please pay Wilmington Trust Co. the $20,000 for the work I did at Hampton Beach, and please send me $2,500 for the deck I built on the Fire Island beach house."

Although Alton Jones had inspected four of the houses at Hampton Beach to his approval, the hurricane destroyed the other four, which he had not inspected.

146. Which of the following statements is most accurate with regard to Owens's assignment "of monies to become due under the March 1st contract" to Wilmington Trust Co.?

(A) Parsons would not be obligated to pay Wilmington Trust, since the contract was nonassignable.
(B) Since personal service contracts of this nature are nonassignable, Parsons would be under no duty to pay Wilmington Trust.
(C) The assignment would constitute a novation, relieving Parsons of liability.
(D) The assignment would be irrevocable if it were reduced to writing.

147. Which of the following is the LEAST accurate statement with respect to the architect's approval of the decks constructed on the Hampton Beach houses?

(A) Parsons would only be obligated to pay for the work on the decks of the four beach houses that Jones approved.
(B) Jones's approval of the decks on the four beach houses destroyed by the hurricane would be excused.
(C) Parsons would be obligated to pay for the deck construction on all of the Hampton Beach houses.
(D) The impossibility of securing Jones's approval would render Parsons absolutely liable for all of the deck construction.

148. What is the probable legal effect of Owens's promise on March 25 to construct the decks on the Fire Island beach houses?

(A) Owens's promise created an enforceable unilateral contract.
(B) Owens's promise created an enforceable bilateral contract.
(C) Owens's promise was voidable, since he could disaffirm at his option.
(D) Owens's promise was illusory, thereby creating an unenforceable contract.

149. Assume that after Parsons returned home and read Owens's letter, he telephoned Owens and told him, "Unless you complete the deck construction on the Fire Island beach houses, I won't pay you a cent." Owens replied, "My letter dated April 23 speaks for itself." In an action for specific performance to compel Owens to complete the decks on the three remaining beach houses at Fire Island, Parsons will most likely

(A) succeed, since Owens's loss of equipment would not excuse his duty of performance.
(B) succeed, since under the doctrine of part performance, Owens's oral agreement would be taken out of the Statute of Frauds.
(C) not succeed, since Owens's performance would be excused by the unforeseeable act of God.
(D) not succeed, since Owens's loss of equipment would render his performance impracticable.

150. Assume for the purposes of this question only that Owens did not assign the "monies to become due under the contract of March 1" to the Wilmington Trust Co. as security for the debt owed by his nephew. What is the maximum amount that Owens may recover from Parsons for the construction that he completed prior to the hurricane?

(A) $10,000 only.
(B) $10,000 plus $2,125 (the amount due for 85% of the completed work on the Fire Island beach house).
(C) $20,000 only.
(D) $20,000 plus $2,125 (the amount due for 85% of the work completed on the Fire Island beach house).

1. (C)

Note that choice (D) is incorrect because, in accord with UCC 2-207, additional terms that materially alter the original bargain will not be included *unless expressly agreed to by the other party*. Since Friedman did not expressly agree to the new terms, they did not become part of the contract. Choices (A) and (B) are wrong because Englishware's written memo was sufficient to satisfy the statute of frauds. The statute does not require that the contract itself be reduced to writing. It merely requires that some note or memorandum be in writing and signed by the party to be charged. Here, Although Friedman did not sign the memo, the UCC also provides that the statute is satisfied where a written confirmation is received and not objected to within ten days. Note that choice (D) is incorrect because UCC 2-207 provides that additional terms that materially alter the original bargain will not be included *unless expressly agreed to by the other party*. Clearly, the vast difference in the quantity of socks would be a material alteration.

2. (D)

With respect to third-party beneficiary contracts, remember the following rule: *intention to confer a benefit on the third-party* is essential to the right of the third-party to enforce the promise. A useful test to determine the necessary intention is to ask yourself, "To whom is performance to be rendered?" If performance is to the third-party, he or she is a protected beneficiary and can sue under the contract. But if the promised performance is to be rendered to the promisee, the contract is for the benefit of the contracting parties, and any third-party is merely an incidental beneficiary. In this particular hypo, performance was to be rendered to Friedman, the promisee (in that he was to receive the socks). In other words, Friedman's intent in ordering the socks was to make a profit on the subsequent sale to Hightower, not to confer a direct benefit on him.

3. (A)

An executory accord is "an agreement that an existing claim shall be discharged *in the future* by the rendition of a substituted performance." Importantly, such an existing claim is usually liquidated and undisputed. For example, C (creditor) writes D (debtor), "I promise to discharge the debt you owe me upon delivery of your black mare if you promise to deliver the horse to me within a reasonable time." D promises to deliver the horse within a reasonable time. Importantly, once *D delivers the horse and C accepts it, there is an accord and satisfaction*. The agreement is the accord. Its performance is the satisfaction. In this hypo, choice (B) is wrong because the accord and satisfaction will not occur until Debtor actually delivers the baseball bat. Choice (C) is incorrect because a substituted compromise agreement usually involves a disputed or unliquidated claim. In such a situation, the creditor enters into a new or substituted agreement because he or she wants to get rid of the uncertainty. Finally, choice (D) is wrong because a **novation** occurs when one contractual duty is discharged and replaced with a new one. Generally, this involves adding a new party to the original agreement. Here, there is no third-party being added to the contract.

4. (A)

In order to have a memorandum sufficient to satisfy the Statute of Frauds, the written memorandum must: (a) identify the contracting parties, (b) identify the subject matter of the contract and its terms, and (c) identify the consideration. "Please be advised that I shall take a 15% discount for cash payment 7 days after installation" fails to disclose any of these essential terms. Consequently, it was insufficient to indicate a contract had in fact been formed.

5. (C)

Under UCC 2-207, additional terms contained in an acceptance do not become part of the contract if they **materially alter** the terms of the contract. Here, the 15 percent discount clearly materially altered the terms.

6. (B)

According to UCC 2-713, the measure of damages for non-delivery or repudiation by the seller is the **difference between the market price at the time when the buyer learned of the breach and the contract price,** together with incidental (and/or consequential) damages as provided under UCC 2-715. Here, Harry learned of the breach on April 1.

7. (D)

As a general rule, in **all unilateral mistake situations**, if the non-mistaken party is aware of the other party's mistake, he or she will not be permitted to "snap up" the bargain. Although choice (C) is also arguably correct, alternative (D) is preferred because the decisive issue is whether the offeree is **aware or should have been aware** of the offeror's mistake.

8. (C)

A modification regarding the sale of goods of $500 or more comes within the Statute of Frauds and must be in writing to be enforceable. Note that under the UCC modifications do not require new consideration. At common law, however, a modification must be supported by new consideration since the parties are under a **pre-existing duty** to perform according to the terms of their original contract. In the present case, Strawbridge's **oral promise** modifying its agreement with Khaki would be unenforceable under the Statute of Frauds since it dealt with the sale of goods of $15,000.

9. (D)

Past actions do not create sufficient consideration to support a contract. Here, Strawbridge is merely making an unenforceable gift promise, rewarding Cheryl for her past action of securing the Khaki contract.

10. (C)

As a general rule, advertisements, circular letters, price lists, and price tags are construed as ***proposals inviting offers.*** However, if the advertisement is definite in its terms, leaves nothing to negotiate, seems objectively reasonable, and is unlikely to be overaccepted, a court may find the advertisement is an enforceable offer. Here, the advertisement appears to meet these requirements. Under *Lefkowitz v. Great Minneapolis Surplus Store*, 86 N.W.2d 689 (1957), it appears that it does not matter whether Roy knew of the "house rule" or not.

11. (B)

Roy's acceptance created a unilateral contract, one in which the offer requested actual performance rather than a promise to perform.

12. (C)

A bilateral contract is a contract in which mutual promises are given as the agreed exchange for each other. A unilateral contract is a contract in which a promise is given in exchange for an actual performance by the other party. Here, one side is promising to fix the speakers, and the other side is promising to pay.

13. (D)

Under the pre-existing duty rule, neither doing nor promising to do that which one is already legally bound to do can furnish consideration for a contract. Here, Ruben was under a pre-existing duty to repair the stereo speakers by the following Tuesday. Note that Tony's promise to forbear to sue would not furnish sufficient consideration because it was not given in exchange for anything.

14. (B)

Ruben is liable to Tony since they had a contract for the repair of the speakers by the following Tuesday, and Ruben failed in his duty to do so. Ruben can only discharge his duties under the contract with a novation, which would require Ruben, Tony, and Pancho to all consent to Pancho's substituted performance. Finally, Pancho is not liable to Tony because he believed the speakers belonged to Ruben, and he was unaware of any prior agreement between Tony and Ruben. Consequently, he could assert a defense of fraud against Ruben for lying to him.

15. (B)

An express promise by a debtor to pay a debt barred by the statute of limitations or by a decree in bankruptcy is legally enforceable without new consideration. However, most jurisdictions require either a writing or a part payment be made before such an agreement can be enforced.

16. (A)

Alarmco is obligated under the terms of its contract with Ohner to install the security system for $12,000, and he mere fact that Supplier refused to perform would not excuse Alarmco from its duties under the original contract. Importantly, by agreeing to perform the installation work, Alarmco assumed the risks attendant with producing that result.

17. (D)

If a subcontractor gives a general contractor a bid, and the general contractor uses that bid in computing the bid it makes to a third-party and informs the subcontractor of that fact, an option contract is created. Importantly, once an option contract is created, the subcontractor cannot withdraw his or her bid.

18. (A)

UCC 2-601 provides that if the goods fail in any respect to conform to the contract, the buyer may (1) reject the whole, (2) accept the whole, or (3) accept any commercial unit or units and reject the rest. Here, Westside can reject the March 10 shipment because the 1/2" refabricated aluminum siding was nonconforming since the contract called for 1/4" siding.

19. (B)

UCC 2-508 permits a seller who has conforming. Here, although Alumalloy initially shipped on March 8, delivery of conforming goods was not due until April 1 delivery within the contract time.

20. (D)

A unilateral offer can only be accepted by performance, not by a return promise. Additionally, mere preparation for performance, no matter how detrimental to the offeree, is not enough to count as an acceptance. Here, Orlando asked for Juan to change the oil, replace the oil filter, and adjust the carburetors. By getting supplies from Pep Boys, Juan has only prepared to perform.

21. (D)

A unilateral offer becomes irrevocable as soon as the offeree has started to perform the act. Once Juan starts the three requested acts, Orlando can no longer revoke his offer.

22. (C)

As a general rule, where the offeree begins the performance contemplated, he or she thereby *impliedly* promises to complete it. By changing the oil and the filter, Juan accepted Orlando's offer and was thus obligated to complete all of his duties under the contract knowledge of it. Note that choice (D) is obviously incorrect because the present action is for breach of contract which is *not* an equitable remedy.

23. (B)

Warhol is obligated under the terms of the April 10 agreement. Wyeth, the offeror, effectively revoked his original offer to sell the painting to Warhol in the written communication of March 15. Thus, the original offer has no effect on any subsequent agreements. The general rule provides that the offeror may terminate his or her offer by revoking it at any time before acceptance. This is true even if the offeror has promised not to revoke for a stated time, *unless the promise is for a consideration.* Here, the original offer was not under seal, nor was there any consideration to keep the offer open. In addition, the "firm offer" rule (UCC 2-205) doesn't apply because Wyeth is an art *collector,* and thus not viewed as a merchant engaged in the sale of goods.

24. (B)

Wyeth's promise to pay his discharged debt is enforceable even if he does not in fact sell the painting because his promise was not conditioned on the sale. A conditional promise is usually prefaced by such words as "provided that," "if," or "on condition that."

25. (D)

Charlene's best argument is that the disciplinary action taken by Bob's is in the form of a penalty and is in excess of any actual loss suffered by Bob's. In general, contract law seeks to compensate for financial losses, not to allow one party to punish another for violating the terms of the contract. (A) is wrong because the smoking policy concerns a material matter in Charlene's continued employment at Bob's. (B) is wrong because permitting Charlene to continue working did not indicate any waiver of the smoking policy. Finally, (C) is wrong because there was no impracticability in Charlene not smoking after the robbery.

26. (A)

Generally speaking, the parol evidence rule provides that when a contract is expressed in a writing that is *intended to be the complete and final expression of the rights and duties of the parties,* evidence of a prior oral or written negotiation or agreement or of a contemporaneous oral agreement that *varies or contradicts the written contract* is not admissible. However, there is an exception if the evidence of the other agreement is used to show that the written contract was not a complete and final expression of the rights and duties of the parties. Here, the parties appear to have made a mistake in translating their oral agreement into a written one.

27. (D)

By making this conditional contract with Tito, Morgana impliedly promised to make a good faith effort to purchase the Westchester house. Tito's best argument would be to claim Morgana breached this implied promise by choosing not to buy the house when it was within her ability to do so.

28. (D)

Since there doesn't seem to be anything unique about this particular piano, specific performance would not be an appropriate measure of the damages to Morgana.

29. (D)

To create a contract, the parties must manifest their mutual assent to the same bargain at the same time.

30. (D)

In interpreting an agreement such as this one where the terms of the agreement are unclear, courts will try to determine the terms of the agreement by looking at the reasonable expectation of the parties, whether one party knew of the other's error in interpretation, and any customary standards or practices.

31. (C)

M was under a contractual obligation to deliver 500 widgets to B. Since M delivered only 490 widgets, he failed to perform part of what was promised in the contract. In this regard, any unjustified failure to perform when performance is due is a breach of contract that entitles the injured party to damages.

32. (D)

The initial communication was an offer, that was then accepted by McCormick's reply. Although the offer requested "prompt shipment," this agreement was a bilateral contract, not a unilateral one. According to Restatement (Second) Contracts, Section 32(c), "an order or other offer to buy goods for prompt or current shipment normally invites acceptance *either by a prompt promise to ship or by prompt or current shipment.*" This view is also adopted by UCC 2-202(b). Ultimately, the later communications between the parties did not change the fact that the first two communications created a contract.

33. (C)

UCC 2-703 provides that "where a buyer wrongfully rejects or revokes acceptance of goods on or before delivery…then with respect to the whole undelivered balance, the aggrieved seller may (a) withhold delivery of such goods, (b) stop delivery by any bailee, (c) resell and recover damages, (d) recover damages for non-acceptance, or (e) cancel." With respect to resale, UCC Section 2-706 entitles the aggrieved seller to sell the goods by either public or private sale.

34. (B)

In accordance with UCC 2-706, a seller may resell goods after the buyer has repudiated or breached the contract. Where the resale is made in good faith and in a commercially reasonable manner, the seller may recover the difference between the resale price and the contract price, together with incidental damages. Since McCormick resold the goods to Western for $50,000 (or the same amount as National promised to pay), McCormick can recover only incidental damages.

35. (C)

Frustration of purpose excuses performance in situations where the purpose of the contract is wholly frustrated by a fortuitous, unforeseeable event. Here, the purpose of renting the hotel room was completely frustrated by the cancelling of Queen Mary's coronation.

36. (B)

The La Valencia was in breach of contract by not renting the Presidential Suite to the Clauses. The Clauses were not obligated to accept Martinez' offer since the Del Mar suite was not comparable to the value of the promised performance. By the same token, even though the Clauses may not have suffered any pecuniary injury, they, would at least be entitled to nominal damages because their expectation interest was staying in the Presidential Suite at the La Valencia, not in the Presidential Suite of another hotel.

37. (B)

Under UCC 2-603, if the rejecting buyer receives no instructions from the seller regarding the rejected goods, the buyer may sell the goods on the seller's account. However, if the buyer does so, he or she is only entitled to reasonable expenses, and those expenses cannot exceed 10 percent of the sale proceeds.

38. (C)

According to UCC 2-607, *the buyer must pay at the contract rate for any goods accepted*. Acceptance made with knowledge of a nonconformity cannot be revoked because of the nonconformity unless the acceptance was made on the reasonable assumption that the nonconformity would be seasonably cured. Here, Feingold's simply accepted the tapestry with no reservations.

39. (C)

According to Restatement (Second) of Contracts, Section 39, "*An offeree's power of acceptance is terminated by his making of a counter-offer.*" When Stokes made his counteroffer, the original offer was terminated, and there was nothing left to accept.

40. (A)

An offeree's power of acceptance is terminated when the offeror takes definite action inconsistent with an intention to enter into the proposed contract and the offeree acquires reliable information to that effect. Thus, Yardley's offer was effectively revoked when Dugan learned that the motorcycle had been sold to Elgin.

41. (A)

According to the Restatement (Second) of Contracts, Section 24, "An offer is the manifestation of willingness to enter into a bargain, so made as to justify another person in understanding that his assent to that bargain is invited and will conclude it." Clearly, Hendrix's letter manifested such a present contractual intent.

42. (D)

Rejection of an offer by the offeree terminates the offer. As a general rule, *rejection is the offeree's refusal to accept the offer as made, and it must be communicated to the offeror.* Here, the mere fact that Jopland talked to Cass (re: renting a cottage) is not a clear indication that she intended to reject Hendrix's offer.

43. (B)

According to Hendrix's letter, the offer was irrevocable for a period of twenty days from the September 2 date. Consequently, Jopland had the power to accept the offer within that 20-day period, or until September 22. Since she did not communicate her acceptance to Hendrix until September 23 (or after the expiration of the "option" period), he had the legal power to revoke the offer.

44. (C)

At common law a promise to keep an offer open, *if supported by consideration,* becomes legally binding. Here, although Jopland never actually paid the $1, the offer acknowledged the receipt of the $1 and courts generally do not inquire into the adequacy of consideration. (D) refers to the Firm Offer Rule under UCC 2-205, which is not applicable here since the offer does not deal with the sale of goods.

45. (B)

In all unilateral mistake situations, if the offeree knows or has reason to know of the offeror's mistake when he or she accepts, then the offeror is not bound. In other words, if the nonmistaken party is or should have been aware of the mistake, he or she cannot "snap up" the offer. Here, since Kirby neither knew nor should have known of Kat's error, the contract was enforceable.

46. (A)

Again, if the offeree is or should be aware of the mistake, there will be no contract. In the present case, since there was a $130,000 difference between Kat's bid and the next lowest offer, Kirby should have known of the mistake in transmission, thereby precluding it from "snapping up" the offer.

47. (A)

A reward offer requires acceptance by actual performance; consequently, acceptance of the offer creates a unilateral contract.

48. (C)

A person cannot accept an offer unless he or she acts with knowledge of the offer. Here, if Archer did not know about the reward, he cannot claim he is entitled to it for providing information leading to the murderer's conviction. See Restatement (Second) of Contracts, Sections 23 & 53.

49. (D)

Linda is suing BRC for breach of contract. Consequently, BRC's best defense is to argue that no contractual obligation existed between Linda and the company. As such, BRC will want to show that Linda's employment was "purely gratuitous" and not supported by consideration. Certainly, the test of a legally enforceable promise at common law is whether it is supported by consideration. Consideration is the price bargained for and paid for a promise. It may consist of an act, a forbearance or a return promise. The consideration must be legally sufficient. The test of a sufficient consideration is whether the act, forbearance or return promise results in a benefit to the promisor or a detriment to the promisee. However, not all promises are legally enforceable. The distinction between consideration and a gift promise depends whether or not the act was bargained for as the agreed price of the promise. If the promisor's motive was no more than to state a condition to a promised gift, there is no contract. *If BRC's motive was merely to confer gratuitous benefits to its employees, then no contractual obligation existed.*

50. (C)

Detrimental action or forbearance by the promisee in reliance on a gratuitous promise, within limits, constitutes a substitute for consideration, or a sufficient reason for enforcement of the promise without consideration, under the doctrine of promissory estoppel. To avoid unjust enrichment, the promisor who induces a substantial change of position by the promisee in reliance on the promise is estopped to deny its enforceability as lacking consideration. Since Linda is seeking to recover on the basis of promissory estoppel as a substitute for consideration, her best argument is to show detrimental reliance.

51. (A)

The majority view is that at an auction, unless a contrary intention is manifested, when goods are put up *without reserve,* the auctioneer makes an offer to sell at any price bid by the highest bidder, and after the auctioneer calls for bids, the goods cannot be withdrawn.

52. (C)

Under UCC 2-715, an aggrieved buyer of goods, such as Mennonite, can recover *incidental damages* resulting from the seller's breach: these damages include "expenses reasonably incurred in inspection, receipt, transportation and care and custody of goods rightfully rejected, and commercially reasonable charges, expenses or commissions in connection with effecting cover and *any other reasonable expense incident to the delay or other breach.*" Note that where Mennonite replied to Amish's phone call by saying, "...be advised that I will hold you liable for any loss I sustain as a result of your failure to deliver the mushrooms on March 1," *Mennonite only waived the delivery date, not Amish's performance.*

Common Law (Covering most legal obligations)	Contracts Reference Chart	UCC (Covering sale of goods)
Consideration Necessary	Option Contracts	No Consideration if Signed Writing by a Merchant
Consideration Necessary "pre-existing duty" rule	Modification	Consideration Unnecessary
Strictly interpreted according to the contract's exact terms	Interpretation	Liberally interpreted based on course of dealing, trade usage, or course of performance
Objective impossibility or Frustration of Purpose	Impossibility	Commercial Impracticability (unforeseeable supervening event)
Determine whether a contract has been made and what are resulting legal relations	Purpose	Liberalize ("de-technicalize") important branches of commercial law and speed of commerce
Complexity & Variation	Basic Distinction	Simplicity & Uniformity

53. (B)

This question deals with the buyer's right to cancel for failure of timely performance. Where the time set for performance has passed, the party awaiting performance may agree to a new commercially reasonable time for performance prior to cancellation. Mennonite could have cancelled the contract for non-delivery on March 1 in accordance with UCC 2-711, which states that "(1) Where the seller fails to make delivery ... the buyer may *cancel* and ... (a) cover ... or (b) recover damages for non-delivery ..." Mennonite nevertheless chose to await performance, although no specific date was set during the February 28 telephone conversation. Under UCC 2-309, "(1) The time for shipment or delivery or any other action under a contract if not provided in this Article or agreed upon shall be a reasonable time." Comment 5 provides "The *obligation of good faith ... requires reasonable notification before a contract may be treated as breached because a reasonable time for delivery or demand has expired.* This operates both in the case of a contract originally indefinite as to time and of one subsequently made indefinite by waiver." Therefore, Mennonite was entitled to cancel provided the email received by Amish on March 6 (i.e., 3-day notice) was a reasonable time.

54. (B)

Where the parties agree that a condition precedent must occur before the contract is effective, it is generally agreed that the failure of the condition to occur may be shown despite what otherwise would be deemed a total integration. Thus, even if there is a merger clause, a party can show that the instrument was handed over to another with an oral condition attached to delivery. The theory is that the agreement is not to take effect until the condition occurs, and thus there is no contract to be added to or contradicted until that time. Here, Toshi will be permitted to introduce evidence of Kifune's refusal to approve the fish since the agreement was subject to this condition precedent.

55. (C)

The promise would be enforceable if a bargained-for exchange was intended. In the present hypo, Marty's return promise to study for five hours per day would constitute adequate consideration since he was under no legal duty to study at all. Under Restatement of Contracts, 2d Section 75, to constitute consideration, a performance or a return promise must be bargained for. A performance or return promise is bargained for if it is sought by the promisor in exchange for his or her promise and is given by the promisee in exchange for that promise. With respect to the requirement of consideration, the performance may consist of (a) an act, (b) a forbearance, or (c) the creation, modification, or destruction of a legal relation.

56. (D)

In a bilateral contract, *both promises must be legally binding,* or the contract is void for lack of consideration. This is the doctrine of *mutuality of obligation.*

Since the exchange for a promise must be something of value and since value is tested in terms of detriment or benefit, it follows that a non-detrimental promise is insufficient consideration. In this regard, if the promise is wholly void for illegality (or is illusory), it is non-detrimental. Here, Marty's promise is void for illegality, so there is no consideration to support the contract.

57. (C)

A contract may be voidable by one party by reason of (a) incapacity, (b) mistake, or, as in the present case, (c) under the Statute of Frauds. A promise to answer for the debt or default of another is required to be in writing under the Statute of Frauds. Since Uncle Homer's promise to answer for Marty's father's debt was never reduced to writing, it constituted a voidable promise.

58. (C)

When two parties have made a contract and have expressed it in a writing as a complete and accurate integration of that contract, evidence of prior understandings and negotiations will not be admitted for the purpose of varying or contradicting the writing. Choice (A) is wrong because it is contrary to the stated rule. Choice (B) is incorrect because Yellin's failure to pay the one dollar consideration is not construed as a modification. A modification alters or changes the parties' duties and obligations under a contract. Here, Yellin's failure to pay the consideration simply contradicts the written contract, and, therefore, evidence of this fact is inadmissible under the parol evidence rule.

59. (C)

At common law, an offer is always revocable up to the time of acceptance, even though it contains a promise not to revoke. However, if the promise to keep the offer open is supported by consideration, it becomes legally binding. Here, the recited consideration of $1 was sufficient consideration. Even in the event the $1 was not in fact paid, because courts do not look into the sufficiency of the consideration, a recital like this is sufficient.

60. (B)

An express promise by a debtor to pay all or part of a debt barred by the statute of limitations or by a decree in bankruptcy is legally enforceable without new consideration. The majority of jurisdictions require that a promise to pay a debt barred by the statute of limitations be in writing and signed by the debtor, but only a few states require the same formality as to the express promise to pay a debt discharged in bankruptcy.

61. (A)

The **contracts of a minor are voidable at the option of the** minor. On the contrary, an adult party to the transaction cannot avoid the contract on the ground of the other's infancy. In other words, the power of avoidance is held by the minor only. ***After reaching the age of majority***, however, the minor may ratify or affirm the contract. In the present case, Rufus's affirmation (namely, his promise to pay Morrisey $10,000) was conditioned upon his financial position improving. Since that condition apparently did not occur (given the fact that the accident took place shortly after the mailing of the letter), Rufus will not be liable under the contract.

62. (C)

When Rufus reached the age of majority, he promised to pay Morrisey $10,000 for the automobile. However, that ***promise was conditioned upon Rufus's financial condition improving.*** Since his financial condition did not appear to improve, this ratification did not create an enforceable promise to pay $10,000.

63. (C)

All duties can be delegated unless the personal skill, expertise, or identity of the actor is a material segment of the contract. In the instant case, the Grimsbys contracted for LeVey to personally undertake the landscaping services.

64. (A)

Assuming, of course, that the value of Grimsbys' property was enhanced by Herman's landscaping, he will most likely recover for the reasonable value of his work on the theory of quasi-contract.

65. (B)

Green, as sub-assignee, does not have any rights against LeVey, the original assignor, since there is no privity of contract between a sub-assignee and the original assignor. However, Green may recover against Herman since the assignee (Herman) who "subassigns" becomes the assignor with respect to that assignment and can be held liable thereon.

66. (B)

The parol evidence rule states that once the parties have reduced their agreement to a writing, evidence of any ***prior oral or written, or contemporaneous oral*** agreements is inadmissible to alter, vary, or contradict the terms of the writing. However, the parol evidence rule does not prevent proof of an oral or written agreement that varies or contradicts the terms of a ***prior written*** contract. Since the oral agreement, which Dr. Dreck claims took place ***during*** the operation, occurred at a point in time ***after*** the written contract, Dr. Dreck will contend that the parol evidence rule is not applicable as applied to a ***subsequent*** oral agreement. Choice (B) correctly states this consideration. Choice (A) is incorrect because the conferral of a clear benefit would be relevant to recovery in quasi-contract for the value of services rendered; however, quasi-contract recovery is unavailable where the parties already have a valid existing contract. Choice (C) is incorrect because the statute of frauds is not a relevant consideration. Even though the statute of frauds may not apply to personal service contracts, the parol evidence rule must be considered whenever an existing written contract is affected by a prior or contemporaneous oral agreement. Choice (D) is incorrect because it states an irrelevant consideration. Regardless of the **nature** of the second procedure, the **payment** for it will be determined by the court's interpretation of the subject matter of the original written contract.

67. (A)

If the court agrees with Dr. Dreck that Zelda may not introduce evidence of any prior oral agreement between the parties concerning the performance of "any additional medical procedures" for the lump fee of $750, it will be because the written contract was construed as a complete integration of the parties' agreement. As a general rule, **where there is complete integration of a writing, no extrinsic parol evidence is admitted**. The rationale is that since the writing embodies the full and final expression of the parties' agreement, it is complete on its face and may not be altered or varied in any way by extrinsic evidence. Choice (B) is incorrect because if the court found the written contract merely to be **partial integration** of the parties' agreement, then the parol evidence would be admissible, and Dr. Dreck's objection would not have been sustained. Choice (C) is incorrect because the doctrine of quasi-contract, or contract implied-in-law, is used to impose a legal obligation and afford a remedy, without which injustice would result, under circumstances where it is clear no promise was ever made or intended. The written contract between the parties clearly evidences that a promise was made. Choice (D) is incorrect because the subject matter required to make an oral agreement **"collateral"** to a written agreement must be so far separate that it is not covered, dealt with, or even mentioned in the writing. Therefore, any oral agreement for free medical services could not have been collateral to a written agreement for similar medical treatment during the course of the same operation.

68. (B)

The key to this question is to realize the effect of the court's admission of **Zelda's** oral testimony. If it is believed that the original written agreement incorporated in its terms the understanding that "any additional medical procedures...would be included in the $750 fee," then Dr. Dreck would be under a **pre-existing duty** to perform the second procedure removing the mole from Zelda's back for no additional charge. Therefore, Dr. Dreck will not be entitled to recover the $150.

69. (D)

The brokerage agreement between Theisman and Crosby provided that Crosby was to be paid a commission "following the consummation of the sale and transfer of title." Thus, the condition (i.e., the consummation of sale) would be viewed as a condition precedent since it must occur before Theisman's duty of performance can arise (i.e., his obligation to pay the commission). However, after Crosby found a buyer who was willing to perform, Theisman decided not to go through with the sale. In this situation, would the broker be entitled to her commission? The answer is yes, because in this case an implied duty of performance is imposed upon the seller.

70. (B)

In a brokerage commission situation like this one, the seller's implied duty to perform does *not extend to bringing an action for specific performance.* Consequently, Crosby cannot sue Theisman for failing to sue Riggins for specific performance.

71. (D)

According to UCC 2-205, "an offer by a merchant to buy or sell goods in a signed writing which by its terms gives assurance that it will be held open is not revocable, for lack of consideration, during the time stated or if no time is stated for a reasonable time, but in no event may such period of irrevocability exceed three months; but any such term of assurance on a form supplied by the offeree must be separately signed by the offeror." Under this "firm offer" rule, Stopler's offer would remain open until October 1.

72. (C)

Under UCC 2-207, "additional terms are to be construed as proposals for addition to the contract. Between merchants, such terms become part of the contract unless: (a) the offer expressly limits acceptance to the terms of the offer, (b) they materially alter it, or (c) notification of objection to them has already been given or is given within a reasonable time after notice of them is received." Here, the additional term regarding October and November delivery did not materially alter the contract. Thus, it will become part of the agreement.

73. (D)

A condition is any fact or event other than lapse of time that must occur before the parties have a duty to perform. Here, Homeowner conditioned the creation of the contract on his ability to get a loan.

74. (C)

Although Graduate was a third-party beneficiary to the original contract, Graduate's rights did not become enforceable ("vest") because Painter and Homeowner effectively modified their agreement *before* Graduate learned of his beneficiary rights.

75. (C)

First, Mia was an intended third-party donee beneficiary under the terms of the December 16 Franco-Mario contract. However, an intended beneficiary can only enforce a contract after his or her rights have vested. The general rule is that a beneficiary's rights vest when: (1) the beneficiary learns of the contract and (2) assents to it by conduct or some other action. In the present case, Mia's rights as an intended third-party donee beneficiary vested when she learned of the Franco-Mario contract and assented to it. Importantly, once Mia's rights are vested, Franco and Mario can't agree to discharge, modify, or vary their duties. Therefore, the May 20 modifying agreement would be ineffective.

76. (D)

Under the pre-existing duty rule, since Franco was legally bound to pay Mario a salary of $1,500 per month, the May 20 agreement between them would be unenforceable as it was not supported by any new consideration. While the UCC does not require new consideration to modify a contract, this is a contract for personal services, and thus does not fall under the UCC.

77. (C)

With respect to statement (I), the bonus provision is unenforceable because it is illusory. A promise to pay a bonus "to be determined by the parties...after the year's profits have been ascertained" would fail for indefiniteness because it is too vague to be capable of enforcement. However, alternative (II) is correct since Franco had a pre-existing duty to pay Mario a monthly salary of $1,500. Consequently, the oral agreement of May 20, 2006, between Franco and Mario (to reduce Mario's salary $500 per month) would be ineffective. Thirdly, alternative (III) is correct since Mia's rights as an intended third-party beneficiary vested at the time she learned of her entitlement of $500 per month under the terms of the original Franco-Mario contract. In addition, Mia materially changed her position in justifiable reliance by assigning her entitlement to the Pine Creek Nursing Home (where she was a patient). Therefore, the subsequent "ineffective" modification between Franco and Mario on May 20 would not adversely affect Mia's rights as an intended third-party beneficiary.

78. (B)

A divisible contract is one in which the parties have divided their respective performances into separate units, so that performance of an installment on one side entities such party to the other's performance of that installment. In this regard, employment contracts are regarded as divisible for the purpose of permitting the employee to recover the agreed price for the number of months of service he or she has put in.

79. (A)

The test of a legally enforceable promise at common law is whether it is supported by consideration. To constitute consideration, *a performance or a return promise must be bargained for.* In the present example, the Browning-Vandeway agreement was clearly supported by consideration. There was a bargained-for exchange in that Browning agreed to sign a coaching contract with the university and, in return, Vandeway promised to pay him a $100,000 salary supplement.

80. (A)

In order to determine whether the university is an intended or an incidental beneficiary, the "key" is to ascertain the primary intent or purpose of Vandeway, the promisee, in exacting his promise from Browning. If the promisee's main purpose is to confer a gift upon the third-party, then the latter is viewed as an intended donee beneficiary. On the other hand, where the promised performance is to be rendered to the promisee, then no inference of a gift promise for the third-party's benefit is possible no matter how much the third-party may collaterally benefit. Here, Vandeway, the promisee's, main purpose is to benefit the university by hiring Browning as its basketball coach. Thus, the university is viewed as an intended beneficiary.

81. (D)

A unilateral offer which invites performance of an act as acceptance, rather than a return promise, becomes irrevocable as soon as the offeree has started to perform the act. Note that choice (C) is wrong because purchasing the materials is mere preparation and not the commencement of performance.

82. (C)

Since the plaintiff completed his side of the bargain, he is entitled to the contract price. *Quantum meruit* (i.e, reasonable value for services rendered) is a restitutionary form of relief. In this particular situation, the plaintiffs proper form of relief is damages for breach of contract, not restitution. Importantly, where plaintiff has fully performed his or her side of the contract, and the defendant's only duty is the payment of the agreed price the remedy of restitution is *not* available to the plaintiff. His or her proper remedy is damages for breach.

83. (D)

Because Electrician made an offer that he should have reasonably expected to induce reliance on the part of the Builder, and the Builder in fact relied upon that promise in making his bid, the offer was binding as an option contract to the extent necessary to avoid injustice.

84. (D)

As a general rule, the offeror may revoke his or her offer at any time before acceptance. This is true even though the offeror has promised not to revoke for a stated time, unless the promise is supported by consideration. ***Revocation takes effect only when communicated to the offeree.*** However, the offeree can learn about the revocation from a third-party. Here, the revocation took effect when Martin learned of Donner's sale of the stamp collection in the newspaper article.

85. (A)

As a general rule, where only one of the parties is mistaken about facts relating to the agreement, the mistake will ***not*** prevent formation of a contract. If the other party forms reasonable expectations based upon the apparent terms of the bargain, the contract is generally enforceable against the mistaken party on those terms.

86. (B)

In the interpretation of a contract, where the intention of the parties clearly appears from the words used, there is no need to go further. In such cases, the words or language in the contract govern; or, as it is sometimes said, where there is no doubt, there is no need for interpretation. Here, the contract clearly stated that the entrance fee was non-refundable.

87. (D)

Under UCC 2-609, if one party has reasonable grounds for insecurity, that party can demand adequate assurances of due performance. These assurances must be provided within a reasonable time not to exceed 30 days, and if they are not, the buyer can cancel the contract, cover, and sue for damages.

88. (D)

The Foodtown-Citrus contract expressly provided that "any modifications must be in writing," any attempt at oral modification would be invalid. Such clauses are specifically allowed under UCC 2-209 (2).

89. (D)

Nikkon's best defense would be temporary impracticability of performance. It is important to note that ***temporary impracticability only suspends contractual duties; it does not discharge these duties.*** When performance once again becomes possible, the duty of performance "springs" back into existence. In personal service contracts, the courts will frequently temporarily excuse performance because of health reasons of the promisor. Therefore, since Nikkon broke his leg and was unable to photograph Starr until October 31, his performance would be temporarily suspended by this unexpected accident.

90. (C)

Nikkon's performance under the contract would be an express condition precedent to Starr's duty to pay Nikkon the $750. An express condition precedent is a fact expressed in a contract that must exist or occur before a duty of immediate performance by the promisor can arise. Here, it was clear that Nikkon had to deliver the photographs before Starr had a duty to pay him.

91. (A)

The most accurate statement is that the performance of Nikkon would have been a constructive condition precedent to the performance by Starr. Where the contract contains no provision relating to the order of the respective performances, and performance on one side will necessarily take time while the other can be performed in an instant, the former is a *constructive condition precedent* to the latter. In other words, the performance which takes time must first be completed before the other party need render his or her performance.

92. (D)

Since the court concluded that the Nikkon-Starr contract required that Starr be personally satisfied with the photographs, Nikkon's injury would not excuse his obligation to produce quality photographs that were satisfactory to Starr. Where the promisee's performance must satisfy the promisor personally a (subjectively) and the promisor in "good faith" is dissatisfied with the performance, his or her duty to pay is discharged.

93. (A)

Under the terms of this personal service contract, Nikkon would not have to assume the risk that Starr would fail to cooperate in arranging for the taking of the photographs. Starr's failure to cooperate with Nikkon would be indicative of "bad faith" on her part. Furthermore, an implied condition exists in a personal service contract like this one that requires both parties to act reasonably in order to carry out their mutual obligations.

94. (B)

Mann's strongest defense is to argue that Mason was not an intended beneficiary under the terms of the Mann-Stone agreement. In which case, Mason would be only an incidental beneficiary, and thus would acquire *no right to enforce the contract between Stone and Mann.*

95. (B)

A contracting party is generally expected to take account of those risks that are *foreseeable* at the time he or she makes the contract. Based upon this rule, damages for Mann's personal injuries were not foreseeable or within the contemplation of Stone and Mason at the time they entered into their contract. Choice (A) is wrong because damages for personal injuries can be recovered in a contract action if such a loss was foreseeable. In fact, in certain situations where breach of a contract is of such a kind that serious emotional disturbance is likely to result, then recovery for such disturbance is even allowed. Common examples are contracts of carriers and innkeepers with passengers and guests. Choices (C) and (D) are wrong because it can be argued that Mann was an intended beneficiary under the Stone-Mason agreement. Certainly, Stone was building the wall to accommodate Mann and alleviate the noise and traffic from the subdivision. As a result, Mann has standing to sue since he would not be viewed as an incidental beneficiary.

96. (A)

Here, Baxter is the guarantor of the loan between First National Bank (the promisor) and the Ajax Company (the promisee). Even though she is a guarantor, is not the same as a donee or creditor beneficiary of the promisee. Third parties who are not donees or creditors of the promisee are incidental beneficiaries, and an incidental beneficiary has no right to enforce the promise.

97. (D)

The written agreement between Calhoun and Sunrise Canyon Video to shoot campaign commercials was a personal services contract. Common law principles as to parol evidence will therefore apply. Calhoun would argue that since the contract made no other reference to compensation other than the "production fee clause," it was completely integrated and no parol evidence should be admitted to vary or contradict the express terms. **Note:** Determination of whether an agreement is fully or partially integrated is a question for the trier of fact. Choice (C) is incorrect because it is incomplete. Parol evidence that contradicts the terms of a writing is barred only when the contract is fully integrated. Choices (A) and (B) deal with exceptions to the parol evidence rule. Extrinsic evidence is admissible to interpret and give meaning to the terms of a contract where there is *ambiguity,* but not where the parol evidence *varies* or *contradicts* the terms. Since evidence of the $50,000 fee to Lindsey Lens would vary the compensation stated in the "production fee clause," any argument as to ambiguity would be irrelevant.

98. (A)

Trade usage can be used to give meaning to, qualify, or supplement an agreement. Trade usage can be used to interpret an agreement if each party knew or had reason to know of the usage and neither party knew or had reason to know that the other's understanding of the agreement was inconsistent with the trade usage. Moreover, there is no requirement that an agreement be ambiguous before evidence of trade usage can be shown.

99. (D)

Here, although Craig, the promisor, promised to pay Asburn the $4,000 debt owed by Thornberry, *Asburn did not suffer any legal detriment by making a return promise in exchange.* Asburn's forbearance to sue Thornberry would have provided adequate consideration, but Asburn only promised to return Craig's golf clubs. Therefore, Craig's best defense in a contract action brought by Asburn would be that since Asburn had a pre-existing duty to return the golf clubs, there was no consideration for Craig's promise to Asburn.

100. (A)

As discussed above, Asburn suffered no legal detriment since he made no sufficient return promise in exchange for Craig's promise to pay Thornberry's $4,000 debt. Therefore, the Craig-Asburn contract would fail for lack of consideration. Since this question asks for Asburn's most persuasive argument, he must attempt to argue that a valid substitute for consideration existed. Such an alternative would be **promissory** *estoppel*. Craig's promise and Asburn's reliance, if proved, could provide a valid claim based on promissory estoppel. Choice (B) is incorrect because it goes against the facts. Asburn never in fact promised to forbear from suing Thornberry; therefore his failure to sue for six months cannot be considered bargained-for consideration as a matter of law because due to expiration of the statute of limitations, his claim was only valid for one day after contracting with Craig. Choice (C) makes no legal sense because consideration must be supplied by a showing of detriment on Asburn's part, not by a mere showing of Craig's intent to be bound—such an intent cannot be transferred. Choice (D) is also incorrect. Even if a surety arrangement had existed between Craig, Asburn, and Thornberry, it would be voidable due to lack of consideration to support Craig's promise.

101. (B)

Jewell was hired by the insurance company to investigate the theft. Since he had a pre-existing duty to perform this service, his promise to Daisy was not supported by consideration and was therefore unenforceable.

102. (B)

An offer which invites performance of an act as acceptance, rather than a return promise, becomes *irrevocable as soon as the offeree has started to perform the act.* However, keep in mind that mere preparation is not enough. Consequently, it was important that Tex actually started to ride the bronco; merely acquiring the saddle was not enough.

103. (D)

Statement I is incorrect because insolvency or bankruptcy of the promisee does not of itself constitute such prospective failure of consideration as will discharge the promisor. See Restatement of Contracts, Section 287. Similarly, neither statement II or III will provide Gallop with justifiable grounds for discharging Sprink after the Sprink had started performance. It is important to note that at no time did Sprink either repudiate his obligations under the contract or disavow his intention to perform. Statement III may also be found to be incorrect because the Gallop-Sprink agreement did not cover the sale of goods. Therefore, it did not need to be in writing.

104. (C)

It is important to point out that Sprink was hired to perform the replacement work at a contract price of $2,400. According to the terms of the agreement, Sprink would be paid **upon completion of the job.** As such, the contract does not appear to be divisible. Therefore, choice (A) is wrong. Although Sprink did not complete performance, he would, nevertheless, be entitled to receive restitution for the part performance that he rendered. A recovery on a **quantum meruit** basis usually applies in situations where the one party has performed such as this services for the other party but he or she cannot recover on the contract (either because there was not full performance or because the contract was unenforceable). Importantly, the reasonable value of the party's services may not be the same asl the price contemplated in the contract.

105. (A)

UCC 2-206(1)(a) provides that offers generally invite acceptance "in any manner and by any medium reasonable in the circumstances." Generally, an offer may call for acceptance by either **(1) a return promise or (2) a specified act.** Here, the Clip Joint's offer expressly called for American to *ship immediately* the scissors. Thus, this is an example of **acceptance by performance.** Here, although American shipped nonconforming goods (by shipping six left-handed scissors), a contract is still formed, although The Clip Joint can sue for breach of contract.

106. (B)

Both UCC 2-601 and 2-608 make it clear that the buyer need not revoke or reject the entire amount of a nonconforming shipment. Instead, the buyer accept and keep "any commercial unit or units and reject the rest." Likewise the buyer may either reject or revoke acceptance and recover damages for nondelivery under UCC 2-713, or he or she may cover and collect damages under UCC 2-712. In any event, a buyer who wishes to reject must "seasonably notify" the seller under UCC 2-602, and UCC 2-608(2) contains a similar requirement for revoking acceptance.

107. (D)

In building contracts, the architect's certificate of completion, if made an express condition to the owner's duty of payment, must be produced or excused before the builder will be entitled to the price. The certificate will be excused where its nonproduction is due to fraud or "bad faith" on the part of the architect. The builder can then recover the contract price on proof of completion of the work without producing the certificate, under the doctrine of substantial performance. Note that choice (A) is incorrect since the majority of courts dispense with the necessity of architect's certificates (excuse their performance as a condition) rather than order their execution. Choice (B) is incorrect since, in most cases, the builder does not attack the validity of the contract's provision for an architect's certificate, as such a tactic would require reformation of the entire contract.

108. (A)

First, it is important to realize that Hoedown and Overalls entered into an enforceable bilateral contract that was supported by adequate consideration. Hoedown promised to pay Overalls a share of the proceeds from the sale of Cornish Acres and, in return, Overalls promised not to sue Hoedown for the improvements he made on the property. Thereafter, Overalls committed a material breach of an implied promise to cooperate on Hoedown's efforts to sell the property by making negative comments to prospective buyers. Where a party to a contract for an exchange of performance ***knowingly prevents, hinders, or makes more costly the other's performance, such conduct is a breach of contract*** for which an action will lie. In this situation, the ***breach is of an implied promise against prevention.*** Note that (B) is wrong because anticipatory repudiation is where one party to an uncompleted bilateral contract repudiates the contract in advance of the time set for performance by announcing that he or she will not perform. Here, Overalls did not anticipatorily repudiate. Choice (C) is incorrect because failure to pay rent for two months is a partial, non-material, breach. Choice (D) is clearly wrong because the Hoedown-Overalls contract does not restrain the alienation of the property.

109. (B)

The most persuasive argument will be the one where Overalls will be deemed not to have breached his contract with Hoedown. Choice (B) is the correct answer. By showing that Overalls made no negative comments to Husker, the actual buyer, there is no evidence that Overalls breached his implied promise to cooperate by preventing Hoedown from realizing the maximum possible sales price. Absent such a breach, Overalls would be entitled to recover the proceeds. Choice (C) is incorrect because Hoedown's promise to pay the sale proceeds was not conditioned on Overalls remaining on the premises, but rather in settlement of Overalls' s claim for compensation for the improvements he made. Likewise, choice (D) is incorrect because, while it is true that Hoedown's promise to pay Overalls a share of the proceeds was an independent covenant from the payment of rent, Hoedown's duty to pay would still be discharged by Overall's material breach of an implied promise to cooperate. Choice (A) is incorrect because the seller is obligated merely to use best efforts to sell at the maximum possible price, not necessarily the appraised market value.

110. (A)

After the right created by a third-party contract has vested in the beneficiary, subsequent rescission and release of the promisor by the promisee is inoperative to affect the right. The cases, however, are in conflict as to **when the right vests.** By the majority view, rescission is possible up to the time the third-party with knowledge assents to the promise, whether he or she is a donee or creditor beneficiary. Here, choice (A) is correct because the Fairmont Hotel (under the majority view) effectively rescinded its $5,000 gift before Cathy Lee's rights (as a third-party donee beneficiary) vested.

111. (D)

The idea that a moral obligation constitutes sufficient consideration has been rejected by the overwhelming majority of jurisdictions. See *Harrington v. Taylor,* 36 S.E.2d 227 (1945), *where a promise by one whose life was saved by the promisee's heroic act to pay compensation for physical injury suffered by the promisee during the rescue was not enforceable.*

112. (A)

According to UCC 2-201 (1), "Except as otherwise noted in this section a contract for the sale of goods for the price of $500 or more is not enforceable by way of action or defense unless there is some writing." Since this section also applies to modifications, choice (A) is clearly the best answer. Choice (B) is wrong because, in contrast to the common law rule, modifications under the UCC do not require new consideration to be enforceable.

113. (B)

The following contracts come within the Statute of Frauds and must be in writing to be enforceable: (1) a contract in consideration of marriage, (2) a contract not performable within one year, (3) a contract of an executor or administrator of an estate, (4) a contract of guarantee or surety, and (5) a contract for the sale of goods of $500 or more. Based on (4), an oral promise to answer for the debt or default of another is unenforceable under the Statute of Frauds. Importantly, an oral contract that does not comply with the Statute is "unenforceable" rather than "void." As a consequence, choice (A) is less preferred.

114. (B)

As noted previously, Humphrey's oral promise to personally guarantee Electro's debt was unenforceable under the Statute of Frauds. As a result, choice (B) is correct because Humphrey was never under a surety duty to pay the debt. Choice (C) is incorrect because, under the "main purpose rule", an oral promise by a promisor to pay the debt of another is enforceable where the party making the promise does so to further his or her own economic advantage. In other words, the consideration for the promise must be beneficial to the promisor either personally or directly. Since Hamilton Humphrey did not stand to directly benefit himself in guaranteeing the corporation's loan, the main purpose rule is inapplicable. On the other hand, if Hamilton was a substantial shareholder in the corporation, then his oral promise may be enforceable, because stock ownership can satisfy the rule.

115. (B)

Since Humphrey was relieved of liability when his surety promise became voidable, Choice (B) is the only correct answer.

116. (C)

If a contract reads *"F.O.B. seller's place of business,"* UCC 2-319(1)(a) indicates that the seller must then: "ship the goods in the manner provided in UCC 2-504 and bear the expense and risk of putting them into the possession of the carrier." Thus, under UCC 2-509(1)(a) *the risk in such a case passes to the buyer when the goods are "duly delivered to the carrier."* Once again, since practically all contracts are assignable the present assignment is in all likelihood valid. However, where one assigns in violation of a non-assignability clause, the assignor is liable for breach of condition, even if the non-assigning party nevertheless must abide by the assignment.

117. (C)

As noted previously, under UCC 2-509(1)(a), where a contract reads "F.O.B. seller's place of business," the risk of loss shifts to the buyer once the seller delivers the goods to the carrier.

118. (C)

The June 2 agreement whereby "Alco agrees to supply all of Reynolds requirements of aluminum sheeting for a period of two years beginning ..." would be an example of a requirements and output contract. With respect to "requirements-output" contracts, UCC 2-306 provides "a term which measures the quantity by the output of the seller or the requirements of the buyer means such actual output or requirements as may occur in good faith, except that no quantity unreasonably disproportionate to any stated estimate or in the absence of a stated estimate to any normal or otherwise comparable prior output or requirements may be tendered or demanded." Moreover, a contract for output or requirements is not too indefinite since it is held to mean the actual good faith output or requirements of the particular party. Nor does such a contract lack mutuality of obligation since the party who will determine quantity is required to operate his or her his business in good faith and according to commercial standards of fair dealing.

119. (A)

UCC 2-202, in stating the parol evidence rule, notes that a party cannot contradict the writing, but he or she may add consistent additional terms unless the court finds the writing to have been intended to be the complete and exclusive statement of the terms of the agreement. In which case, the writing alone constitutes the contract. Here, the parties did *not intend the writing to be the final written expression of their contract* because Reynolds agreed to supply White Owl with the 20,000 containers to cover White Owl's promotional requirements. Therefore, parol evidence can be offered to show subsequent modification of the written contract.

120. (D)

In compliance with UCC 2-305, the parties, if they so intend, can conclude a contract for sale even though the price is not settled. In such a case, the price is a "reasonable price" at the time of delivery if (a) nothing is said as to price, or (b) the price is left to be agreed by the parties and they fail to agree, or (c) the price is to be fixed by some agreed market or other standard as set or recorded by a third person or agency, and it is not so set or recorded.

121. (A)

The June 23rd agreement between Reynolds and Alco would constitute a validly enforceable modification of their June 2nd contractual agreement. In accordance with UCC 2-209 (1), an agreement modifying a contract subject to the UCC needs *no consideration* to be binding. However, such modifications must meet the test of good faith A bad faith attempt to escape performance on the original contract terms is barred, and the extortion of a "modification" without legitimate commercial reason is ineffective as a violation of the duty of good faith.

122. (D)

The probable legal effect of the U.S. Government's embargo on Brazilian imports would be to excuse the duties of performance of the parties through impossibility due to a supervening illegality. Where performance of a contract has become illegal by change in law after the time of contracting, impossibility excuses a party's duty unless he or she has assumed the risk of it or unless his or her fault has contributed to the prohibition. If the embargo had been *temporary,* then choice (C) would be correct.

123. (D)

In accordance with the parol evidence rule, when a contract is expressed in a writing that is intended to be the complete and final expression of the rights and duties of the parties, parol evidence of prior oral or written negotiations or agreements of the parties, or of their contemporaneous oral agreements, *that varies or contradicts the written contract, is not admissible.* Avis's contemporaneous oral promise to extend Heckler's sick leave to 15 days would clearly vary the terms of the written employment contract, and therefore, Heckler would not be permitted to introduce parol evidence of Avis's oral promise (since to do so would contradict the terms of the written contract).

124. (B)

As a rule, in the case of an unliquidated or disputed obligation, if a tender is made by the debtor of money or some other thing as full satisfaction of his or her debt, the acceptance by the creditor of that tendered constitutes a complete discharge of the debt. Thus, where the debt is unliquidated or the amount is in dispute, a payment on condition that it be accepted in full discharge of the debt constitutes an accord and satisfaction.

125. (C)

In bilateral contracts for an exchange of performances, even if the promises are absolute and unequivocal in form, the law regards them as constructively conditional in order to avoid an unjust result. Here, Duke was obligated to travel to Las Vegas and wager $10,000 (for Dexter). After the bet was "laid," Duke would then receive $500 for his efforts. When Duke arrived in Las Vegas, he discovered that The Diamond Head casino was closed. Unable to contact Dexter, Duke went ahead and placed the wager at another casino. In this situation, the law would find that Duke's placing the bet was a constructive condition precedent (an implied-in-fact condition) to his being paid the $500. In the present example, what was the bargained-for-exchange? Briefly, Dexter wanted Duke to wager $10,000 (for him) and in return Duke would receive $500. Since Duke in fact bet the money, he essentially performed his principal obligation under the contract. As a result, he should be entitled to receive that which was promised him, i.e., $500.

126. (D)

As a general rule, No right that is limited in its nature to the personality of the promisee alone is capable of assignment without the assent of the promisor. If X has a contract that Y shall paint his portrait, X may not effectively assign his right to Z so as to enable Z to compel Y to paint Z's portrait. Consequently, an employer's right to an employee's services, where the employee is to work under the personal direction of the employer, is not assignable without the employer's assent because the duty is impliedly conditioned to render the service to the promisee alone. In this regard, it is often said that personal service contracts are not assignable.

127. (C)

Dexter's best defense would be that Duke's telling his girlfriend about the bet constituted a material breach of their agreement. Under the express terms of their written agreement, Duke was forbidden to tell anyone about the bet. Generally, a breach is material wherever the failure of performance defeats the purpose of the contract either wholly or in some vital aspect. However blameless the party may be in failing to perform his or her promise, if the result of the breach is to deprive the other party of an essential part of the agreement, the non-breaching party performance for which he bargained he is not required to undertake his own performance. Note that even where one party has completed part performance, the portion remaining unperformed may be so important as to deprive the other party substantially of what he or she bargained for. If so, the breach is material and non-breaching party is excused from his or her duty to render his or her counterperformance.

128. (C)

A suit for *specific performance will not lie if there is an adequate remedy at law.* It will only lie where the loss cannot be compensated in damages. In the present case, since Stabler does have an adequate remedy at law, choice (C) is the preferred alternative.

129. (A)

Under the modern view, where performance of a contract has become illegal by change of law after the time of contracting, impossibility excuses the promisor's duty unless he or she has assumed the risk of it or unless his or her fault has contributed to the prohibition. Since Ahmat, the promisor, neither assumed the risk nor contributed to the prohibition, his obligation to lend Stabler (promisee) the $50,000 would be excused by supervening illegality. However, if the promisee has already rendered performance (as in the present case when Stabler entered into his contract with Paycheck), then he or she may rescind and recover it back, or its value. Consequently, choice (A) is the best of the given alternatives.

130. (A)

Ahmat's promise to lend Stabler $50,000 is a condition precedent in form because this obligation was expressed in the contract *before* any reference was made to Stabler's obligation to enter into a construction contract on the adjoining lot. However, students should note that Ahmat's promise was subsequent in substance because he would not be obligated to lend Stabler the money *until* after the latter entered into the construction contract.

131. (A)

A purported assignment of a right expected to arise under a contract *not in existence* operates only as a promise to assign the right when it arises.

132. (A)

As noted in the previous explanation, an assignment of future rights under a contract not in existence is unenforceable. In the present hypo, since Amesway had not entered into a valid contract with Seven Brothers Studio at the time, or prior to the time, of his assignment to Lady Buffington, his assignment was ineffective.

133. (C)

In light of the preceding answer, since Amesway's assignment to Lady Buffington was ineffective, the creditors acquired a superior possessory interest to the proceeds from the movie royalties.

134. (C)

Here, the duties of performance are independent and each party may sue the other for breach even though he or she is in default on his or her own promise. So, even though the insured is also in default on his or her promise to pay the premium at the time his house burnt, he can, nevertheless, recover for the loss on the *un*cancelled policy. Note that only when the insurer has expressly conditioned his or her performance on prompt payment of the premium is his or her duty a dependent one.

135. (B)

The contract provisions with respect to (a) the covenant not to compete and (b) the penalty and forfeiture clause would be severed from the contract because the restrictive covenant barring Reynolds from engaging in "any aspect of the hardware business for a period of two years within a 50 mile radius" would be construed as an "unreasonable restraint of trade." Therefore, choices (A) and (C) are incorrect. Choice (D) is wrong because the provisions regarding salary and termination notice would not be objectionable as against public policy. It is important to note that the termination provision requiring the sixty day notice is valid.

136. (C)

A contract clause intended as a penalty in excess of any loss likely to be sustained is unenforceable, and the recovery will be limited to the loss actually sustained.

137. (D)

The assignment of a future right to payment expected to arise out of an existing employment or other continuing business relation is effective in the same way as an assignment of an existing right. Here, Farmingham's assignment (of his right to liquidated damages, upon Reynold's breach of their employment contract) to the Senior Citizen's Center would be effective as a gratuitous assignment even though the potential action did not exist at the time of the assignment. Choice (C), though correct, is the less preferred alternative. In accordance with Restatement (Second) of Contracts Sec. 164, a gratuitous assignment is irrevocable if the assignment is in a signed writing that is delivered to the assignee. In effect, the present assignment is an example of an irrevocable gratuitous assignment of a future right.

138. (A)

In this situation, Workout will not be obligated to perform its duties under the contract (namely, admit Joan to any further exercise classes) *until* she makes the installment payment. Thus, Joan's duty to pay the $500 installment is viewed as a condition precedent to Workout's being obligated to perform its duties under the contract. In other words, Workout may bar Joan from attending any further classes until such time she makes the installment payment.

139. (D)

According to Restatement, the promisee has the following remedies available after the promisor has repudiated the contract *in advance of the time for its performance:* (1) sue at once for anticipatory breach, (2) treat the repudiation as an offer of mutual rescission and accept it in discharge of the contract, (3) treat the repudiation as excusing his or her own further duty of performance, or (4) ignore the repudiation and urge the promisor to perform. Students should also be aware that the *promisor may retract his or her repudiation up to the time the promisee has elected any one of the first three alternatives, but not after.*

140. (B)

Choice (A) is wrong because subjective impossibility will not excuse the promisor's duty of performance under a contract. The mere personal inability of a promisor to perform is no excuse. This is subjective impossibility. At common law, *only objective impossibility (i.e., where because of the supervening event, the performance cannot be rendered by anyone) will excuse the (promisor's) duty of performance.* Choice (D) is incorrect because Joan's duty to make the second installment payment is not regarded as a covenant. Choice (B) is correct because *frustration of purpose* will excuse the promisor's duty where (1) the value of the performance bargained for by the promisor is destroyed by the supervening event and (2) the frustrating event was not foreseeable at the time the parties contracted.

141. (D)

Students should be aware that voluntary waiver (of condition) by the promisor is only effective to eliminate a condition that is not a material part of the agreed exchange. *A condition, however, which is all or a substantial part of the agreed exchange can only be waived by a substituted contract on sufficient consideration.* Here, the condition of the payment of the second installment was a substantial or material part of the agreement between Workout and Fonda. Consequently, that condition could not be waived or extinguished. Choice (C) is wrong because the situation here is one in which there is a present breach (not an anticipatory breach). An anticipatory repudiation occurs when one party repudiates the contract *in advance of the time set for performance by announcing that he or she will not perform it.* In the present case, Joan did not inform Workout prior to January 7 of her intention to repudiate the contract.

142. (B)

UCC 2-612(1) defines an installment contract as one that requires or authorizes the delivery of goods in separate lots to be separately accepted, even though the contract contains a clause that each delivery is a separate contract or its equivalent. Thus, the original agreement would be interpreted as a single installment contract.

143. (B)

When does the breach of part of an installment contract constitute a breach of the whole? When a specific default or nonconformity substantially impairs the value of the entire contract. Here, it is unlikely this nonconformity substantially impairs the value of the entire agreement.

144. (C)

Woody would not be entitled to reject Jones's offer to cure since the nonconformity in plywood size would not constitute a material breach (i.e., substantial nonconformity). Rather, the delivery of the 7' by 6-1/4' sheets, as opposed to the 7' by 6' sheets, would likely be regarded as an insubstantial nonconformity curable by price adjustment.

145. (A)

The forest fire would temporarily suspend Jones's duty to deliver the August shipment. Note that temporary impossibility suspends contractual duties; it does not discharge them. When performance once more becomes possible, the duty "springs back" into existence. Therefore, Timberlane's contractual obligations (with regard to the September, October, November, and December shipments) would not be excused by the temporary impossibility (i.e., forest fire).

146. (D)

Unless a contrary intention is manifested, a gratuitous assignment is irrevocable if the assignment is in a signed writing that is delivered by the assignor.

147. (A)

Under the general rule, impossibility of performance of a condition that is not a material part of the exchange (e.g., architect's certification) will excuse the condition. Where the promisee (i.e., Owens) has already given the promisor (i.e., Parsons) the substantial performance that was bargained for, but because of supervening impossibility has not performed some incidental thing made an express condition of the promise, the condition may be excused (and the liability of the promisor becomes absolute).

148. (B)

On March 25, **by agreeing to construct the decks** on the Fire Island beachhouses, Owens's return promise created an enforceable bilateral contract. **A bilateral contract is a contract in which mutual promises are given** as the agreed exchange for each other. On the contrary, a unilateral contract is a contract in which a promise is given in exchange for an actual performance by the other party.

149. (A)

Owens and Parsons had an enforceable bilateral contract whereby Owens was obligated to build decks on four beachhouses that Parsons owned on Fire Island. Although Hurricane Zelda would excuse Owens's completion of the deck construction on the one house that was demolished on the Island, he would still be required to construct the decks on the other three. Importantly, the washing away of Owens's equipment will not excuse his duty to perform (under the doctrine of subjective impossibility) because Owens, by entering into the contract, has assumed the risk of his ability to perform. In short, to constitute an excuse through impossibility of performance, the thing promised must be impossible of performance by *anyone*.

150. (C)

As per the terms of their agreement, Parsons was only obligated to pay Owens $2,500 per deck upon completion. As a result, Owens will recover $2,500 for each of the eight decks that he constructed on the Hampton Beach properties = $20,000. However, Owens will not be entitled to recover for the *partial* work that he performed on the one Fire Island beachhouse, since it is generally held that a builder has accepted the attendant risks inherently involved in completing the contract.

Your first-year exams will most likely consist of several essay questions. Use the following essay questions to practice spotting issues and to reinforce your knowledge of the law. Remember, your professor cannot read your mind; consequently, if you don't write it down, you didn't think it.

When writing your essay answer, use a clear structure (either IRAC, CRAC, TRRAC, or whatever other template you learned in your Legal Writing course—they are all basically the same thing). Because your professor will be looking at dozens of exams, make yours easy to read (and give a good grade to) by breaking your answer into paragraphs with headings before you discuss each issue. Most of your points will come from your analysis, so make sure your analysis of any issue makes up about 70 percent of your answer.

The most important thing to remember is to actually answer the question. Avoid the "brain dump," where you write down everything you know about contracts, no matter what the question is. The professor wants to see how you deal with the particular issues at hand; importantly, a law school exam is not a memorization contest.

Imagine a client comes into your office and asks you if his or her acceptance was effective when mailed—would you also tell him or her about consideration under the UCC, special rules regarding general contractors, and anticipatory repudiation simply because you could? If you did, you would probably find yourself with one annoyed former client.

Questions 1–3 refer to the following fact pattern:

Without seeking bids from other contractors, Owen entered into a written contract on March 1 with Cobb, a contractor, whereby Cobb was to remodel Owen's house for $20,000. The remodeling was such that Owen could continue to live in his home while Cobb worked on it.

Owen paid Cobb $2,000 when the contract was signed. The contract called for payment of the $18,000 balance upon completion of the work, and for completion of the work by November 1 of the same year. The contract also provided that, in the event of delay in completion, the amount due Cobb from Owen would be reduced by $500 for each month, or part thereof, for delay.

When Cobb had completed 50% of the work, he informed Owen that he would not finish the remodeling at the contract price. He told Owen that he had underestimated labor costs by $4,000 as a result of a mathematical error made by his bookkeeper. Owen refused to agree to pay a higher amount, and Cobb refused to proceed with the remodeling.

Owen promptly obtained bids from two other contractors for completion of the work. He accepted the lower of the two bids—$15,000. Included in this bid was $1,500 to remove and replace paneling Cobb had installed in the family room. Cobb had installed a much lighter-weight paneling than that called for by the contract. The substitute contractor completed the remodeling, including replacement of the paneling, on December 1.

Cobb sued Owen to recover the value of work he did up to the time he stopped performance. Owen counterclaimed for damages stemming from Cobb's refusal to fulfill the contract and for $500 based on late completion of the work.

After receiving evidence of the above facts, the trial judge, sitting without a jury, ruled that:

1. **Cobb had breached the contract but could recover $8,000 on his claim;**

2. **Cobb's recovery would be offset by $5,000, as damages owing to Owen based on Cobb's breach of the contract; and**

3. **Owen could not recover any amount based on the liquidated damages clause in the contract.**

Were the rulings of the trial judge correct? Discuss.

Question 4 refers to the following fact pattern.

Sam owned Blackacre and Whiteacre, two unimproved vacant tracts of land. The county assessor's records listed each tract as containing 10 acres. Without having seen either tract, but having checked the assessor's records, Bob telephoned Sam and said, "I offer to buy Blackacre and Whiteacre for $20,000, $10,000 now and $10,000 in one year." Sam responded, "O.K., I'll have the papers ready tomorrow." The following day Bob paid Sam $10,000, and the parties signed a land sale contract prepared by Sam's lawyer. The contract described the property as "Blackacre, containing 20 acres, more or less," and did not mention Whiteacre. The contract was otherwise consistent with oral communications between Bob and Sam.

The contract did not contain language making time of the essence. During the next twelve months, the following events occurred:

A. Bob sold his interest in the contract to Cal for $10,000. Cal notified Sam of his purchase.

B. The announcement of proposed freeway construction increased land values in the area from $1,000 per acre to $3,000 per acre.

C. Bob, Sam, and Cal each learned that while Blackacre contained 10 acres, Whiteacre contained only 7 acres.

On the date the final payment was due, Cal tendered $7,000 to Sam and demanded deeds to Blackacre and Whiteacre. Sam rejected the tender, and two days later notified Cal that the purchaser's interest in the contract was "terminated because of nonpayment."

Land values in the area are continuing to increase rapidly.

4. **What rights and remedies, if any, does Cal have?**

Questions 5–10 refer to the following fact pattern.

Buyer, a builder of industrial plants, requested Seller, one of his regular suppliers, to submit a proposal for supplying a turbine for a plant Buyer was building for Carlson. Several days later, Seller phoned Buyer and offered to produce and install a turbine, pursuant to the specifications Buyer had supplied, at a price to be agreed upon at a later time when all of Seller's costs were known. During this telephone conversation, Buyer accepted this offer, "so long as the price does not exceed $400,000," and emphasized that delivery by February 15 was essential because the turbine was vital to Buyer's completion of the plant. Seller assented to Buyer's requests.

The next day, Buyer sent Seller a written confirmation that referred to the specifications Buyer had given Seller, stated the price as "not to exceed $400,000," required delivery by February 15, provided for damages of $1,000 per day for any delay in delivery, specified "the usual warranties," and stated that "any changes in the terms of this agreement must be in writing." Shortly after receiving this confirmation, Seller began producing the turbine.

On January 15, Buyer received a letter from Seller requesting a one-month extension in the delivery date. Buyer phoned Seller and, after hearing Seller's reasons for the request, said that a one-month delay in delivery would be acceptable.

On February 20, Buyer learned from a reliable source that Seller had completed the turbine and was about to sell and deliver it to Ted, another builder, for $430,000.

5. **Is the contract sufficiently definite?**

6. **Is the contract enforceable under the Statute of Frauds?**

7. **Did Buyer effectively waive the original delivery date?**

8. **Did the liquidated damages clause become part of the contract?**

9. **Can Buyer successfully sue for specific performance and/or damages?**

10. **Can Buyer successfully sue Ted?**

Questions 11–14 refer to the following fact pattern.

Art and Betty own adjoining farms in County, an area where all agriculture requires irrigation. Art bought a well-drilling rig and drilled a 400-foot well from which he drew drinking water. Betty needed no additional irrigation water, but, on January 1, she asked Art on what terms he would drill a well near her house to supply better-tasting drinking water than the County water she had been using for years. Art said that because he had never before drilled a well for hire, he would charge Betty only $10 per foot, about $1 more than his expected cost. Art said that he would drill to a maximum depth of 600 feet, which is the deepest his rig could reach. Betty said, "OK, if you guarantee June 1 completion." Art agreed and asked for $3,500 in advance, with any additional further payment or refund to be made on completion. Betty said, "OK," and paid Art $3,500.

Art started to drill on May 1. On May 10, Art reached a depth of 200 feet when his drill struck rock and broke, plugging the hole. The accident was unavoidable. Up to that point, it had cost Art $12 per foot to drill to 200 feet. Art said he would not charge Betty for drilling the useless hole, but he would have to start a new well close by, and could not promise its completion before July 1.

Betty, annoyed by Art's failure, refused to let Art start another well, and, on June 1, she contracted with Carlos to drill a well. Carlos agreed to drill to a maximum depth of 350 feet for $4,500, which Betty also paid in advance. Carlos could not start drilling until October 1. He completed drilling and struck water at 300 feet on October 30.

In July, Betty sued Art seeking to recover her $3,500, plus the $4,500 paid to Carlos.

On August 1, County's dam failed, thus reducing the amount of water available for irrigation. Betty lost her apple crop, worth $15,000. The loss could have been avoided by pumping from Betty's well if it had been operational by August 1. Betty amended her complaint to add the $15,000 loss.

11. **Is Art relieved of his obligations to Betty under the mutual mistake doctrine?**

12. **Was Art discharged from his obligations by reason of the impossibility or impracticability of performance doctrines?**

13. **Did Betty materially breach the agreement when she refused to permit Art to complete the drilling?**

14. **Assuming Betty prevailed on the foregoing issues, to what damages would she be entitled?**

Question 15 refers to the following fact pattern.

John Doe recently formed the Smith Company. Its purpose was to carry on a ready-mix concrete business. Robert Jones, owner of a tract of land possessing a very large gravel deposit, agreed in a signed writing with the Smith Company to sell it "all gravel the Smith Company's mixing plant, now under construction, will require for the next 25 years." However, the maximum weekly purchase was to be 50 tons. The Smith Company agreed to buy and pay for the gravel at the rate of "$1.25 per ton, payment to be made at the close of business on Friday for all gravel delivered by Jones during the preceding week." The gravel was to be weighed by an employee of Smith Company upon Smith Company scales.

For six months, Jones delivered gravel to the Smith Company pursuant to the contract. Deliveries of 100 tons per week were requested and made during this six-month period. At the end of this period, Smith Company sold its ready-mix concrete business to Two Ton Corporation and transferred to Two Ton "any and all contract rights of Smith Company." Two Ton was a much larger and, more prosperous entity than Smith Company. Two Ton immediately sent Jones a letter informing him of the sale.

One day after receiving this letter from Two Ton, Jones asked John Doe to have the Smith Company release him from the gravel contract because a municipality had offered to buy his gravel for $2.00 per ton. John Doe agreed and the Smith Company received $500 from Jones for the release.

15. **Two Ton has sent orders for gravel to Jones at the rate of 125 tons for several weeks, but Jones has refused to deliver anything. Two Ton now seeks your advice as to its rights against Jones. Discuss.**

Question 16 refers to the following fact pattern.

Clark is a wholesale distributor of office supplies. Jones operates a novelty supply company. On May 1, Clark received a written order from Jones for 30,000 pens at 50 cents each. This was the price listed in Clark's catalogue. Jones's order stated that these pens must be specially imprinted with a particular political slogan, as they were purchased for resale to Davis, a candidate for the U.S. Senate. The order required delivery of half of the pens by August 1, and the remainder by October 1.

On May 5, Clark sent to Jones a written confirmation acknowledging the quantity, price, delivery dates, and purpose of the purchase. Both the order and the confirmation were on forms containing a number of printed clauses that were substantially the same, except that Clark's confirmation included a clause stating that any disputes were to be resolved by arbitration.

On June 30, Jones telephoned Clark and told him another distributor had offered to sell him the same pens at 45 cents each and that he intended to switch his order to the other distributor unless Clark agreed to lower his price. Rather than lose the sale, Clark grudgingly told Jones that he would accept the 45 cents per pen.

On July 30, Clark shipped the first 15,000 pens. On August 2, Clark received Jones's payment for them at 45 cents each. On August 10, Jones wrote to Clark canceling the second half of the order because Davis had withdrawn from the Senate race due to health problems. When he received the letter of cancellation, Clark had not yet ordered the second shipment of pens from the manufacturer.

16. **Clark has sued Jones for breach of contract, seeking damages based on the original 50-cent price for all of the pens. How should the case be decided? Discuss.**

Question 17 refers to the following fact pattern.

Owner ("O") wished to build a summer house on his mountain lot. He retained Architect ("A") to draw the plans and specifications and to supervise construction of the house. The contract between O and A stated, in part: "The total fee for Architect's work is $4,000, payable on completion of the construction, provided that *no amount is due* to Architect if the plans and construction fail to meet Owner's personal satisfaction."

Plans and specifications were prepared by A and were approved by O. O then entered into a contract with Contractor ("C") to build the home for $45,000, payable on completion. This contract incorporated the plans and specifications as an exhibit and contained the following provision:

> "Architect shall be the interpreter of this contract and judge of its performance. The $45,000 shall be due and payable when Owner receives a certificate from Architect stating that the work required by this contract has been completed."

O did not see the house during construction. C finished the work and requested A's certificate. When A and O visited the site, they noticed that the siding was different than that specified in the contract. It gave an appearance to the exterior different from that which O had desired. A refused to issue his certificate of completion.

C refused to remove and replace the siding. C explained that a severe shortage of the specified lumber had increased its cost to the extent he could not afford to use it, and that the lumber substituted was equal in quality and durability. These matters were confirmed by A.

When A demanded payment of his fee. O refused and stated; "The plans were great, but I hate the siding. I'm personally dissatisfied with the construction."

O then wrote C: "Although I do not owe you anything, in view of the effort and money you have expended, I am giving you $35,000 in full payment." O enclosed a check for $35,000 with these words clearly written on the back: "Accepted in full settlement of all claims to date."

C endorsed and cashed the check, but has now demanded that O pay him the balance of $10,000.

17. What are C's rights against O? Discuss.
    What are A's rights against O? Discuss.

CONTRACTS

Question 18 refers to the following fact pattern.

Owner offered in a signed writing to sell Greenacre, a five-square-acre parcel of unimproved realty, to Byer for $50,000 on January 3. Byer was to pay $5,000 on February 1. The remainder of the purchase price and the deed were to be exchanged on April 1. Byer verbally accepted Owner's offer.

On January 17, Byer, in a signed writing, assigned all his rights under the contract to Ellis. Ellis, in a signed writing mailed to Byer, agreed to pay the entire contract price of $50,000 to Owner. Byer then notified Owner via letter that he had assigned the contract to Ellis, that Ellis had agreed to pay the entire contract price, and that Byer therefore considered himself "free and clear of any further obligations under the contract." Owner received, but didn't respond to, this communication.

On February 1, Owner accepted the $5,000 installment paid to him by Ellis. On March 15, Owner notified Byer and Ellis that he had just discovered that he did not own a three-feet wide strip along the western edge of Greenacre.

On April 1, Owner tendered to Byer and Ellis a deed to Greenacre, excluding from the description of the property the three-foot strip. Both Byer and Ellis refused to accept the deed or pay the remaining $45,000. Owner thereupon commenced a suit for specific performance against both Byer and Ellis. Ellis cross-complained against Owner for restitution of the $5,000 installment.

18. **What will be the result of Owner's suit against Byer, Owner's suit against Ellis, and Ellis's cross-complaint against Owner? Discuss.**

Question 19 refers to the following fact pattern.

In early December, A (a widget manufacturer) telephoned B (a widget vendor) and asked, "How would you like to buy all of your requirements of widgets for the next calendar year at $7.00 per widget?" When B replied, "Yes." A said "OK, I'll send you the papers." Six days later, B received A's preprinted agreement, which contained the following handwritten statements by A:

> "In confirmation of our telephone conversation, I agree to sell you all widgets required and ordered by you for the next calendar year at $7.00 per widget. If the foregoing is acceptable, please sign and mail this contract back to me within five business days."

This contract was signed by A.

At a dinner party the evening after B had received A's contract, B met C, a good friend of A. To B's surprise, C said that A had told him that very morning "only a fool" would enter into a long-term contract for the sale of widgets in the present economic environment. The very next morning, at 10:00 A.M., B sent a telegram to A, accepting the contract. At 10:30 A.M., A sent a telegram to B, stating, "My offer to you is hereby revoked." Each telegram reached its destination two hours after it was sent. At about 2:00 P.M. that same day, B signed and mailed the contract back to A.

19. A has refused to make any deliveries, and B is now threatening to sue A. A has consulted you with respect to this matter. What would you advise A? Discuss.

Question 20 refers to the following fact pattern.

Mechanic operates an automobile repair shop. He entered into a two-year written contract with Renter, who operates a car rental service. This agreement stated that Mechanic would:

(1) Provide all service and repairs for all of Renter's cars at a charge of $20.00 per hour for labor.
(2) Supply all parts and materials at Mechanic's cost plus 10%.
(3) Supply gasoline for all of Renter's cars at a cost of 2 cents per gallon below the prevailing retail market price.

The contract also required Renter to purchase all of its repairs and gasoline from Mechanic.

During the first eight months of the contract, inflation caused Mechanic's expenses to rise about 50%. Meanwhile, Renter's fleet of cars tripled with a proportionate increase in the amount of repairs needed. As a result, Mechanic informed Renter that he would refuse to continue to perform, unless Renter agreed to an increase in charges for the remainder of the contract period to $25 per hour for labor, and cost plus 15% for parts and materials. These increases would offset the rise in Mechanic's expenses.

Renter sought, but failed, to find another repair shop willing to do the work. Renter and Mechanic then entered into a new written agreement. For the remainder of the two-year period, the charges for labor and parts and materials would conform to Mechanic's demands.

Renter now consults you. He informs you that:

(1) He has now found an automobile repair shop that will do his work for the same prices set forth in the original agreement with Mechanic.
(2) Mechanic has informed Renter that due to global gasoline shortages, Mechanic must limit each of Renter's cars to 10 gallons a week.

20. Renter wants to know about his rights against, and obligations to, Mechanic. What advice would you give Renter? Discuss.

Question 21 refers to the following fact pattern.

Safari hired Clyde to negotiate sales to American zoos of animals that Safari had trapped in Africa. It was orally agreed that Clyde would be paid $500 per month for his services. He would also receive 10% of the gross sales by Safari, on the condition that sales exceeded $150,000 per year. All sales were subject to approval of Safari. Clyde agreed to bear his own transportation expenses so long as he could drive to the particular zoo involved. Clyde and Safari discussed expense arrangements in the event it became necessary for Clyde to travel by air, but were unable to arrive at an understanding. They agreed to leave that point unresolved until they could observe how the arrangement worked out. Clyde's employment was for a period of two years.

Safari gave Clyde the first $500 in advance, and asked him to start by finding a sale for five rare albino impalas at an aggregate price over $35,000. Within the first month after their agreement, the following events took place:

1. Clyde negotiated a sale of the impalas to the Bronx Zoo for $50,000, but Safari refused to approve, stating he did not like the zookeeper.

2. Clyde then negotiated a sale of the impalas to the Lincoln Park (Chicago) Zoo for $40,000. Safari approved this and the sale was consummated.

3. Safari asked Clyde to fly to San Francisco to negotiate a sale for a pair of zebras for an aggregate price of $5,000 or more. Clyde flew there and his round-trip airfare was $400.

Before Clyde had contacted the San Francisco Zoo, he received a call from Safari notifying him that the zebras had been sold to Woodland Park in Seattle for $6,000, and that his services were no longer required. Safari also advised Clyde that he owed him nothing more than the $500 previously advanced.

21. **What are Clyde's rights against Safari? Discuss.**

1. Is Cobb entitled to recover $8,000?

Where a person substantially performs the terms of a contract, he or she is entitled to recover under the agreement, less an offset equal to the damages suffered by the non-breaching party. Cobb probably asserted that his breach was not material (i.e., he had substantially performed), since he had completed 50% of the contract. Therefore, he is entitled to 50% of the agreed-upon fee. However, Owen probably argued in rebuttal that Cobb had not substantially performed, since (1) completing 50% of the required work ordinarily does not constitute substantial performance (especially where the breach is deliberate), and (2) Cobb did not even complete this portion, since the paneling in the family room was too lightweight. Owen should have prevailed on this point, and therefore Cobb should not have been permitted to recover under the contract.

Alternatively, Cobb may have asserted that he was entitled to recover $8,000 under quantum meruit. Under this theory, a party is entitled to recover the value of the benefit bestowed upon another, provided the former's services were rendered with the justifiable expectation of payment. However, even if the second contractor was able to utilize the work previously done by Cobb, the benefit bestowed would only be $6,500 (since $1,500 of the additional $5,000 Owen was obliged to pay resulted from Cobb's use of incorrect paneling).

Thus, the trial court erroneously ruled that Cobb could recover $8,000 in damages.

2. Should Cobb's recovery be offset by $5,000?

A non-breaching party is usually entitled to be made "whole" (i.e., put in the position he or she would have been in had the other side fully performed). Owen probably contended that, since he was required to pay an additional $5,000 to the substitute contractor, the offset was proper.

Cobb could have argued in rebuttal, however, that where an offeree should have realized that the offeror had made a calculation error, the former cannot "snap up" the offer. However, Owen probably asserted in rebuttal that there was no reason for him to have realized that Cobb had made an error in calculation. Presumably, Owen had no experience with respect to prices normally charged for remodeling homes. Additionally, since no other bids were obtained when Owen accepted Cobb's offer, there was no basis for the former to recognize that Cobb had made an error in calculation.

Thus, the court was probably correct in concluding that Owen was entitled to a $5,000 offset.

3. Should Owen have been entitled to recover liquidated damages?

Liquidated damages are appropriate where (1) the non-breaching party's damages would be difficult to calculate; (2) the damages prescribed were, at the time of contracting, a reasonable forecast of the losses that the non-breaching party would be likely to suffer as a consequence of the other party's breach; and (3) the damages bear a reasonable relationship to the damages actually incurred by the non-breaching party.

Since (1) Owen was able to remain in the house while the remodeling was being undertaken, and (2) there is nothing to indicate that Owen would lose potential business (or suffer any other type of loss) as a consequence of the completion of the work in less than a timely manner, the liquidated damage clause appears to be an invalid penalty.

Thus, the court was correct in not permitting Owen to recover under the liquidated damages clause.

4. What rights and remedies, if any, does Cal have? Discuss.

Reformation

An initial issue is "can the contract be reformed to reflect the purchase of both Blackacre and Whiteacre?" Under the parol evidence rule, evidence that is inconsistent with an integrated agreement is not admissible. Since the writing pertains only to Blackacre, Sam might argue that Cal is precluded from introducing proof that the original transaction also covered Whiteacre.

However, an integrated contract can ordinarily be reformed to reflect the parties' actual agreement, where there is clear and convincing evidence that a term was inadvertently omitted. Cal could probably satisfy this burden of proof, because (1) the contract alludes to "... 20 acres, more or less" (it is unlikely that the land would actually be only about one-half as large as they had thought); (2) at the time the contract was made, land in the area was only worth $1,000 per parcel (it is unlikely that Bob would have agreed to pay twice the fair-market value of the land); and (3) Sam may have advised his attorney that the transaction was to cover both Blackacre and Whiteacre (the lawyer presumably overlooked the fact that the final agreement did not reflect his client's instructions). Thus, the contract would probably be reformed to cover Blackacre and Whiteacre.

Constructive Condition Precedent

Sam could contend that payment of the entire purchase price was a condition precedent to his performance. While there was no express condition precedent to this effect, there is a constructive (i.e., implied) condition precedent that where the performances of each party are to occur concurrently, each side's tender is a condition precedent to the other side's obligation to perform. Since delivery of the deeds and payment of the $10,000 balance could happen concurrently, Cal's failure to deliver the entire balance arguably released Sam from his duty to deliver the deeds.

Abatement

Cal could argue in rebuttal that where a buyer learns that land that is to be conveyed to him is less than that anticipated by the parties, the purchaser (if he or she chooses to consummate the transaction) is entitled to an abatement in the purchase price equal to the diminished value of the property. Because Sam owns 15% less acreage than indicated in the assessor's records and contract, the $7,000 tender was appropriate.

Sam could contend in rebuttal, however, that (1) the acreage alluded to the contract was an approximation, (2) he is not responsible for the misstatements in the public record made by the county assessor, (3) Cal should have performed his own survey to verify the precise acreage being conveyed, and (4) because Cal was aware prior to the closing date that Whiteacre embodied only 7 acres and (apparently) made no effort to reconcile this variance with Sam, Cal cannot unilaterally determine the proper amount owing to Sam at this late date. Sam's argument should be successful.

Termination

Sam could next argue that because the due date for payment of the balance has passed, his obligation to perform has expired. However, assuming the closing date did not occur too long ago, Cal is probably not yet in material breach of the agreement (especially as there was no "time is of the essence" clause). Thus, Cal should either (1) tender $10,000 to Sam, but reserve his right to sue for abatement under quasi-contract principles or (2) immediately commence an action for specific performance, coupled with a request for an abatement in the purchase price.

If Cal is unable to tender the entire purchase price to Sam or commence a lawsuit, he might be entitled to recover the $10,000 paid to Sam one year ago under a quasi-contract theory (i.e., Sam would be unjustly enriched if allowed to retain the land and the initial $10,000 payment too). However, if the contract contained a valid liquidated damages clause, Sam would probably be permitted to retain the original down payment.

Cal v. Bob

It is unlikely that Cal has any rights against Bob. Cal is probably charged with notice of the terms contained in the contract that was assigned to him.

5. Is the contract sufficiently definite to be enforceable?

A contract must be definite as to its material terms to be capable of enforcement. Seller could initially contend that (1) there never was agreement as to price (it was merely the understanding of the parties that the price would not exceed $400,000), and (2) nothing was said as to place of delivery. However, Buyer could probably successfully contend in rebuttal that under UCC 2-305, where the parties agree that the price would subsequently be "agreed upon," a reasonable price at the time and place of delivery will be implied into the contract. Additionally, the price term might be determinable from the parties' prior course of dealing (i.e., if Seller usually obtained a profit of 20% above its costs, a similar profit could be allowed to Seller in this transaction). The place of delivery is also probably determinable by the prior course of dealing between the parties (i.e., were the goods delivered to Buyer's premises in the past, or had Buyer picked them up at Seller's plant?).

6. Is the contract enforceable under the Statute of Frauds?

Seller might next argue that any purported agreement is unenforceable under the Statute of Frauds (where a contract involves the sale of goods with an aggregate price of $500.00 or more, it must be embodied in a writing signed by the party against whom enforcement is sought), because he never signed a writing indicating that a contract had been made. However, under UCC 2-201(2) if (1) the transaction is between merchants, (2) a confirmation is sent that would meet the Statute of Frauds requirements against the sender, and (3) the confirmation is not objected to within 10 days after it is received, the Statute of Frauds is deemed to be satisfied against the recipient.

Seller could nevertheless argue that Buyer is not a merchant under UCC 2-104 (one who deals in goods of the kind involved). Buyer's business is the building of industrial plants, not the buying or selling of turbines. However, Buyer could probably successfully respond in rebuttal that he did "deal" in turbines in the sense that he frequently purchased them for subsequent integration into structures which he had agreed to construct. Assuming Buyer signed the confirmation and prevails on the "merchant" issue, Buyer would overcome Seller's Statute of Frauds defense.

7. Did Buyer effectively waive the original delivery date?

Assuming an enforceable contract existed, Buyer would contend that the one-month extension of the delivery date can be retracted since (1) the contract contains a clause that specifically makes verbal modifications of the agreement unenforceable, and (2) the contract, as modified, is still within the Statute of Frauds, and therefore any purported modification must be embodied in a writing signed by Buyer to be enforceable.

Seller could argue in rebuttal that (1) clauses prohibiting non-written modifications are usually held to be waivable, especially where the waiver was actually relied upon by the party who sought it (as Seller presumably did in this instance by entering into a new agreement with Ted), and (2) Buyer is estopped from asserting the Statute of Frauds. However, since the alleged waiver was obtained deceitfully (presumably Seller offered an excuse other than he needed extra time to fill an order for Ted), it is arguably invalid. Thus, Buyer can probably retract the waiver and insist upon delivery on the initially agreed-upon date.

8. Did the liquidated damages clause become part of the contract?

Seller could initially contend that the liquidated damages clause calling for damages of $1,000 per day never became part of the contract because it was merely a proposal made by Buyer after agreement had been reached on the telephone (without mention of such a clause). However, under UCC 2-207(2), where a transaction is between merchants, additional terms set forth in a written confirmation become part of the contract unless they "materially alter" the agreement. Buyer could argue that the liquidated damages clause does not materially alter the contract since it merely affects the recoverable damages (as opposed to changing a party's substantive rights pertaining to liability).

However, Seller could probably successfully argue in rebuttal that such a drastic change in the ordinary rules for recovery does constitute a "material change." Thus, the liquidated damages clause probably did not become part of the contract.

Even if Buyer prevailed on the preceding issue, under UCC 2-719, a liquidated damages clause is valid only if (1) it provides for a recovery that is reasonable in light of the actual harm caused by the breach and, (2) it was not otherwise feasible for the aggrieved party to obtain an adequate remedy. While it is conceivable that Buyer could show that, if the turbine were not received on time, (1) he could become liable for damages to others, or (2) goodwill would be permanently lost, since Buyer had accepted a month's delay in the delivery of the turbines, it is likely that the normal UCC remedies for breach are adequate. Thus, the liquidated damages clause is invalid.

9. Can Buyer successfully sue for specific performance and/or damages?

Specific performance is warranted where the goods involved are unique or "other appropriate circumstances exist." UCC 2-716. Although the turbine was manufactured according to specifications furnished by Buyer, it does not appear to be "unique" (i.e., another vendor could build a similar turbine). It is unclear from the facts if Buyer could forcefully contend that "other appropriate circumstances" exist (i.e., that Buyer would lose goodwill if the turbine is not acquired immediately). If Buyer could show that goodwill would be permanently diminished by failure to receive the turbine in a timely manner, his assertion that "other appropriate circumstances" are present would be strengthened. Even without such proof, Buyer might be able to persuade a court that Seller's deceitful conduct constitutes "appropriate circumstances."

If specific performance is denied, Buyer should "cover" (i.e., purchase a similar item from another vendor), and then sue Seller for the difference between the cover price and contract price.

10. Can Buyer successfully sue Ted?

The facts are silent as to whether Ted was aware of the outstanding contract with Buyer when he contracted to purchase the turbine from Seller. If (1) he was aware of the outstanding contract, and (2) this jurisdiction views the offer of a higher price for a specific item as being improper, Buyer could probably (1) restrain the sale of the turbine to Ted, and (2) recover any damages resulting from the transfer to Ted under an interference with contract theory.

11. Is Art relieved of his obligations to Betty under the mutual mistake doctrine?

Where there is a mutual mistake of fact existing at the time the contract was made, and that mistake goes to the essence of the transaction, the adversely affected party can avoid the agreement (provided the risk of such mistake was not borne by him or her). Art will contend that since neither side was aware of the rock that subsequently caused the drill to break, thereby making it impossible for him to complete the job by June 1, Art may avoid the agreement. Betty would contend in rebuttal, however, that (1) this doctrine is not applicable because (1) the burden of the existence of the rock was borne by Art, because he could have made the necessary subsoil investigation, and (2) the incident that prevented Art's performance (the collision with the rock) occurred subsequent to the time the contract was made. Betty should prevail on this issue.

12. Was Art discharged from his obligations by reason of the impossibility or impracticability of performance doctrines?

Where, as a consequence of some unforeseeable, post-contract event, one of the parties (through no fault of his or her own) cannot possibly perform his or her prospective obligations,that party is relieved of his or her obligations until the impossibility ceases to exist. Art could contend that as a consequence of the drill unexpectedly breaking after it struck the rock, his performance by the due date (June 1) became impossible, and thereafter Art's obligations were completely discharged when Betty advised him that he would not be permitted to finish the contract. However, Betty could argue in rebuttal that many states require that it must be objectively impossible for the breaching party to perform (i.e., no one in the Art's position could have rendered the requisite performance), and one with unlimited funds could (presumably) have acquired new equipment that could have drilled to a depth of 600 feet by June 1. Thus, this defense will probably not be successful.

Some jurisdictions follow the rule that where a party's performance is merely made impracticable as a consequence of some unforeseeable, post-contract event (which occurred through no fault of his or her own), that party is relieved of his or her obligations until the impracticability ceases to exist. If this jurisdiction adheres to this view, Art would contend that his obligation was suspended when the drill unexpectedly broke as a result of impacting upon the unknown rock, and that such obligation was discharged entirely when Betty advised Art that she would not permit him to finish the drilling. However, it is unclear from the facts as to whether Art should have recognized that a subsurface rock could be strong enough to break his drill. If such an impediment had previously been encountered by persons in the area, it would be difficult for Art to satisfy the "unforeseeability" element. Thus, unless Art can demonstrate that the rock and its effect upon the drill were unforeseeable, Betty should prevail with respect to this contention too.

13. Did Betty materially breach the agreement when she refused to permit Art to complete the drilling?

Where a material breach occurs, the non-breaching party is relieved of any further obligations under the agreement. Art could argue that when Betty advised him that he could not commence another well she materially breached the contract. It is an implied obligation in all contracts that neither party will undertake any conduct that prevents the other side from performing his or her obligations under the agreement.

Betty could assert the anticipatory repudiation doctrine in rebuttal. An anticipatory repudiation occurs where one party unequivocally advises the other that his or her performance will not be forthcoming. Where an anticipatory repudiation has occurred, the aggrieved party can treat the agreement as terminated and sue for damages. Thus, Betty could contend that when Art advised her that performance was unlikely prior to July 1 (a full month subsequent to the contractual due date), his statement constituted an anticipatory repudiation (thereby discharging Betty from the obligation to permit Art to complete the drilling). While Art could claim in rebuttal that he only advised Betty that he "could not promise" that the drilling would be completed before July 1 (not that he absolutely couldn't perform by June 1), Art's statement that performance could not be assured even one month after the agreed-upon date for completion would probably constitute an anticipatory repudiation. Thus, Betty did not materially breach the agreement by refusing to permit Art to re-commence the drilling.

It should be mentioned that Betty would probably be unsuccessful in arguing that Art materially breached the agreement at the moment his drill impacted upon the rock and broke. The facts indicate that this occurrence was unavoidable, and therefore Betty's mere annoyance with Art's failure to complete the job expeditiously would not constitute a material breach by Art.

14. Assuming Betty prevailed on the foregoing issues, to what damages would she be entitled?

Betty would assert that the damages sought in her complaint are necessary to put her in the position she would have been had Art performed in a timely manner.

Art would initially argue that the $15,000 loss reflecting the ruined apple crop is not recoverable since it was not foreseeable at the time the contract was made. Betty had advised Art that the new well was for the purpose of obtaining better drinking water (rather than cultivation) and the likelihood of the dam failing was probably minimal. Additionally, Art could contend that the loss was avoidable. Had Betty permitted Art to finish the contract, the well would presumably have been completed within 30 days (the period of time that it took Carlos to complete the job) after the drill broke. Since Betty appears to have no effective means of countering these arguments, the $15,000 apple crop loss is probably not recoverable.

Whether Betty could recover the remaining $8,000 claimed as damages would depend upon whether the fee charged by Carlos was reasonable or not. Where one side fails to complete a personal services agreement, the non-breaching party is permitted to retain another to finish the breaching party's performance. Thus, assuming the fee charged by Carlos was reasonable, Betty would be entitled to recover $8,000 from Art.

15. Two Ton has sent orders for gravel to Jones at the rate of 125 tons for several weeks, but Jones has refused to deliver anything. Two Ton now seeks your advice as to its rights against Jones. Discuss.

Robert Jones ("J") would probably raise the following issues if Two Ton ("2T") attempts to enforce the contract ("K") against him.

Definiteness

J might initially contend that the K is not sufficiently **definite as to all material terms,** since the quantity term is indefinite. It is impossible to estimate how much gravel 2T would order over the next 24½ years. However, 2T could probably successfully argue in rebuttal that this argument will fail, as requirements contracts like the one here ("all gravel the Smith Company … will require") do not need quantity terms to be sufficiently definite. Moreover, the quantity term and 2T's requirements are easily discernible, because (1) 2T is attempting to purchase the maximum amount available under the K, and (2) once J's liability has been established, 2T's requirements can be proven by showing how much gravel it purchased from other suppliers.

Material Increase in Risk (UCC §2-210(2))

J might next contend under UCC 2-210(2), all rights of either seller or buyer can be assigned unless the assignment would materially increase the burden or risk imposed on the other party. J will argue that the assignment was invalid because its risk would be materially increased in that (1) there is a credit term (gravel is to be paid for **at the end** of each week), and (2) the weighing was to be done by Smith's employees, whom J trusts. However, 2T could probably successfully argue in rebuttal that (1) the credit term is relatively minor (100 tons times $1.25 is only $125.00 per week), and, in any event, 2T (apparently) has a greater net worth than Smith Company, and (2) there is no truly subjective aspect involved in weighing the gravel (the scales must be functioning and honestly read).

Release

Where a party is validly released from a contract, he or she has no further liability. J might contend that he was **released** by the Smith Company, and so has no liability to 2T. However, 2T could successfully argue in rebuttal that once an assignment is made, the assignor (Smith Company) no longer has any rights in the underlying K. Consequently, the K is still enforceable by 2T.

Waiver

2T could contend that the limitation of 50 tons per week was **waived in its entirety** by J's conduct in fulfilling Smith's orders of 100 tons for six months. In some cases, conduct may constitute a waiver, but a written waiver is preferable to an implied one. There is nothing to indicate that J intended this result (or that his conduct should have been interpreted in this manner). At most, the underlying agreement was impliedly modified to recognize a maximum of 100 tons per week (rather than the original 50).

Extent of Modification

J could contend that, since the K contained a maximum of 50 tons per week, this is all 2T is entitled to receive. In most contract disputes, the court will look to the plain language of the contract. While 2T could argue in rebuttal that J *waived* this term by supplying 100 tons to Smith for six months, J could respond (probably successfully), that (1) modifications to a written K are rarely found by conduct, but only by express agreement, so J's 100 ton orders should be viewed as requesting his K maximum, plus an offer to purchase an additional 50 tons, and (2) since the K as modified cannot be performed within one year and involves a sale of goods over $500, the modification must satisfy the Statute of Frauds (i.e., there would have to be a writing signed by J) to be valid. J should prevail on this point.

Therefore, 2T can enforce the K against J in the amount of 50 tons per week only.

Remedies/Damages

2T can obtain specific performance only if the goods are unique or other appropriate circumstances exist. Gravel is not a unique good. While 2T could contend that appropriate circumstances exist because it would have to institute a multiplicity of suits (a new lawsuit would arise each time J was obliged to purchase gravel from another party), this argument is *not* likely to prevail.

I would therefore advise 2T to cover (purchase the gravel from another source) up to 50 tons, and sue J for the difference between the cover price and K rate.

16. Clark ("C") has sued Jones ("J") for breach of contract, seeking damages based on the original 50-cent price for all of the pens. How should the case be decided? Discuss.

Can C insist upon arbitration?

Under UCC 2-207(2), where a transaction is between merchants, additional terms set forth in a written confirmation become part of the agreement unless they "materially alter" the contract. C could argue that an arbitration clause is not a material alteration because it merely changes the forum in which the controversy is heard (rather than any substantive rights). However, case law favors J. Since some evidentiary rules and the right to a jury trial are relaxed in an arbitration proceeding, such a clause is usually considered "material." Thus, C probably has to pursue his rights against J through normal judicial channels.

Is the modification enforceable?

C would initially contend that the purported modification of the contract from 50 cents to 45 cents per pen is unenforceable, since (1) it is violative of the *pre-existing duty rule* (i.e., C received no additional consideration for lowering the price by 5 cents), and (2) it is unenforceable under the Statute of Frauds ("S. of F.") provision pertaining to the sale of goods with an aggregate price of $500 or more. As the pen order would cost $15,000 at the 50-cent price and $13,500 at the 45-cent price, either price would place the K squarely within the S. of F.

In rebuttal, J could assert that, since the transaction involves a sale of goods, no consideration is necessary for the modification of an existing agreement. UCC 2-209(1). However, the UCC comments do require that such modifications be made in good faith. Since J threatened repudiation of the agreement simply because he had received a more profitable offer, the "good faith" requisite is probably lacking. Under this analysis, the modification may not be valid.

Assuming he prevails on the pre-existing duty rule issue, J could also contend that the S. of F. was waived by reason of C's acceptance of the 45-cent-per-pen payment with respect to the initial installment. UCC 2-209(4). However, C could assert in rebuttal that a *waiver* can ordinarily be retracted upon reasonable notice, provided the other side has not relied upon it to his detriment. UCC 2-209(5). Since the facts fail to indicate reliance by J upon the lower price, C could probably successfully assert non-payment by J at the rate of 50 cents per pen as to the entire 30,000 pens.

Can J successfully assert the frustration of purpose doctrine?

Where one of the parties has a special purpose for entering into a contract (of which the other side is aware) and that purpose is frustrated by an unforeseeable, post-contract event, the former is relieved of his or her prospective obligations. J could contend that since C knew the pens were for Davis ("D"), and that purpose was frustrated by his withdrawal from the Senate race, J was relieved of any obligation to pay C for the final 15,000 pens. However, C could argue in rebuttal that withdrawal from the race by D (for any reason) was a risk of which J was always aware. J could have protected himself from this situation by insisting upon a provision precluding liability in this eventuality. Thus, this defense would probably fail.

Is J relieved of liability as a consequence of an implied condition subsequent?

A condition subsequent may be implied into an agreement where, had the parties considered an event that later occurred, the parties would almost certainly have agreed that its occurrence would relieve them of their prospective obligations. J could contend that implied into their agreement was that a decision by D to not run would extinguish J's obligation to pay for the pens. However, C would assert in rebuttal that (1) courts are ordinarily reluctant to imply conditions subsequent, and (2) J could have explicitly provided for discharge of his contractual obligations in the event that D abandoned his campaign. C would probably prevail on this issue also.

The commercial impracticability doctrine is not applicable. It pertains only to situations where a seller is seeking to avoid liability, not a buyer.

Damages

Under the UCC, an aggrieved party is entitled to be placed in the position he or she would have occupied had the other side performed. See UCC 1-106. Therefore, C could probably recover its lost profits (based upon 50 cents per pen) on the remaining 15,000 pens, and an additional 5 cents per pen with respect to the original 15,000.

17. What are C's rights against O? Discuss.
What are A's rights against O? Discuss.

C vs. O

C's rights against O depend upon resolution of the following issues:

Did an accord and satisfaction occur?

Where there is a bona fide dispute as to the amount due and one party offers the other less than full performance in full satisfaction of his or her obligation, acceptance by the latter discharges the former's obligation. This is called an accord and satisfaction. C will argue that no bona fide dispute existed because (1) the lumber substituted was at least equal in quality and durability as that required, and (2) this is a "summer house" on a "mountain lot," and so very few people would even see it. O would contend in rebuttal that giving a different appearance to a home, a highly personal object, is a good faith basis for non-performance on his part and that specifications were included in the C/O contract. O should prevail on this point.

Was A's certificate a condition precedent or merely a covenant to C's receiving payment?

Where a condition precedent fails to occur, neither party has any obligation to the other. However, where a covenant is breached, the non-breaching party can still recover, provided substantial performance has been rendered. O will argue that A's certificate was a condition precedent because the contract specifically stated that the $45,000 was due "when A issued that certificate." C will contend in rebuttal, however, that this language merely alluded to the timing of the payment, and point out that where O intended a condition precedent, he specifically stated that to be the case, as evidenced by his contract with A ("**no amount** shall be due to A if the plans and construction fail to meet O's satisfaction").

Assuming A's certificate was only a covenant, did C materially breach the contract by utilizing different siding? (If C's breach was material, he has no right to recover from O.)

O will argue that C's breach is material because (1) the appearance of a home is very significant to an owner, and (2) C intentionally used lumber different than that specified in the contract. C would contend in rebuttal that: (1) only a mountaintop, summer residence is involved, and (2) C was obliged to purchase the different lumber because this was all he could afford. O should prevail. Under contract law, C had no right to substitute a different kind of lumber merely because the contract would otherwise be less profitable for him, and C made no effort to modify the specification

Did O waive C's use of the different lumber?

Where one party does not insist upon strict performance by the other, the former may be deemed to have waived that breach. O could contend that A's failure to object to the different lumber during construction, which presumably was fairly obvious, constituted a waiver of this right. However, O would argue in rebuttal (probably successfully), that he had no contractual obligation to be on the site and the specifications were clear.

Assuming A's certificate was merely a covenant and that he had substantially performed, what is he entitled to recover?

The non-breaching party should be placed in the position he or she would have been if the breaching party had performed. O will thus contend that he should be able to deduct from the contract price the cost that will likely be incurred in removing and replacing the present lumber with the specified type. This would presumably exceed $10,000. C would argue, however, that since this damage remedy is grossly disproportionate to the loss actually suffered, O is only entitled to the diminishment in value to the house resulting from the use of a different siding, and this would only be a nominal amount because the siding is similar to the siding that was included in the contract. However, the appearance of a home goes to the essence of the contract, and O should prevail.

Assuming A's certificate was a covenant and C's breach was material, can C obtain recovery in quasi-contract?

If a breach is material, the breaching party is ordinarily entitled to recover nothing from the non-breaching party. Under the doctrine of quasi-contract, however, where one accepts a benefit from another knowing that the latter expects compensation, the former is liable for the reasonable value of that benefit. Importantly, the contract rate may be evidence of the reasonable value of services rendered, but it is not conclusive. Since C rendered services with the expectation of payment, and O was aware of these services, C should be able to recover for the value of his work.

A vs. O

Since the contract between A and O clearly stated that A was to receive nothing if the construction failed to meet the "personal satisfaction" of O, O's satisfaction is a condition precedent to A's payment.

A major factor in determining whether a condition precedent based upon "personal satisfaction" has been met is determining whether a subjective standard (what O himself believes) or an objective standard (what a reasonable person would believe) applies? The a subjective standard is usually used where the performance involved is personal in nature. The appearance of a house, even a summer home on a mountain top, is probably personal in nature. Therefore, its different appearance is a good faith reason for O's refusal to pay anything to A.

18. What result in Owner's suit against Byer, Owner's suit against Ellis, and Ellis's cross-complaint against Owner? Discuss.

Owner ("O") v. Buyer ("B")

Before it can be determined if O can compel B to specifically perform, it must first be decided if O could successfully sue B for breach of contract.

Did a novation occur?

A novation occurs where one party agrees to release the other party from his or her contractual duties and accept a new party in lieu thereof. B might contend that since O accepted the $5,000 down payment from Ellis ("E"), and B had advised O that (1) the contract had been assigned to E, and (2) he no longer considered himself bound by the original agreement (a statement that O did not protest), O impliedly accepted a novation. However, there would probably have to be more affirmative conduct by O indicating he viewed E as the sole obligor under the contract.

Can B successfully assert the Statute of Frauds ("S of F")?

Contracts pertaining to the transfer of an interest in land must be memorialized in a writing and signed by the party against whom enforcement is sought. Since B only verbally agreed to buy Greenacre ("G/A"), he wouldn't be liable to O absent any other documentation. However, under the *aggregation of documents rule*, several writings (whose inter-relationship is reasonably apparent) may be combined to satisfy the S of F. B's letter to O and E's letter to B probably satisfy the S/F with respect to B.

Can B successfully assert the material breach doctrine?

Where one of the parties to an executory contract has committed a material breach, the non-breaching party is relieved of his or her obligations. B could contend that since O didn't actually own the westernly three-foot-wide strip of G/A, O had materially breached the contract. However, O could argue in rebuttal that the three-foot-wide strip was, in relation to a sale of 25 acres, a very minor aspect of the agreement. There is no indication that this strip of land was crucial to B's purpose in acquiring G/A. So, O's innocent breach (there is no indication that O was aware of this problem when he offered G/A to B) was probably not material.

Assuming O prevailed on the previous issues, can he obtain specific performance ("SP")?

While some states permit an aggrieved seller of realty to recover only his out-of-pocket expenses, other jurisdictions permit this party to obtain SP (i.e., obtain a judgment for the contract price, contingent upon giving the buyer a deed to the land when full payment is made). This remedy puts the vendor in the position he would have been in if the buyer had performed. If this state follows the latter view, B would be entitled to an abatement in the purchase price equal to the loss of the strip.

O v. E

While E has agreement with O, O could probably successfully contend that he is a third-party beneficiary of the B-E agreement. E expressly agreed (with B) to pay O. So, assuming O prevailed with respect to each of the issues described above (E could also raise the same arguments against O, since a promisor can assert any defenses against a third-party beneficiary that could have been utilized by the promisee), O can also obtain a judgment against E. Of course, O is permitted only one recovery.

E v. O

As discussed above, if E or B could successfully assert the S of F, or that there was a material breach by O as a result of the strip, E is entitled to rescind the assignment contract and recover back the $5,000 paid to O. Otherwise, this action would fail.

19. A has refused to make any deliveries, and B is now threatening to sue A. A has consulted you with respect to this matter. What would you advise A? Discuss.

There are two possible ways in which a contract ("K") could have been formed: (1) the initial telephone conversations (when B replied "Yes" to A's statement), and (2) when B telegraphed (and later mailed) his acceptance to A's written K.

I.   The Telephone Conversation

Was A's statement an offer or mere invitation?

Whether a statement is an offer or merely an invitation depends upon how a **reasonable offeree** would construe it. A could argue that the words "how would you like" constitute a mere invitation. In rebuttal, B might contend that he reasonably took A's words to be an offer, since it was specific as to term and price. Additionally, A subsequently sent B a writing, which confirmed A's intent to be bound.

Assuming A's statement was an offer, was it sufficiently definite as to the material terms?

A would also contend that his alleged offer was not **sufficiently definite as to material terms** because (1) the quantity term is indefinite (it is not known what B's requirements will be), and (2) nothing was said as to place of delivery or payment terms (e.g., cash or credit). However, B could probably successfully argue in rebuttal that (1) the quantity can be determined by ascertaining how many widgets A purchased from other vendors during this period, (2) that requirements contracts (like this one) do not need a quantity term, and (3) when nothing is said as to place of delivery and payment terms, delivery is at the seller's place and payment must be in cash.

Statute of Frauds ("S. of F.")

Although the K pertains to goods with an aggregate price of $500.00 or more and could *not* be performed within one year from the date it was made, the subsequent written K signed by A to B would satisfy the S. of F.

II. The Written K

To the extent the issue is not cured by the writing, the discussion above as to *definiteness* would again be applicable.

Was the K illusory?

A could contend that the written K was *illusory* (B could *unilaterally avoid his obligations*) because, while A agreed to sell all widgets required "and ordered by" B, B was arguably not obliged to order any. However, B could probably successfully assert that this was simply awkward language (i.e., A wasn't trying to create an "illusory" issue) and, in fact, B is prepared to purchase all of his requirements from A.

Was A's offer revoked at the party?

Under the indirect revocation rule, A might next argue that B received *reliable information* that his offer had been revoked at the party, since C stated that A was opposed to long-term contracts. However, B could probably successfully contend in rebuttal that he had *not* received reliable information because (a) C was merely a friend (not someone at A's business), and (b) the language spoken to B didn't repudiate A's offer (it was merely a general economic comment).

Was A's offer revoked by his telegram to B?

Under the mailbox rule, acceptance is effective when *validly dispatched*. A could contend that B's purported acceptance was *not* valid, since A stipulated that the K had to be signed and mailed back to him. B initially telegraphed his acceptance. Since A's telegram was received by B before he signed and mailed the K back to A, A could argue his revocation was timely.

However, B could argue that the K merely said "please" sign and mail it back; it didn't stipulate that this was the sole mode of acceptance. Consequently, B's telegram to A was therefore a reasonable and probably valid means of acceptance.

Advice

B should prevail in a breach of contract action against A. Thus, unless A performed, B can cover and sue A for the difference between the cover price and the K price ($7.00 per widget). Specific performance seems unlikely. There's no suggestion that A's widgets are unique.

20. Renter wants to know about his rights against, and obligations to, Mechanic. What advice would you give Renter? Discuss.

Based upon the following analysis, I would advise Renter that (1) the contractual modification is probably valid, and (2) Renter can probably recover for his gasoline costs to the extent that any of these purchases exceed the contract price.

Is this transaction governed by the UCC?

The answer to this inquiry will depend upon (1) whether the contract ("K") is divisible, and (2) if not, is it predominantly a sale of goods or a service agreement?

A. Is the K divisible?

Whether a K is divisible or not usually depends upon the parties' bilateral intent and whether performance can be divided into discrete units. The parties in this instance probably did **not** envision a divisible K. Mechanic presumably would not have sold Renter gasoline at 2 cents below the prevailing rate if it were not performing the service and repair functions on its fleet. I would advise Renter that the K is not divisible.

B. Is the K predominantly a sale of goods or a sale of services?

Where an indivisible K involves both the sale of goods and rendition of services, whichever aspect predominates is usually controlling. I would advise Renter that the UCC probably applies, since the sale of goods (the parts and gasoline) probably accounts for a significant majority of the payments to be made by Renter under the agreement.

Was the modification to the original K valid?

Mechanic could assert three theories upon which to uphold the modification.

A. Was the modification of the original K obtained in good faith?

UCC 2-209(1) provides that modifications to an existing K need not be accompanied by consideration to be valid. However, such modifications must be obtained in good faith. Mechanic will contend that he only demanded an increase in prices necessary to offset higher costs. Renter could argue in rebuttal that since it was confronted with a "take-it-or-leave-it" proposition, the modification wasn't in good faith.

B. Are Renter's increased needs "unreasonably disproportionate" vis-a-vis the original K?

Where the needs of a purchaser in a requirements contract become unreasonably disproportionate with those existing at the time the K was made, the supplier need not accommodate those additional needs. UCC 2-306(1). Mechanic will contend that there was consideration for the modification, since it was under no obligation to supply Renter's increased number of vehicles. The facts do not indicate the size of

Renter's fleet at the K's inception. However, assuming it had several cars, Mechanic's assertion is probably correct.

C. Was Renter discharged from his obligations under the original K by the commercial impracticability doctrine?

A party is relieved of his or her obligations under a K for the sale of goods if (1) a contingency occurs, (2) the non-occurrence of which was a basic assumption upon which the K was made, and (3) that party's performance became "commercially impracticable" as a result. Mechanic would argue that he was discharged from his obligations under the initial agreement since the dramatic rate of inflation was an unforeseeable contingency that made his performance commercially impracticable. Renter could argue in rebuttal that inflation is always foreseeable and a K is not "commercially impracticable" merely because it's less profitable than anticipated, or even unprofitable (if the supplier is still financially capable of performing). Assuming the economic consequences to Mechanic would *not* be devastating, Renter should prevail as to the latter point. Thus, this argument will *not* succeed.

Ultimately, however, the modification is probably valid.

Can Mechanic limit Renter to 10 gallons a week per car?

Whether Mechanic could limit Renter to 10 gallons per week per car depends upon whether the "commercial impracticability" doctrine is applicable. Assuming the gas shortage is a sufficient "contingency," that was not foreseeable at the time the K was made, Mechanic is entitled to make "fair and reasonable" allocations. UCC 2-615(b). However, if it's possible for Mechanic to buy the gasoline necessary to fulfill its obligations to Renter, and these purchases would not seriously impact upon Mechanic's solvency, Mechanic's performance is not "commercially impracticable."

It should be noted that the other repair shop can apparently acquire the gasoline necessary to service Renter. So, additional facts (should the shortage have been foreseen, is the allocation fair, what's the economic effect on Mechanic, etc.) are necessary to determine whether Mechanic can limit its sales to Renter.

21. What are Clyde's rights against Safari? Discuss.

Safari could assert that no contract ("K") was ever formed, and, even if it were, he has a defense to Clyde's action.

Was the K definite as to all material terms to be enforceable?

Safari might contend that no K was ever formed since (1) reimbursement for air travel was never agreed upon, and (2) material terms are missing (e.g., when will Clyde be paid, how much effort does Clyde have to expend in finding zoos for the animals, etc.). However, the reimbursement question is arguably a relatively minor point and does not have to be settled for a K to exist. The other points may be implied (e.g., Clyde will be paid no later than the end of the K, Clyde will use his reasonable best efforts to find zoos for the animals, etc.). Clyde should prevail on this issue.

Was the K illusory?

A K is illusory where one party can unilaterally avoid his or her obligations. Safari might argue that the contract was illusory since all sales were subject to his unrestricted approval. Since he could reject all prospective sales, he arguably had no duties under the K. However, Clyde could respond that Safari must impliedly exercise good faith in making such determinations. Consequently, Clyde should prevail on this issue.

Is the Statute of Frauds (S of F) applicable?

Ks that by their terms are not capable of performance within one year from the time they are made are ordinarily within the S of F, and therefore unenforceable unless evidenced by a writing signed by the party against whom enforcement is sought.

Since Clyde's employment was for two years, Safari could assert this defense. Clyde might argue that the doctrines of substantial performance and estoppel can negate the S of F. However, the K is probably not sufficiently performed for this contention to be successful. Clyde's estoppel contention is that, based upon the time and money he has expended in performing the K, an "injustice" would result if Safari were permitted to avoid it. However, Clyde's efforts to this point are probably inadequate for estoppel to apply, and so Safari should prevail. Nevertheless, Clyde's potential damages will be analyzed from both possibilities (i.e., that a K did, and did not, exist).

Remedies

A. Breach of contract

A non-breaching party is usually entitled to recover all losses occasioned by the other's breach. Clyde will therefore argue that he should receive $5,000 for arranging the sale of the impalas to the Bronx Zoo because, Safari unreasonably withheld his approval. Alternatively, he's entitled to $4,000 for the sale of those impalas to Lincoln Park, $400 for flying to San Francisco, and the compensation that Clyde would have earned had the K been fulfilled.

Safari can make several counter-arguments. First, damages must be reasonably susceptible to estimation, and it's impossible to determine the compensation that Clyde would have received over the next two years. Specifically, there is no way to estimate who would have purchased Safari's animals and for how much. However, Clyde can (probably successfully) contend in rebuttal that, since the matter might not come to trial for two years, the measure of damages should be 10% of all sales that Safari makes during the two-year period that would have been covered by the K.

Safari might also argue that he owes Clyde nothing since the agreement was terminated prior to the time Clyde's sales exceeded $150,000. However, where one party prevents fulfillment of the terms of a K, the other party is excused from performing those terms. Thus, this contention should be unsuccessful. Finally, it should be noted that Clyde has a duty to mitigate Safari's damages by accepting similar employment, if it's available.

B. Quasi-contract

If Safari successfully asserted the S of F, Clyde might still recover in quasi-contract.

Under the doctrine of quasi-contract, even though the parties' agreement is not enforceable, if one accepts a benefit from another knowing that the latter expects compensation, the former is normally liable for the reasonable value of that benefit. Thus, Clyde could alternatively contend that he should receive at least $5,900 (10% of the sales of the impalas and zebras, and $400 for flying to San Francisco). The contract rate is ordinarily evidence of the reasonable value of the services rendered. Of course, Safari will argue that only the sale of the impalas should be allowed and that he never agreed to pay the plane fare. However, under an unjust enrichment analysis, Clyde would probably prevail on these points.

C. Specific performance

Finally, it is highly unlikely that Clyde could obtain specific performance. Courts virtually never require the performance of personal service contracts because of the difficulty in supervising enforcement and compelling a continuing relationship between antagonistic parties.

Flowchart 1 OFFER AND ACCEPTANCE

O = Offeror   E = Offeree   Kt = Contract

OFFER
— Statement which (1) reasonably appears to indicate a willingness (2) to be presently bound (3) to a definite commitment (4) upon E's acceptance.

PRESENTLY BOUND
- **REASONABLE APPEARANCE** – objective test, applies even to offers made in jest or anger
- **NOT EXPRESSION OF FUTURE INTENT OR INTEREST (e.g., request for quotation).**
- **ADVERTISEMENTS** – generally deemed to be "invitations to an offer" unless quantity is specific and language of promise is present.

DEFINITENESS
- **AMBIGUITIES** – construed against O.
- **ESSENTIAL TERMS**
  - **Parties** – only E can accept (rewards are generally offers for unilateral Kt).
  - **Subject Matter**
  - **Quantity**
  - **Price** – if unstated, UCC implies reasonable price at time of delivery, payment due at time and place buyer receives goods.
  - **Time for Performance** – if unstated, UCC implies reasonable time at seller's place.

MANNER OF ACCEPTANCE

OFFEREE'S ACCEPTANCE – formation of the Kt in the hands of E; no further act by O required.

- **MEDIUM** – unless O unambiguously indicates otherwise, offer may accepted by *any medium*.
- **PERFORMANCE**
  - **BILATERAL CONTRACT** – where offer may be accepted by a promise, E may also accept by performing, but must inform O that he is doing so.
  - **UNILATERAL CONTRACT** – if offer specifically calls for performance (not a mere promise), E may also accept by performing, but must inform O that he is doing so.
    (modern view forms Kt upon *commencement*, but some courts say O may revoke any time prior to completion.)
- **PROMISE TO PERFORM** – an offer may be accepted by *dispatch* of a promise to perform unless offer specifically calls for performance.

SILENCE – valid acceptance if:
- E INTENDS TO ACCEPT BY SILENCE *AND O PRESCRIBES SILENCE,* or
- PREVIOUS DEALINGS IMPLY ACCEPTANCE, or
- TAKING BENEFIT OR EXERCISING CONTROL – if E has opportunity to reject offer but instead takes benefits or exercises dominion over goods offered.

OFFEREE'S RESPONSE

UNEQUIVOCAL ACCEPTANCE – unequivocal acceptance (even if "grumbling") forms Kt upon *dispatch*.

EQUIVOCAL ACCEPTANCE: PROPOSING NEW TERMS
- **COMMON LAW** – proposal of new terms (not mere inquiries for a better offer) makes acceptance invalid and acts as *counteroffer* (i.e., a rejection).
- **UCC** – a "definite and seasonable" acceptance which proposes new but *not inconsistent* terms forms a Kt on O's terms if E's acceptance is *in writing*; O may accept or reject new terms.
- **UCC MERCHANT'S RULE** – *between merchants*, if E proposes new but *not inconsistent* terms along with a "definite and seasonable" acceptance, Kt *includes new terms unless*: (1) O expressly limited to O's terms acceptance, Kt includes new terms, or (2) new terms materially alter original offer, or (3) offer expressly limited to O's terms

REJECTION – terminates offer when *received* by E.

COUNTEROFFER – operates as a rejection when *received* by O and terminates original offer.

INDECISION – offer remains open until terminated by O or lapse of time.

TERMINATION OF OFFER

- **REVOCATION** – offer terminates when E receives notice of O's revocation in spite of express promise not to revoke unless:
  - **Paid-for Option** – promise to keep offer open supported by consideration.
  - **UCC Firm Offer** – promise to keep offer open is enforceable without consideration if: (1) *made by merchant*, (2) *signed writing for the (3) sale of goods and (4) E accepts within three months*.
- **REJECTION** – an express rejection or counteroffer terminates an offer *upon receipt*.
- **INDIRECT REVOCATION** – unaccepted offer terminates when E *learns* of acts by O inconsistent with offer.
- **LAPSE OF TIME** – unaccepted offer expires upon lapse of time stated in offer or by a "reasonable time."
- **DEATH OR INSANITY** – unaccepted offer terminates when E *learns* of O's death or insanity.
- **DESTRUCTION OF SUBJECT MATTER** – offer terminates when subject matter of offer is destroyed.
- **INTERVENING ILLEGALITY** – offer legal when made terminates if made illegal before acceptance.

multistate issue graph

Flowchart 2   THIRD PARTY BENEFICIARIES

DEFINITIONS

Promissee-Benefactor (X) ⟵ **Promisor (Y)**

Third Party Beneficiary (Z)

ISSUE SPOTTING SEQUENCE

(1) *What was X's intent with regard to the benefit conferred upon Z?*

(2) *What rights does Z have to enforce the contract?*

STATUS OF BENEFICIARY
What was X's intent with regard to the benefit conferred upon Z?

INCIDENTAL BENEFICIARY — if X had no specific intent or motive to confer a benefit on Z.

DONEE BENEFICIARY — if X intended to confer a gratuitous gift on Z.

CREDITOR BENEFICIARY — if X was conferring a benefit on Z to satisfy a pre-existing debt or obligation.

THIRD PARTY BENEFICIARIES:
Contractual rights created in a third person at the time of formation:

RIGHTS OF BENEFICIARY
If Y fails to perform for Z's benefit, what rights does Z have?

INCIDENTAL BENEFICIARY — no right against either Y or X.

DONEE BENEFICIARY — Z's rights *vest* upon knowledge of X-Y contract (some states require reliance), thereafter Z has the following rights:

Against Y — Z stands in shoes of X in suit against Y.

Against X — Z may prevent X from rescinding X-Y contract but may not sue X if Y fails to perform.

CREDITOR BENEFICIARY — Z's rights vest upon his reliance on X-Y contract.

Against Y — Z stands in shoes of X in suit against Y.

Against X — Z may sue X on original obligation disregarding X-Y contract (unless there was a novation).

multistate issue graph

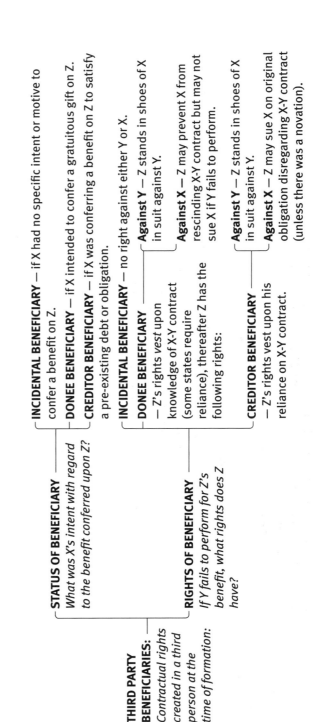

KAPLAN *pmbr*

Flowchart 3   CONTRACT REMEDIES

MONEY DAMAGES — normal remedy; should place non-breaching party in position he would have been in had the contract been performed.

- **Restitution** — recovery of money already paid to breaching party (less possible *quantum meruit* offset).
- **Reliance Costs** — recovery of out-of-pocket expenses in preparing to perform.
- **Incidental Costs** — recovery of costs necessitated by breach directly relating to the contract itself (e.g., shipping, storage, inspection, reselling or repurchasing).
- **SALES CONTRACTS** — difference between the market price at the time of breach and the contract price.
  - **SERVICE CONTRACT**
    - **Employee** — full contract price *if* she has performed or stands ready to do so (*less* mitigation).
    - **Employer** — recovery limited to costs of replacement.

- **Expected Bargained For Benefit** — *not* including anticipated profits (see consequential costs).
- **FORESEEABLE** — *Hadley v Baxendale* — reasonably foreseeable costs and losses contemplated by both parties at the time of the contract may be recovered.
  - **MITIGATION** — non-breacher's recovery must be reduced by amount yielded or yieldable by reasonable efforts to reduce costs of breach.
- **Consequential Costs and Losses** — money damages resulting from special situation of non-breaching party (*not* including mental anguish or inconvenience).
- **REASONABLE AMOUNT** — amount must be reasonable in light of parties' contemplations at the time of contract.
  - **NECESSARY** — amount of actual damages must be difficult to ascertain.
  - **TAILORED TO CONTRACT** — provision must be tailored to nature of contract (i.e., *not* boilerplate).
- **Liquidated Damages** — contractual provision setting the total amount of all money damages in the event of breach (does *not* bar non-monetary remedies); if invalid, non-breacher may prove and collect actual damages.
- **Punitive Damages** — only available in extreme cases of malicious or intentional breach (like a separate tort recovery).

SPECIFIC PERFORMANCE — court may order breaching party to perform the contract.

- **Contract Must be Valid and Enforceable**
- **Money Damages Must Be Inadequate**
  - **UNIQUE SUBJECT MATTER** — land, stock of close corporation, one-of-a-kind item.
  - **AMOUNT NOT ASCERTAINABLE**
- **No Special Problems of Enforcement** — (e.g., personal service contract may *not* be specifically enforced).
- **Subject to Equitable Defenses** — look for (1) *unclean hands*, (2) *laches*, (3) *estoppel*.

RESCISSION — cancellation of the contract to put parties as they were before the contract.

- **Grounds**
  - **MUTUAL MISTAKE IN FORMATION**
  - **FRAUD** — knowing misrepresentation of material fact relied upon by non-breacher.
  - **MAJOR BREACH CHANGING NATURE OF AGREEMENT**
- **Requirements**
  - **NON-BREACHING PARTY MUST HAVE CLEAN HANDS**
  - **NOTIFICATION WITHIN REASONABLE TIME**
  - **RESTORATION OF BREACHER TO STATUS QUO** — *non-breacher* must return all consideration unless alteration or change made in good faith reliance that breacher would perform.

REFORMATION — court may reform contract to accurately describe the actual agreement if there was a mutual mistake.

QUASI-CONTRACT — if no formal contract and work has been partly or fully performed, plaintiff may collect reasonable value of services *from the actor's point of view*; if an express contract was breached, P may sue on the contract or, if there are grounds for rescission, rescind it and sue for the reasonable value of services performed or goods transferred using the quasi-contract theory. This is actually an alternative theory for money damages based on equity rather than contract.

multistate issue graph

KAPLAN) *pmbr*

NOTES

KAPLAN) *pmbr*